MULTI-AGENCY WORKING IN CRIMINAL JUSTICE

Control and care in contemporary correctional practice

Edited by Aaron Pycroft and Dennis Gough

This edition published in Great Britain in 2010 by

The Policy Press
University of Bristol
Fourth Floor
Beacon House
Queen's Road
Bristol BS8 1QU
UK

Tel +44 (0)117 331 4054
Fax +44 (0)117 331 4093
e-mail tpp-info@bristol.ac.uk
www.policypress.co.uk

North American office:
The Policy Press
c/o International Specialized Books Services (ISBS)
920 NE 58th Avenue, Suite 300
Portland, OR 97213-3786, USA
Tel +1 503 287 3093
Fax +1 503 280 8832
e-mail info@isbs.com

© The Policy Press 2010

British Library Cataloguing in Publication Data
A catalogue record for this book is available from the British Library.

Library of Congress Cataloging-in-Publication Data
A catalog record for this book has been requested.

ISBN 978 1 84742 453 2 paperback
ISBN 978 1 84742 454 9 hardcover

The right of Aaron Pycroft and Dennis Gough to be identified as editors of this work has
been asserted by them in accordance with the 1988 Copyright, Designs and Patents Act.

Cover design by Qube Design Associates, Bristol.
Front cover: image kindly supplied by www.istock.com
Printed and bound in Great Britain by Hobbs, Southampton.
The Policy Press uses environmentally responsible print partners.

For our beautiful families:

Nicky, Samuel, Barnabas and Lydia Pycroft

Caroline, Eleanor and Tom Gough

Contents

List of boxes and tables

Boxes

Tables

Notes on contributors

Suzie Clift works as a Senior Lecturer in the Institute of Criminology at the University of Portsmouth. Her areas of interest and research concern risk, sex offenders and public protection. Suzie is a qualified probation officer and as such has experience in the assessment, supervision and management of high-risk offenders, including sexual and violent offenders. She is currently researching her PhD, which considers the shaping of risk within criminal justice.

Rachel Goldhill qualified as a Probation Officer in 1984 and then worked in Court and Case Management, Resettlement, Brighton Bail Hostel, the Thames Valley Sex Offender Groupwork Programme (TVSOGP) and as a Practice Development Assessor. She left probation in 2004 to take up the post of Senior Lecturer/Regional Tutor on the Diploma in Probation Studies at the University of Portsmouth. Her particular research interests are women offenders and reflective practice.

Dennis Gough is Senior Lecturer in Penology in the Institute of Criminal Justice Studies at the University of Portsmouth. He teaches and researches in the broad fields of punishment, prisons and their respective alternatives. He is co-author with Professor Carol Hayden of *Implementing Restorative Justice in Children's Residential Care* (The Policy Press, 2010). In addition, his PhD research is concerned with the governance of corrections.

Bernie Heath is a regionally based Senior Lecturer at the University of Portsmouth. Formerly a Senior Probation Officer, she has a long and varied experience, which includes seven years as a manager of an Approved Premises and two years as a regional manager for substance misuse. Effective multi-agency liaison has been a crucial area of practice throughout her career. Particular interests include substance misuse, offenders with mental health problems and the management of high-risk offenders.

Sarah Hilder is a Senior Lecturer at De Montfort University and course director for the BA Hons in Community and Criminal Justice/Diploma in Probation Studies for trainee Probation Officers. Previously she held a senior lecturer post with Portsmouth University and prior to her move to academia in 2004 she worked both as a main grade and then Senior Probation Officer in a variety of different specialisms. Her teaching and research interests centre around issues of race equality and justice in work with offenders.

John E. Howard worked for 27 years in the Probation Service as a practitioner and senior manager. From 2002 to 2009 he was a regional tutor on the Probation Studies Programme at Plymouth and Portsmouth and is currently an Associate

Lecturer with The Open University on the social work degree programme and the youth justice effective practice certificate.

Mark Mitchell is Course Director for the BA (Hons) in Community Justice Studies at the University of Portsmouth. He has published extensively in the fields of migration, asylum and citizenship in Europe; race, ethnicity and identity in the UK; and anti-racism, diversity and professional practice. He is active in the local community and is a former chair of the Portsmouth Racial Harassment Forum and a former trustee of the Portsmouth Area Refugee Support Group.

Mike Nash is Head of Department and Reader in Criminology at the Institute of Criminal Justice Studies, University of Portsmouth. He has taught, researched and published on public protection issues for many years. Recent books include *Public Protection and the Criminal Justice Process* (Oxford University Press, 2006) and *The Anatomy of Serious Further Offending* (with A. Williams) (Oxford University Press, 2008). He is presently editing with A. Williams a *Handbook of Public Protection* (Willan Press, 2010).

Francis Pakes is Reader in Comparative Criminology at the University of Portsmouth. He studied psychology in his native Netherlands and holds a PhD from Leiden University. His main research interests are in comparative criminology, crime and justice in the Netherlands and the intersections of criminal justice and mental health. In particular, Francis has extensively researched the workings of criminal justice mental health teams that operate at police stations or Magistrates' Courts. He is currently elected treasurer of the British Society of Criminology.

Nicholas Pamment is a Lecturer in the Institute of Criminal Justice Studies at the University of Portsmouth and has also worked for a Youth Offending Team in various roles. His main area of interest lies within youth justice and he is currently undertaking doctoral study into the impact of reparative community service on young offenders.

Gerry Parkinson is currently a Probation Officer. Prior to this he worked as a Senior Lecturer at the University of Portsmouth on the BA (Hons) Community Justice Studies programme. His main interests include the legal framework underpinning probation practice; enforcement; resettlement; and the role of motivational interviewing and pro-social modelling in the supervision of offenders.

Aaron Pycroft is a Senior Lecturer in Addiction Studies in the Institute of Criminal Justice Studies at the University of Portsmouth. Before joining the university he worked for 15 years in the non-statutory sector as a practitioner and senior manager in substance misuse services and has worked extensively with a range of organisations in providing and developing services. His primary teaching and research interests are in the application of complexity theory to policy and practice, particularly in relation to substance misuse. His book *Understanding and Working with Substance Misusers* (2010) is published by Sage Publications.

Anne Rees – following a lengthy career as a Probation Officer, Anne is now a Senior Lecturer and Regional Tutor for the University of Portsmouth. She is based in the North West Region of England and has specific interest in the areas of risk assessment, dangerousness, drug misuse, women in the criminal justice system and mental health.

Carrie Skinner was formerly a Probation Officer and for the last six years has been a Senior Lecturer/Regional Tutor for the University of Portsmouth. Her practitioner expertise has been in case management and group offender programmes. Her teaching and research interests are in resettlement, risk and dangerousness and the politics of community justice.

Jacki Tapley is a Principal Lecturer in the Institute of Criminal Justice Studies at the University of Portsmouth. Her main interests lie in victimology and the role of victims in the criminal justice system. Prior to joining the Institute in 2000, Jacki worked as a Probation Officer in Dorset. She has retained her links with Dorset and is the Independent Facilitator for the CPS Hate Crime Scrutiny Panel and is a member of the Dorset Criminal Justice Board Consultative Committee.

Aileen Watson is a Senior Lecturer in Criminology in the Institute of Criminal Justice Studies at the University of Portsmouth. Her current role is teaching students on the BA (Hons) Community Justice programme, part of the recognised training programme for Probation Officers. Prior to working in higher education she worked as a Probation Officer in Greater Manchester. Her particular interests are working with sex offenders, gender and crime, and safeguarding children.

Jane Winstone is a Principal Lecturer in the Institute of Criminal Justice Studies at the University of Portsmouth. In addition to obtaining postgraduate degrees in sociology and psychology, Jane is a qualified Probation Officer and for the past 10 years her role at the University of Portsmouth has been to support the delivery of the probation qualification. Jane's research interests include youth penology, the subject of her PhD, and the management of mental health in criminal justice settings in which she has been contributing to the debates in the area of mental health provision through publication and research since 2004.

Introduction

Aaron Pycroft and Dennis Gough

Aims of the book

- To provide an introductory text for students and practitioners involved in correctional work, through the Probation or Prison Services, or other statutory and non-statutory agencies.
- To outline the legislative and policy framework for a 'mixed economy of service provision' in the criminal justice system.
- To highlight key offender groups, issues associated with rehabilitation and the necessary conditions for helping those people to desist from crime.
- To discuss multi-agency arrangements in the management and control of high-risk offenders.
- To discuss key skills involved in multi-agency working.
- To offer a critique of some aspects of multi-agency working.
- To critically discuss and evaluate professional and organisational conflicts within multi-agency contexts.

This text for the first time brings together theory, policy and skills relevant to working in a multi-agency setting within the criminal justice system. It comes at an important time when the qualifying arrangements for probation officers are changing, and with the emergence of the National Offender Management Service (NOMS) and the implementation of the Offender Management Model.

All of the contributors to this book have been involved in delivering professional qualifying courses for probation officers since 2001. The inspiration for this book has arisen from our involvement in the teaching of trainee probation officers over the last six years. The majority of the contributors have extensive practitioner experience and the editors both have substantial practitioner and management experience in the Probation Service (Dennis Gough) and the non-statutory sector (Aaron Pycroft).

One of our core messages to students has been that there is not a guide book to multi-agency working. Well, there still isn't, as this is not a guide book, in the sense of how to do it! Good and effective multi-agency working essentially stems from 'practitioner wisdom', and the development of contacts and networks. The aim of this book is to contribute to the development of that 'wisdom' by discussing some of the key issues within the broader and general policy context, and to examine the key developments with particular reference to the concept of multi-agency working. Within the recent developments in criminal and community justice is the rise of a more punitive crime control and risk management agenda, running alongside a considerable investment in programmes of rehabilitation; this book aims to discuss some of the issues and tensions that arise from this. Throughout you will be invited to reflect upon the text and to make links with your own understanding and experiences; you will also be guided towards other useful resources.

Structure of the book

Chapter 1 – 'Consensus, complexity and emergence: the mixed economy of service provision' – by Aaron Pycroft, explores the post-war consensus around the development of the welfare state as a 'mixed economy' of welfare provision, the various approaches to public service provision since 1945 and the rationale behind New Labour's approach to capacity building within public services. It argues that, despite a huge financial investment in the public services, along with commensurate performance targets and increased accountability, the approaches taken by New Labour have not produced the desired results because they have been based on simplistic notions of cause and effect. The chapter therefore discusses the idea of organisations and multi-agency arrangements as complex adaptive systems that are essentially interactive in nature and give rise to emergent (unintended) issues that appear as random and unforeseen. The implications of this for policy makers, practitioners and service are discussed.

Chapter 2 – 'Multi-agency working in corrections: cooperation and competition in probation practice' – by Dennis Gough, discusses the recent multi-agency approach to the delivery of public policy in a broad criminal justice context. It traces the history of multi-agency working in direct work with offenders, from the origins of 'partnership' to public and private alliances, which more recently have formed the bedrock of the NOMS project. It then moves on to discuss how the values and ethics behind multi-agency working have shifted from an approach based on cooperation and mutuality to one of competition in a mixed market of corrections. Finally, it situates the corrections policy agenda against recent criminological theory, offering insights from works such as Garland's (2001) adaptive strategies of responsibilisation agendas and the growth of a multiplicity of actors in criminal justice, and Jonathan Simon's (2007) work *Governing Through Crime*.

There are a number of implications for both service users and probation staff in multi-agency working and Chapter 3 – 'Clients or offenders? The case for clarity of purpose in multi-agency working' – by Carrie Skinner, is concerned with examining the case for a 'major reconstruction of practice' in order to establish the authenticity of its claim to improve practice outcomes. The counterargument over the loss of professional knowledge needed to work with difficult individuals with complex needs along with the fragmentary experiences of service users is examined against the backdrop of recent research on what supports desistance from crime.

Chapter 4 – 'Diversity and the policy agenda in criminal justice' – by Mark Mitchell, gives a brief history of diversity as a shift away from anti-discrimination, which had been the focus of policies in the 1960s and 1970s. In relation to criminal justice agencies and diversity, the impact of the Macpherson Inquiry and the 2000 Race Relations (Amendment) Act is discussed along with the rapid emergence of diversity as a strategic objective in criminal justice agencies. The questions of whether this diversity agenda promotes effective partnership working across the criminal justice system and whether current approaches to diversity can reduce social exclusion and promote social inclusion are addressed. The importance of the Cantle Report (Home Office, 2001) and the role of the Equality and Human Rights Commission are considered in detail. The chapter concludes with a discussion of whether there is a conflict between a diversity agenda and an equality and human rights agenda.

Chapter 5 – 'Multi-agency work with black and minority ethnic offenders' – by Sarah Hilder, outlines the opportunities presented by multi-agency working to increase the creativity and 'responsivity' of offender interventions. It takes as its example black and minority ethnic offenders and outlines current criminal justice initiatives to provide meaningful and engaging interventions with an important offender group. The chapter highlights contributions from beyond the formal criminal justice system and reflects on 'what works' with black and minority ethnic offenders from a multi-agency perspective.

Chapter 6 – 'From pillar to post: multi-agency working with women offenders' – by Rachel Goldhill, explains the different pathways into crime for women offenders and how this impacts on criminal justice agency interventions. It examines the feminist literature on chivalry and double deviance, which has tended to focus on police and sentencers' prejudices within the court setting, but shows that such attitudes may apply equally to offender managers in statutory and voluntary services. Renewed interest in women offenders has come about recently backed by legislation and ministerial support and so the final part of the chapter considers the organisational difficulties in effecting improved multi-agency working.

Chapter 7 – 'Working together to manage risk of serious harm' – by Suzie Clift, considers multi-agency arrangements in relation to managing risk. It explores definitions around risk and the agencies most likely to be concerned with this and potential conflicts and tensions in definition. It also considers the Multi-Agency Public Protection Arrangements (MAPPA) framework and the potential issues in adopting a multi-agency approach where there are (potential) competing goals and cultures. The duties of agencies (both statutory and voluntary) to comply are considered, along with what this means in practice. Key sections consider definitions of risk, methods of assessment and methods of managing risk, with the main emphasis being on MAPPA. However, other methods and processes are also considered, highlighting the need to still adopt a multi-agency approach when offenders do not meet criteria for MAPPA.

Chapter 8 – 'Singing from the same MAPPA hymn sheet – but can we hear all the voices?' – by Mike Nash, follows on from the previous chapter on MAPPA. It explores the legal context of the duty to collaborate and sets this within wider explorations of multi-agency working in child protection and health fields. It then narrows down to focus very specifically on a 'slice of MAPPA' life in one county area using the author's own empirical research. It goes on to explore cultural transference and merger, facilitators and barriers to effective multi-agency working and examines which agencies collaborate the most and with whom, while identifying those with less willing participation and a greater degree of distrust.

Chapter 9 – 'Sharing or shifting responsibility? The multi-agency approach to safeguarding children' – by Aileen Watson, considers the role of multi-agency working in safeguarding children and identifies current policies and statutory arrangements in relation to multi-agency working. Its focus is on the Laming Reports that followed the deaths of Victoria Climbié and Baby Peter (Laming, 2003, 2009) with a discussion of the professional issues involved and highlighting the aspects of multi-agency working that can enhance or impede the safeguarding of children.

Chapter 10 – 'Working together to tackle domestic violence' – by Jacki Tapley, explores the shift in attitudes over time towards violence in the home on the part of both the public and politicians. It charts the development of services for victims of domestic violence, and through an examination of research into services in one particular area of the country looks at the ways in which those services have been improved through the development of multi-agency arrangements.

Chapter 11 – 'Unlocking prisoners: does multi-agency working hold the key to the successful resettlement of released prisoners?' – by Gerry Parkinson, outlines the policy framework provided by the NOMS *Agency Framework Document* (2008) and the National Action Plan for Reducing Reoffending (Home Office, 2004) as well as the local reducing reoffending strategies, all of which emphasise the role of a variety of corporate, civic and voluntary/faith groups in reducing reoffending. The focus of the chapter is on ex-prisoners, with a brief examination of the neglect of, particularly, short-term prisoners and the disadvantages they face, as detailed in a report by the Social Exclusion Unit (SEU, 2002). This neglect has resulted in high reconviction rates among those released following short-term prison sentences and a response from the government that focuses on seven reducing reoffending pathways. The chapter provides an examination of these pathways, how they were identified, with examples from specific regional strategies and the nature of the multi-agency response in addressing the relevant pathways. The chapter concludes with a discussion of the difficulties faced by the offender manager in balancing the above approaches/models in the supervision of ex-prisoners within the prescriptive Offender Management Model.

Chapter 12 – 'Offenders with mental health problems in the criminal justice system: the multi-agency challenge' – by Francis Pakes and Jane Winstone, critically considers those aspects of multi-agency work that support the delivery of both justice and health outcomes for those passing through the criminal justice system with mental health needs. It opens with a brief history of delivery of services to people with mental health needs, defines key concepts such as 'mentally disordered offender', 'effective practice' and 'diversion' and locates a definition of multi-agency work within these. The chapter concludes with an analysis of the current state of provision for the diversion of mentally disordered offenders and considers the likely impact of the implementation of the 2007 Mental Health Act and the Bradley Review (Bradley, 2009).

Chapter 13 – 'The partnership approach to drug misuse' – by Bernie Heath, looks at the historical context and particularly the Tackling Drugs Together approach of the Major government, which was then developed by New Labour for the strategic delivery of drug treatment via Drug Action Teams, the National Treatment Agency and the Drug Intervention Programme. This chapter defines partnership working in drug services and considers some of the ethical and value dilemmas in relation to coerced treatment and the implications for the range of agencies involved. In particular, notions of drug-related harm are considered along with the challenges for services in responding to diverse needs, for example is the case management model a hindrance or a help in addressing some of these issues? The chapter draws on case examples and service user perspectives.

Chapter 14 – 'Dual diagnosis and issues and implications for criminal justice partnerships' – by Anne Rees, focuses on service provision for those experiencing difficulties related to the combination of mental health problems and substance misuse. The areas of focus includes theoretical perspectives on dual diagnosis and their implications for policy and practice; a review of policy in relation to mental health legislation; and guidance from the Department of Health and the National Treatment Agency for Substance Misuse on working with dual diagnosis issues. The development of separate services provision, the lack of integrated approaches and the implications for service users and practitioners alike are discussed, as well as what the research evidence suggests is effective practice in working with dual diagnosis.

Chapter 15 – 'Youth Offending Teams: a multi-agency success or system failure?' – by Nicholas Pamment, considers the policy background and the multi-agency arrangements in place within the youth justice system. The impact of this in relation to performance and efficiency is discussed. Particular emphasis is placed on the latest research that explores Labour's youth justice reforms and which shows that every target set by the government has been missed (Soloman and Garside, 2008). The strengths and weaknesses of multi-agency arrangements within youth justice, with competing requirements for differing agencies, as well as differences of professional cultures, are explored. A key part of the chapter focuses on service user perspectives on the youth justice system.

Chapter 16 – 'The beauty of reflection and the beast of multi-agency cooperation' – by John E. Howard, begins by considering what constitutes effective multi-agency working in a criminal justice context. It discusses the nature of reflective practice as a fundamental tool for professional development. It moves on to consider the essential skills and professional attributes necessary for the development of effective practice. It argues that while there may be a *core* set of skills for effective partnership working, the *emphasis* is likely to be different for different workers at different grades in different agencies involved in different kinds of partnerships. The chapter then considers the obstacles and challenges to effective partnership working and how skilled practice can help to overcome some of these challenges. It argues that, in terms of practice skills, effective communication is crucially important.

The final chapter – 'Conclusion: does multi-agency working equate with effective practice' – by Aaron Pycroft and Dennis Gough, invites the reader to reflect on some of the key themes raised in the book, and the implications for the Offender Management Model in the light of these debates. The chapter considers the wholesale changes to the Probation Service brought about by the introduction of a mixed economy of corrections, and considers some of these issues given the evidence base from other areas of social policy and service delivery.

References

Bradley, Lord (2009) *Lord Bradley's Review of People with Mental Health Problems or Learning Disabilities in the Criminal Justice System*. London: Department of Health.

Garland, D. (2001) *The Culture of Control, Crime and Social Order in Contemporary Society*. Oxford: Oxford University Press.

Home Office (2001) *Community Cohesion: A Report of the Independent Review Team Chaired by Ted Cantle* (Cantle Report). London: Home Office.

Home Office (2004) *Reducing Re-offending: National Action Plan*. London: Home Office.

Laming, H. (2003) *The Victoria Climbié Inquiry: Report of an Inquiry by Lord Laming*. Cm 5730. London: The Stationery Office.

Laming, H. (2009) *The Protection of Children in England: A Progress Report*. London: The Stationery Office.

NOMS (National Offender Management Service) (2008) *Agency Framework Document*. London: NOMS.

SEU (Social Exclusion Unit) (2002) *Reducing Re-offending by Ex-prisoners*. London: Office of the Deputy Prime Minister.

Simon, J. (2007) *Governing through Crime: How the War on Crime Transformed American Democracy and Created a Culture of Fear*, Oxford: Oxford University Press.

Solomon, E. and Garside, R. (2008) *Ten Years of Labour's Youth Justice Reforms: An Independent Audit*. London: Centre for Crime and Justice Studies.

CHAPTER 1

Consensus, complexity and emergence: the mixed economy of service provision

Aaron Pycroft

Aims of the chapter

■ To provide an overview of the development of a mixed economy of public service delivery in the UK, and to provide a context for the ensuing chapters.

■ To utilise insights from organisational theory to explain and analyse the evolution of the approaches involved, and their strengths and weaknesses.

■ To make suggestions for future developments.

Introduction

In 1997, the incoming New Labour government placed partnership working at the centre of its modernisation agenda; for the purposes of this chapter, Sterling's (2005: 139) definition of partnership will be used, denoting 'a relatively formalised arrangement between two or more organisations in order to achieve a set of objectives, generally with a degree of independence from any one partner'. Over the course of the Blair administrations, partnerships became a key feature of public service delivery, with some 5,500 partnerships in the UK by 2005, accounting for £3 billion of public expenditure (NAO, 2005). Many of those partnerships involved organisations from the public, private or voluntary sectors. In particular, New Labour continued a trend of previous governments both Conservative and Labour in seeking to harness the potential of the third sector, seeing that it had 'much to contribute to the Government's goals for public services, communities and the economy ... [and] has taken significant steps since 1997 to promote, enable and grow the ... sector' (HM Treasury, 2005: 3).

This partnership approach was initially focused in the arenas of health and social care (see Leathard, 2005) but developed along with National Service Frameworks (NSFs) (see below) in other policy areas. All areas of social policy and government intervention have experienced the process of outsourcing key services to the private and not-for-profit sectors and the growth of private finance in public sector building projects (eg schools and hospitals). In addition, there have been significant changes in professional roles and identity, with an expansion of non-professionally qualified staff (eg care managers, teaching assistants, nursing assistants, Probation Service officers).

The key to understanding the current developments in criminal justice lies in these broader debates in social policy and political economy, which over time have affected all the professions, which have developed in tandem with the welfare state post 1945. That the creation of the National Offender Management Service (NOMS) and the advancement of a mixed economy of correctional services are the most significant developments in the delivery of criminal justice in recent times is beyond doubt. Other authors in this volume (Gough and Skinner) attest to this reality but then predominantly from a Probation Service perspective. It is my intention to argue for the evolutionary rather than revolutionary nature of those changes and to make the case for taking this broader view to see how and why these changes are deemed to be necessary and desirable. These balances between the notions of justice, democracy and accountability and value for money are complex and difficult areas, but nonetheless provide the everyday context for punishment and rehabilitation within the criminal justice system. This chapter will argue that it is this complexity that gives rise to unintended consequences in service delivery, which means that organisations do not necessarily work in the ways that they are intended to do so by their managers or political masters. In practical terms, the very nature of service delivery within a multi-agency context increases the complexity of the tasks at hand in terms of the numbers of people and processes involved, and as we shall see, an increase in complexity leads to an increase in unintended or unpredictable outcomes.

The 'mixed economy' of service provision

A 'mixed economy' refers to the idea of balancing market forces with some degree of planning (see Jessop, 1999). Powell (2007) identifies the range of component agencies involved in a mixed economy such as the state, private ('for-profit') organisations, voluntary organisations ('not-for-profit' charities) as well as informal help and assistance (family, friends and neighbours). But importantly, Powell (2007) argues that despite discussions about the mix of agencies involved, there also needs to be an analysis of the balance between them, as well as their dimensions. He argues that the dimensions to be considered are 'between countries; over time; between services; and between components of services' (2007: 9). He argues that it is through this level of analysis that account can be given to the different strategies used by the state in the planning, commissioning and financing of public services. This might involve contracting out services, creating internal and quasi markets and voucher schemes, for example, with the emphasis being less on provision and who provides, and more on the quality of the service provided, value for money and best outcomes. In response to Powell's argument for a comparative dimension to an analysis of the mixed economy, Sterling (2005: 140) makes the point that this process is not restricted to the UK alone but is being utilised in a range of policy areas, and is a global phenomenon.

–

The post-1945 social democratic settlement saw that the majority of services that constituted the new welfare state would be provided by the state, with voluntary sector agencies filling the gaps that the state could not or would not provide for. This left a residual role for the private sector (mainly in private healthcare). In turn, the state as provider and producer of services was also crucially dependent on the development of professional groupings that were licensed by the state to practise, for example doctors, nurses, social workers and teachers. This dependency is best highlighted by the role of doctors within the National Health Service (NHS), with private beds still being provided in NHS hospitals and doctors engaging in both private and NHS work, very often on the same ward. The argument has been made (see Walshe and Benson, 2005) that this failure to regulate the profession has prevented radical reform of the NHS. This argument has been a consistent theme of the New Right and neoliberals – that professional power and self-interest are blocks to reforming services, which are seen to be acting primarily in the interests of the professionals rather than their service users.

If, as is argued by Powell (2007: 2), 'the mixed economy of welfare or welfare pluralism is a vital but relatively neglected part of social policy', then it is certainly a truism in debates concerning the delivery of criminal justice at the beginning of the 21st century. One of the consequences of changes in the Probation Service to a more punitive and correctional approach has been to sever links with wider social policy agendas. Prior to 1996, probation officers were social work trained and were the key links to areas of social policy that provided the context in which the problem of crime was to be understood. This removal of crime from context, and the creation of the pathological 'offender' (see Hudson, 2003), have created an artificial and damaging schism between these two areas. Encouragingly, there are important debates now emerging about the relationship between criminology and social policy (see Knepper, 2007; Rodger, 2008). Within criminology, multi-agency responses to crime as expressions of community regeneration and accountability have been key themes in left realist criminology, which has sought to address the problems caused by crime in local communities. Since the publication of the Carter Report (Carter, 2003) (see Gough in the next chapter) and the development of the Offender Management Model (see Skinner, this volume) the consequent reforming of the role and identity of the Probation Service is starting to have a profound impact on the criminal justice system, the people who work in and alongside it, and the lives of offenders as well.

In linking theory to practice, left realism along with communitarian and so-called third way thinking (see Giddens, 1994; see below) certainly seemed to influence the early policies of the incoming New Labour government in 1997, at least in the rhetoric that was used (Newburn, 2007). Certainly, the rhetoric of efficiency, choice, accountability, democracy and community were key themes in New Labour's plans to modernise public services (see Powell, 2008) and tackle social exclusion. Although relatively small in comparison with other criminal justice agencies the Probation Service with its pivotal role in linking punishment, rehabilitation and social policy agendas meant that it seemed to fit the approach signalled by the totemic slogan 'tough on crime and tough on the causes of crime'.

Despite the New Labour agenda seeming to chime with left realism in arguing that a multi-agency response is required to respond to the varied nature of crime itself and the multifaceted nature of crime control, Walklate (2007: 63) argues that 'much of the work to date around multi-agency intervention has neglected to pay attention to the complex processes that may inhibit or facilitate such working, under what conditions, and with what kind of support from the public'. As a consequence of this neglect, within criminal justice itself the actual mechanics of 'multi-agency' service delivery and the issues arising from them have been reduced to technical competencies or taken-for-granted practices in the lives of correctional workers. These everyday practices exist within an increasingly mixed economy of correctional services drawn from statutory, not-for-profit and profit-making organisations and also have profound implications for those agencies providing services for the criminal justice system itself or services for offenders. If these issues are viewed only through a 'taken-for-granted' lens of technical competency, then we miss a much richer discussion that only a process of detailed abstractedness can offer. This deeper analysis is able to highlight the links between theory, policy and practice in a way that ultimately benefits service users and the practitioners involved as well as radically informing notions of what constitutes 'quality' and 'effectiveness'.

When considering both the mix and the dimensions of a mixed economy of criminal justice provision, an important point needs to be made, namely that the shift in identity for the Probation Service to law enforcement and public protection has also had a major impact on the range of agencies that it needs to work with to achieve its newly defined mission. That multi-agency working or a mixed economy of service provision has always been a feature of probation work is also beyond doubt. The Probation Service has always provided some support services of its own in the form of housing, hostels, alcohol and drug interventions, and seconded staff to other agencies, for example. However, what has changed is the nature of those relationships with the external organisations involved and the impact that contractual arrangements have on 'partner' agencies (see Charity Commission, 2007).

The evolution of public service provision post 1945

The implementation of the Beveridge Report (Beveridge, 1942) into legislation that set up the key institutions of the welfare state was a defining moment in the political and social history of the UK. Building on the reforms of the 1902 Liberal government, the experience of total war and the need to rebuild not only the country but also the continent of Europe, the report ushered in some new political imperatives. The report had also been commissioned by the war-time coalition government of National Unity, and so from its beginning the idea of a welfare state that looked after people 'from the cradle to the grave' enjoyed a fair degree of political consensus from both Left and Right. However, it is argued (by Mishra, 1984, among others) that it is possible to overplay this consensus. The welfare state and a mixed economy of service provision has always had its critics, with the control and delivery, and ultimately the legitimacy, of what the state could and should provide over and above that received from individuals, their families and other community groups being a matter of constant debate between Left and Right (see Mishra, 1977). However, from the point of view of electoral politics, the defining concerns were about how to govern the so-called 'centre ground' with a series of incarnations of consensual politics emerging.

The post-war consensus between Labour and the Conservatives that turned the Beveridge Report into statute and sustained it, was initially defined by 'Butskellism', which emerged from the response of the Conservative Party to the legislative agenda set by Attlee's Labour government (Cole, 2005). R.A. Butler (a Conservative) and Hugh Gaitskell (Attlee's successor) shaped the centre ground of British politics until the 1970s. This consensus was predicated on demand-side economics, full employment, and 'welfare statism' as a defining feature of liberal democracy. However, despite the apparent Thatcherite and Blairite revolutions in 1979 and 1997, which abandoned this statist approach in favour of New Right market solutions, 'small government' and the rolling back of the state, these changes can be viewed as rapid developments of evolutionary processes rather than radical junctures in policy and practice; the classical mix of agencies is still obvious. The Thatcher government of 1979 was required to provide state services for the increasing number of people claiming state benefits due to economic recession. Despite 'third way' thinking (see below), there are debates as to whether Butskellism gave way to 'Blatcherism' (Thatcher and Blair), because of the strong neoliberal individualist influences inherent within their policies. At the time of writing, with a current world economic and banking crisis, and a forthcoming general election in the UK, a key question concerns the emergence of 'Camerownism' (Cameron/Brown) and what form this might take (see Powell, 2008) in terms of levels of investment in public services to stimulate growth or a return to a more free market solution.

The management of scarce public resources, consequent levels of taxation and public spending and ultimately democratic legitimacy are at the heart of countries facing 'the challenge of redefining state–citizen relationships' (Johansson and Hvinden, 2005: 113). Current welfare governance focuses on a utilitarian, means–ends relationship with commensurate performance management, management by clearly defined objectives and market-driven solutions (see Johansson and Hvinden, 2005). This current position has emerged over time but stands in contrast to the founding principles of the welfare state; so how have we arrived at this position, indeed how do we define the current position, and can we tell whether it will evolve further? In examining these incarnations of consensus and their contribution to the developing 'mix' of the mixed economy, it is useful to utilise a model developed by Ouchi (1980, cited in Kernick, 2004) and further developed by Kernick (2004), which highlights the key themes prevalent in the management of organisations during the periods of time in question. Within the Ouchi/Kernick model, four historical approaches to the delivery of services are identified (see Table 1.1). From the perspective of organisational theory, these developments represent a move from 'mechanistic' to 'organic' modes of organisational delivery; multi-agency networks are an example of the latter.

Table 1.1: Changing models of service delivery

Approach	Key features	Mixed economy of welfare	Drivers for change	Examples of evolutionary change
Managerial command, survived until 1970s (Labour government, 1974–79)	Statism, hierarchy, central control	State as main provider, bureaucratic control, residual role for non-statutory agencies. Charities and action groups respond to gaps in service provision	Economic crises, inefficiency, need to cut public spending, loss of legitimacy	The 1972 Housing Finance Act increases role of housing associations as 'third arm' of housing policy to address housing problems. Economic crisis leads to free market approaches under Callaghan government, leading to … ↵
↳ Market (Conservative governments, 1979–97)	Competition, state as enabler, purchaser/provider split, targeting scarce resources	Through contracts, state enables more providers, competition drives up standards	Inefficiency, postcode lottery	The 1990 NHS and Community Care Act creates purchaser/provider splits and opens service provision to agencies from all sectors, creates increased inequities, leading to … ↵
↳ Integrating cooperation and competition (New Labour, 1997–2010)	State as enabler, central direction and local autonomy	Increased capacity from engagement with all sectors. All contracting agencies subject to inspection and control	Over-emphasis on competition, and centrally defined performance targets. Economic crisis	National Service Frameworks and 'evidence-based practice' but poor outcomes. Search for paradigm shift (see Pawson, 2006; Orford, 2008)
Agencies as complex adaptive systems	Agency as eco system	Soft systems methodology. Outcomes emerging from worker–service user interactions		

On coming to power, New Labour proposed a 'third way' that was, it claimed neither left–wing nor right–wing, but used the power of the market to regenerate local communities and take the best from both. However, New Right and neoliberal thinking and the consumerist language of the marketplace is evident within this approach, as outlined by Office of Public Service Reform (OPSR) (2001), which highlighted the importance of putting the customer first, through standards and accountability. The OPSR made clear that this was to be achieved through devolution and delegation, flexibility and incentives and the expansion of choice. But importantly, on coming to power New Labour had also established the Social Exclusion Unit, the remit of which was to ensure that social exclusion was addressed across all social policy areas. In 1979, the Conservative government had tried to suppress the Black Report (DHSS, 1980), which had been commissioned by the Callaghan government to look into inequalities in healthcare. The report had effectively found the existence of an inverse care law in the sense that those people who need the most services get the least, with huge inequities across the country. As in healthcare, so in a range of service provision across social welfare, which made up the key components of social exclusion and poverty. For New Labour, NSFs were the key to the social inclusion agenda (see Pycroft, 2005) and the end of the 'postcode lottery', the existence of which meant that the quality and/or quantity of services experienced became the 'geographies of life and death'.

These inequalities inherent within the system had been exacerbated by the creation of competitive tendering processes and internal markets under the Conservatives, which had invariably seen contracts awarded on the basis of best price, without consideration of the quality of the services provided. The intention of NSFs was therefore to have strong regulatory components that determine quality, alongside occupational standards designed to ensure a properly trained workforce. The NSFs were created across all social policy areas including, for example, health and mental health, education, criminal justice, housing and drugs. Alongside these regulatory components, the government set ambitious targets that had to be met in order to secure funding. To meet these targets, there had to be an increase in service capacity and efficiency, thus leading to enhanced multi-agency arrangements.

Ostensibly, in its eschewing of ideology, New Labour was concerned with 'what works' and evidence-based practice (see Pawson, 2006), and took the view that if an organisation could provide a quality service, at the right price and with the right outcomes, then it made no difference whether it was a statutory, non-statutory or private agency. While the Conservatives had promoted the benefits of the private sector (see DHSS, 1983) there had also been increased recognition by government of the role of not-for-profit agencies in improving public services. Many such organisations had developed in the absence of statutory services, and had achieved considerable influence in policy networks (for example, MIND in mental health, and the women's refuge movement). In tackling social exclusion, it was thought that some of these groups may have expertise in specialist areas and be best placed to deliver some services, particularly with difficult-to-reach groups. It was seen that in the right circumstances non-statutory agencies can deliver more effective services and provide better value for money (NAO, 2005) than statutory agencies.

The third way approach was also a partnership between central government and local communities, with the centre setting standards, and providing resources in return for increased efficiency and performance. This remaking of governance (see Newman, 2005) based on the dismantling of the post-war social democratic settlement, and the recasting of the social contract based on responsibility and choice, looked to organisations to respond to the voices of their consumers in shaping the services provided. All of the NSFs except the one for criminal justice have an emphasis on service user participation in the planning and delivery of services (see Pycroft, 2005, 2006), and all organisations have had to demonstrate how service user views have informed practice. To meet the needs of a regulated marketplace and to direct central funds into local service provision, a host of virtual organisations have developed to commission services based on local need. These include, for example, Primary Care Trusts, Hospital Trusts, Drug Action Teams, Supporting People consortia, and Crime and Disorder Partnerships. These organisations often have complex and overlapping existences, with, for example, Drug Action Teams having no statutory basis but still providing the conduit for the National Treatment Agency for Substance Misuse to channel its resources. Some Drug Action Teams are merged with Crime and Disorder Partnerships that do have statutory powers under the 1998 Criminal Justice Act, while some are not.

As an example and in relation to the modernisation agenda of New Labour and the NHS, Kernick (2004: 98) summarised the proposed changes as follows:

- The clinical discretion of doctors was to be reduced with the application of scientific knowledge deduced from expert research and translated into clinical guidelines that all practitioners had to adhere to.
- A culture of continuous professional development was to be established based on performance management and the achievement of clearly defined targets.
- Services were to be redesigned drawing on the experiences of all sectors, with an emphasis on the patient's experience and their care pathway.

In reality, all professional groupings delivering social policy objectives would recognise these changes, the criminal justice system included. For the criminal justice system, the establishment of a national service and the 'what works' agenda has followed the same process, and in the same ways that 'what works' has had disappointing outcomes (see Pycroft, 2010), then the ability of the NHS to influence performance has been limited (Kernick, 2004).

These disappointing outcomes are, however, nothing new. In seeking to provide value for money to the taxpayer, and a quality of service to the service user that is efficient and targeted, successive governments have been perplexed at their inability to produce the best outcomes. From the restructuring of social services departments in the early 1970s following the publication of the Seebohm Report (1968) through to the creation of the National Offender Management Service public sector reform has been continuous; a key question then becomes why organisations do not appear to work in the ways in which they are intended to. If we take the example of the New Labour approach, why, for example, does multi-agency working provide so much promise, but raise so many problems and issues, which the contributors to this book attest to?

Complexity theory – a new paradigm?

Increasingly, approaches based around ideas of complexity theory are being used in the study of organisations and the delivery of services (see Guastello et al, 2009). In varying levels of abstractedness, complex multi-agented systems are a ubiquitous feature of our lives and the universe in which we live (although we are probably more used to identifying them in 'nature' than in the realities of our everyday lives). However, various academic disciplines, including physics, chemistry, biology, psychology and the social sciences, whether studying the behaviour of atoms, eco systems, planets, families, societies or governments, are all increasingly attesting to the complex and interrelated nature of life itself. It is beyond the scope of this chapter to examine complexity theory and its various offshoots in detail, but it is important to note that this approach has clear implications for people, groups and organisations that seek to influence the complex nature of organisational delivery and to improve the lives of service users.

Complexity theory is concerned with non-linearity and the findings from a range of scientific inquiries, which show that change is not (necessarily) proportional to inputs (Guastello and Liebovitch, 2009). We tend to think in a linear and traditional medico-scientific way in which a problem is identified, the components are separated and are treated with the aim of an overall effect. Within this framework, ideas of dosage and appropriate intensity of treatment are seen to be important. Typically, politicians want to allocate a certain amount of money to, for example, the National Probation Service and demand specific performance measures on the basis of that investment in enforcing orders, and the numbers of people rehabilitated and desisting from crime. In the words of Kernick (2006: 385), 'the confident assumption is that a simple relationship exists between cause and effect in a system that can be understood by reducing it into its component parts'. This assumption underestimates the complexity of the environments in which social policy objectives are delivered and begs the question of how to best address that complexity.

In considering some of the social problems that governments and societies have to contend with and which present the biggest challenges to organisational responses, it can be seen that the problems themselves are multi-agented. They very often combine medical, psychological and social problems, with addictions, mental health problems and obesity being obvious examples (see Pycroft, 2007). It is clear from the above that a multi-agency approach as a response to those problems is not unproblematic; it is an approach that has strengths and weaknesses whereby proposed solutions can become part of a problem, and apparent problems (from a commissioner's or politician's point of view) may also provide solutions. These responses mirror the inherent complexity of the problem by having a range of services and interventions to meet what are seen as its component parts.

It is argued by Burns and Stalker (1961, cited in Dooley, 2009: 436) that mechanistic organisations are best suited to stable environments whereas organic modes of delivery are appropriate to volatile environments. This judgement is based on the idea that a control system must have at least the same level of complexity or greater than the system it is controlling. The organic approach is characterised by 'distributed knowledge and authority; local and lateral interactions leading to constantly changing tasks; the loosening of bureaucratic constraints; a network structure of control, authority and communication; and task over obedience, expertise over rank' (Burns and Stalker, 1961, cited in Dooley, 2009: 436).

The trick perhaps is to find a balance between accountability and creativity, and the use of smarter performance measures that do not become an end in themselves and thus run the risk of distorting service delivery. This 'soft systems' approach places the worker–service user relationship at the heart of the organisation, which evolves around the resolution of known and emerging issues. An example of the importance of this can be taken from both core correctional practices (Dowden and Andrews, 2004) in working with offenders and motivational work with problems of addiction (Miller, 2006), both of which demonstrate the importance of empathic, trusting relationships. In implementing multi-agency solutions, the work of Partridge (2004) demonstrates that offenders are happy to access a range of services as long as they have an established relationship with their offender manager, who is a central point of contact.

A case example

A well-established charity provided a range of services in its local area, had strong links with the local community and was seen as an important community resource. The charity provided a purpose-built residential detox and rehabilitation centre and worked very closely with other agencies to plan and provide services. The bulk of the funding for the detox and rehabilitation came from jointly commissioned contracts with the local health authority and social services department. The area in which the service was located was the last to implement the 1990 NHS and Community Care Act with a required purchaser/provider split. Up until then the service had carried out its own assessments 24 hours a day, 365 days a year and achieved 100% capacity for detox and 95% for rehabilitation. The intended changes were that all referrals would come through the community alcohol and drugs team, who would assess each referral for suitability, and operate on the basis of client choice. The detox service would be purchased by the Primary Care Trust as this was seen as a medical issue (requiring general practitioner assessment), and rehabilitation (a psychosocial service) would be purchased by social services (requiring a care management assessment).

When these new arrangements were implemented, assessments could only be carried out by care managers working 9am to 5pm, Monday to Friday (closed bank holidays, etc). The net result was empty detox beds and an increase in people accessing Accident & Emergency services. Also, despite being in the same building it was not possible to go straight from detox to rehabilitation without further assessment, which meant being discharged, being put on a waiting list, being assessed, then being put on a further waiting list. A consequence of this was that relapse rates increased, with people undertaking several detoxes before accessing rehabilitation. Occupancy fell significantly for both detox and rehabilitation and the service is now closed. Despite demand, there is no longer a local residential detox centre.

> The pros and cons of these changes can be argued from a number of different perspectives, but what do you see as the intended and unintended consequences of these policy changes?

In the example given of implementing a required purchaser/provider split to provide value for money and to drive up standards and service user choice, the net consequence was to increase the complexity of the service delivery. It was an essentially mechanistic response to the problem of drug and alcohol addiction, which, because it is a dynamic issue, gave rise to a whole host of unintended outcomes. Within a complexity framework it is not possible for external managers, commissioners or politicians to act like 'puppeteers' and manipulate a social system at will from outside the system. Despite having differing linkages, resources and motivations, they are all part of the same system in which organisation and environment co-evolve (see Dooley, 2009).

Conclusion

The use of this type of analysis is not intended to provide easy linear answers to complex non-linear problems. Systems that are highly coupled (with strong links between its component parts) can stifle creativity and the ability to respond to emergent problems. In this sense the charitable sector continued post 1945 and flourished outside of bureaucratic state control, thus gaining a reputation for innovation. Systems that are loosely coupled may be more creative and responsive, but may lack consistency and longevity as in market solutions to social problems. The history of the mixed economy in the UK has seen the emergence of differing approaches to trying to hold onto and control organisations, as well as defining their performance. The reasons for this are of course laudable: as taxpayers we demand that our democratic representatives ensure value for money and equality of access and service delivery from our health and social welfare agencies. However, as our understanding of the behaviour of complex systems (of which the mixed economy is but one example) emerges, then we may have to review the standards by which we make those judgements.

Summary of key points

■ Multi-agency working is a key facet of the mixed economy of service provision. This mixed economy has continued to evolve over the last 60 years.

■ Changes in criminal justice service delivery are commensurate with changes in other areas of social policy delivery.

■ All forms of service delivery experience intended and unintended consequences from their implementation.

■ Complexity theory helps us to analyse the reasons for these consequences.

Further reading

Guastello, S., Koopmans, M. and Pincus, D. (eds) (2009) *Chaos and Complexity in Psychology: The Theory of Nonlinear Dynamical Systems*. Cambridge: Cambridge University Press.

Powell, M. (ed) (2007) *Understanding the Mixed Economy of Welfare*. Bristol: The Policy Press.

Powell, M. (ed) (2008) *Modernising the Welfare State: The Blair Legacy*. Bristol: The Policy Press.

Pycroft, A. (2010) *Understanding and Working with Substance Misusers*. London: Sage Publications.

References

Beveridge, W. (1942) *Social Insurance and Allied Services*. London: HMSO.

Carter, P. (2003) *Managing Offenders, Reducing Crime: A New Approach: Report of the Correctional Services Review*. Carter Report. London: Prime Minister's Strategy Unit.

Charity Commission (2007) *Stand and Deliver: The Future for Charities Providing Public Services*. Liverpool: Charity Commission.

Cole, M. (2005) 'Quangos: the debate of the 1970's in Britain', *Contemporary British History*, 19(3), 321-52.

DHSS (Department of Health and Social Security) (1980) *Inequalities in Health: Report of a Research Working Group*. London: HMSO.

DHSS (1983) *NHS Management Inquiry Report*. London: DHSS.

Dooley, K.J. (2009) 'Organizational psychology', in Guastello, S., Koopmans, M. and Pincus, D. (eds) *Chaos and Complexity in Psychology: The theory of Nonlinear Dynamical Systems* (pp 434-46). Cambridge: Cambridge University Press.

Dowden, C. and Andrews, D. (2004) 'Importance of staff practice in delivering effective correctional treatment: a meta-analytic review of core correctional practice', *International Journal of Offender Therapy and Comparative Criminology*, 48(2), 203-14.

Giddens, A. (1994) *Beyond Left and Right: The Future of Radical Politics*. Cambridge: Cambridge University Press.

Guastello, S., Koopmans, M. and Pincus, D. (eds) (2009) *Chaos and Complexity in Psychology: The Theory of Nonlinear Dynamical Systems*. Cambridge: Cambridge University Press.

Guastello, S. and Liebovitch, L.S. (2009) 'Introduction to nonlinear dynamics and complexity', in Guastello, S., Koopmans, M. and Pincus, D. (eds) *Chaos and Complexity in Psychology: The Theory of Nonlinear Dynamical Systems* (pp 1-36). Cambridge: Cambridge University Press.

HM Treasury (2005) *Exploring the Role of the Third Sector in Public Service Delivery and Reform: A Discussion Document*. London: The Stationery Office.

Hudson, B. (2003) *Justice in the Risk Society: Challenging and Re-affirming Justice in Late Modernity*. London: Sage Publications.

Jessop, B. (1999) 'The changing governance of welfare: recent trends in its primary functions, scale and modes of coordination', *Social Policy and Administration*, 33(4), 348-59.

Johansson, H. and Hvinden, B. (2005) 'Welfare governance and the remaking of citizenship', in Newman, J. (ed) *Remaking Governance: Peoples, Politics and the Public Sphere* (pp 101-18). Bristol: The Policy Press.

Kernick, D. (2004) 'The search for the correct organizational solution for the NHS', in Kernick, D. (ed) *Complexity and Healthcare Organization: A View from the Street* (pp 93-104). Oxford: Radcliffe Publishing.

Kernick, D. (2006) 'Wanted – new methodologies for health service research: is complexity theory the answer?', *Family Practice*, 23, 385-90.

Knepper, P. (2007) *Criminology and Social Policy*. London: Sage Publications.

Leathard, A. (2005) 'Evaluating interagency working in health and social care: politics, policies and outcomes for service users', in Taylor, D. and Balloch, S. (eds) *The Politics of Evaluation: Participation and Policy Implementation* (pp 135-52). Bristol: The Policy Press.

Miller, W. (2006) 'Motivational factors in addictive behaviors', in Miller, W. and Carrol, K. (eds) *Rethinking Substance Abuse: What the Science Shows and What We Should Do About It* (pp 134-52). New York: Plenum.

Mishra, R. (1977) *Society and Social Policy: Theories and Practice of Welfare*. London: Macmillan.

Mishra, R. (1984) *The Welfare State in Crisis*. Milton Keynes: The Open University.

NAO (National Audit Office) (2005) *Working with the Third Sector*. London: The Stationery Office.

Newburn, T. (2007) *Criminology*. Cullompton: Willan Publishing.

Newman, J. (ed) (2005) *Remaking Governance: Peoples, Politics and the Public Sphere*. Bristol: The Policy Press.

OPSR (Office of Public Service Reform) (2001) *Reforming our Public Services: Principles into Practice*. London: The Stationery Office.

Orford, J. (2008) 'Asking the right questions in the right way: the need for a shift in research on psychological treatments for addiction', *Addiction*, 103(6), 875-85.

Partridge, S. (2004) *Examining Case Management Models for Community Sentences*. London: Home Office.

Pawson, R. (2006) *Evidence-based Policy: A Realist Perspective*. London: Sage Publications.

Powell, M. (2007) 'The mixed economy of welfare and the social division of welfare, in Powell, M. (ed) *Understanding the Mixed Economy of Welfare* (pp 1-22). Bristol: The Policy Press.

Powell, M. (2008) 'Introduction: modernising the welfare state', in Powell, M. (ed) *Modernising the Welfare State: The Blair Legacy* (pp 1-16). Bristol: The Policy Press.

Pycroft, A. (2005) 'A new chance for rehabilitation: multi agency provision and potential under NOMS', in Winstone, J. and Pakes, F. (eds) *Community Justice: Issues for Probation and Criminal Justice* (pp 130-41). Cullompton: Willan Publishing.

Pycroft, A. (2006) 'Too little, too late? Service user involvement and the Probation Service', *Community Justice Matters*, 64, 36-7.

Pycroft, A. (2007) 'The psychology of addiction: are there more questions than answers?', in Pakes, F. and Winstone, J. (eds) *Psychology and Crime* (pp 131-47). Cullompton: Willan Publishing.

Pycroft, A. (2010) *Understanding and Working with Substance Misusers*. London: Sage Publications.

Rodger, J. (2008) *Criminalising Social Policy: Anti-Social Behaviour and Welfare in a De-civilised Society*. Cullompton: Willan Publishing.

Seebohm Report (1968) *Report of the Committee on Local Authority and Allied Personal Social Services*. London: HMSO.

Sterling, R. (2005) 'Promoting democratic governance through partnerships?', in Newman, J. (ed) *Remaking Governance: Peoples, Politics and the Public Sphere* (pp 139-58). Bristol: The Policy Press.

Walklate, S. (2007) *Understanding Criminology: Current Theoretical Debates*. Maidenhead: McGraw-Hill/Open University Press.

Walshe, K. and Benson, L. (2005) 'Time for radical reform', *British Medical Journal*, 330(7506), 1504-6.

CHAPTER 2

Multi-agency working in corrections: cooperation and competition in probation practice

Dennis Gough

Aims of the chapter

■ To trace the development of partnerships and multi-agency approaches to professional practice in the Probation Service.
■ To highlight the changing ethos of multi-agency cooperation in the sector, highlighting its move from cooperative practice to working in competition.
■ To highlight key overarching themes regarding multi-agency working.

The Probation Service has a long and proud history of relationships with a range of statutory and non-statutory organisations (Nellis, 2002; Rumgay, 2003). Indeed, the Probation Service's unique position within the criminal justice system has made effective working relationships essential with sentencers, police and prison officers, and a whole host of organisations in the voluntary and community sector. As Rumgay (2003: 195) suggests, the Probation Service has traditionally operated simultaneously within the formalised and statutory criminal justice system and localised, community environments. Probation officers have a long tradition of occupying professional space that involves advising sentencers on the most appropriate punishment and working with offenders in their localities to improve their social position and with community organisations in order to impact upon the risk factors that fuel offending behaviour.

In contemporary times, multi-agency working has enjoyed a new impetus in the era of criminal justice modernisation, shared strategic aims and 'joined-up justice' under New Labour (McLaughlin et al, 2001). 'Partnership mania' (Crawford, 1999: 58) has characterised the recent development of the Probation Service culminating in the new vision from Carter's (2003) review of correctional services. As a result of Carter's vision we have witnessed the introduction of a new ethos in the nature of the relationship between the statutory, the private and the third sector. The central idea from the review of correctional services is that working relationships between the Probation Service and voluntary and private organisations could be characterised by contestability or competition, whereby the state would compete with other providers to win contracts to deliver services to offenders. This signals a change in our understanding of the terms of engagement between the state and multi-agency providers from the non-statutory sector. Carter's end vision could be that the Probation Service would be reduced to being merely one of a number of competitors in a 'mixed economy of corrections' involving the voluntary and private sectors.

The development of multi-agency arrangements in probation

The Probation Service's history of multi-agency working or partnership arrangements entered a new phase in the 1990s in England and Wales. Rumgay (2003) has noted that this time represented a 'heyday' for partnership approaches, with the idea appearing for the first time in probation strategic documents. This characterised a move from ad-hoc multi-agency arrangements and local informality to such arrangements becoming key strategies or business plans. In the Home Office's (1990) document *Partnership in Dealing with Offenders in the Community*, the government's clarion call was to promote and extend the relations with the private and voluntary sector. Partnership was defined as 'relations between the Probation Service and the private and voluntary sectors, whether on the basis of grants of payments, or services in kind or joint working relationships' (Home Office, 1993). In emphasising the benefits of multi-agency working and partnership in terms of efficiency and effectiveness, the new strategic direction for the Probation Service was seen clearly in terms of moving away from its monopoly in terms of interventions with offenders in the community. Now the energies of other providers could be harnessed to complement and work cooperatively with the statutory provision of services to offenders.

Within probation, the development of partnerships and cooperative practice as a key policy has arguably two key drivers. First, the strategic direction of the New Labour government elected in 1997 accelerated the desire for a 'joined-up' criminal justice system. Second, during the 1990s, the changes to probation professional assessment and practice from a holistic and welfarist stance to a crime reduction agency responsible for identifying and eradicating a whole gamut of individual 'risk factors' that underpin offender criminal behaviour, necessitated the development of a strategy to build capacity in the number of interventions offered to offenders.

This move from in-house provision to the contracting of offender interventions from outside the statutory sector reflected the more radical broker/provider of service split in health and social care under the 1990 NHS and Community Care Act. Similar if not quite so radical developments in probation strategy clearly represented a muted attempt to 'roll back the frontiers of the state' when it came to the provision of certain interventions with offenders. As such, after discussion documents such as *Partnership in Dealing with Offenders in the Community* (Home Office, 1990), local Probation Service began to fund and second staff to voluntary organisations such as Victim Support in order to begin to understand and shape probation interventions with this new and increasingly important 'client group'.

The development and implementation of structured Third Wave assessment tools such as the Offender Assessment System resulted in the Probation Service and probation officers identifying and assessing a complex amalgam of criminogenic needs. Such developments in the quality and thoroughness of assessments of offending behaviour necessitated a larger number of specialist agencies and professionals to deal effectively with substance misuse, housing problems, mental health problems, financial difficulties and other 'criminogenic needs' (McGuire, 1995). In light of this, the probation officer during the late 1990s found themselves removed from their role as an agent of personal change. Rather, the role became reduced to case 'managing' and ensuring compliance with court orders, with other providers actually engaging with the offender to change their lives (Home Office, 1990). This process of partnership working and collaborative endeavour initially was centrally allocated from the Supervision Grants Scheme before being devolved to local Probation Areas, who were informed they should spend at least 5% (then later raised to 7%) of the Area budget on partnership activity with the independent sector.

The high watermark for multi-agency working as the overarching approach to crime control has to be the 1998 Crime and Disorder Act. This Act placed a legal duty on the police and local authorities to undertake detailed crime audits and to work in collaboration with the voluntary and private sectors to address such concerns. As Crawford (1999) notes, probation officers joined a whole host of other 'responsibilised' (Garland, 2001) organisations and specialists such as town planners, teachers, youth workers, health service workers and business people to reduce crime in localities. In addition, in relation to youth crime, the creation of multi-agency Youth Offending Teams signalled a further criminalisation of the raison d'être of a range of organisations and professions traditionally outside the formal criminal justice system who would have new responsibilities to manage and reduce youth crime.

While the 1998 Crime and Disorder Act can be seen as the pinnacle of the development of the multi-agency approach to crime control in England and Wales, the impact of the Crime Prevention and Community Safety agenda has had limited impact on probation's core focus. As Crawford (1999) notes, for an organisation that government sought to change throughout the 1990s with calls for a merger with the Prison Service and an abandonment of its social work values that underpinned its work with offenders, crime prevention was seen as a way of resisting the increasing correctionalist and punitive demands for the service. Probation's work in the crime prevention field offered a new-found legitimacy and professionalism at a time of threats and profound change.

Clift (this volume) notes that even in terms of public protection work which has developed and remained the Probation Service's core professional terrain, the field is marked by a multi-agency approach involving statutory players and organisations with a 'duty to cooperate' with the Multi-agency Public Protection Procedures. Even here, where the Probation Service, the Prison Service and the police work in a highly politicised and controlling penal agenda, we see health professionals, social workers and in some cases private sector tagging providers working together in a sort of 'risk complex' to share information, make shared decisions and ensure that the aims of the state for protection and security are met (Garland, 1997).

The incorporation of private sector electronic monitoring as a form of punishment in the community, originally espoused in the 1991 Criminal Justice Act, exposed the Probation Service to the realities of working in tandem with the private sector security companies. Although originally the Probation Service had great misgivings about the relationship between partial incapacitation and its traditional rehabilitative approaches to working with offenders through the use of Home Detention Curfew, the Service quickly muted its opposition and arguably now views such private providers as Group 4 Security Services and Premier Monitoring Services as legitimate partners in the supervision of court orders with an electronic monitoring component. Indeed, in relation to the management of dangerous offenders, probation officers have actively sought the use of technology by private providers as a key defensible approach to securing control and 'hawk-like' supervision in the community.

The creation of the National Probation Service in 2001 further cemented the position of multi-agency working and partnership as a key value of the new national service. In *The New Choreography* (NPS, 2001), the conceptualisation of partnership focuses on the roles that other non-statutory organisations can occupy to ensure that the National Probation Service achieves its outcomes. As a result, the stated aim is to 'build capacity' in probation work and add value by 'using a highly collaborative approach to add value to the capacity of the NPS [National Probation Service] to achieve its expected outcomes' (NPS, 2001: 8).

Multi-agency working in 'NOMS world'

The creation of the National Offender Management Service (NOMS) has renewed interest in the dominance of multi-agency working in probation. With the 2007 Offender Management Act, NOMS represents what amounts to probation's own NHS and Community Care Act nearly two decades later. The merger with the Prison Service aimed to break down the silos of the two organisations and encourage closer working relationships encapsulated in the creation of a unified correctional agency. This closer alignment of working culture and practices had already been achieved with the Probation Service's closer working relationships with police officers within public protection and persistent and priority offender work. Carter (2003) called for a split between offender management (and the management of court orders) from programmes and interventions designed to effectively reduce recidivism. In Carter's new approach this split between the management function of probation from treatment or rehabilitative service delivery echoed the purchaser/provider split in adult social care. Offender managers would therefore broker a range of interventions provided by a mixed economy of statutory, voluntary and private service delivery to offenders. The call from Carter, which was subsequently adopted by the government, was for greater use of multi-agency arrangements in work with offenders. This picture of multi-agency arrangements was slightly more developed in Carter's vision in that it also necessitated an element of competitiveness and loss of probation's monopoly of managing court punishments. For Carter and for Blair the issue was who offered the most effective intervention and value for money rather than ideological concerns with regard to which sector delivers.

Therefore, for Carter (2003), the Probation Service becomes only one of a range of competitors in the offender management and interventions market. Helen Edwards, Chief Executive of NOMS in 2006, sums up Carter's central proposals of competition and contestability by saying:

> We want to get a wider range of partners involved in managing offenders and cutting re-offending. Therefore, we will legislate to open up probation to other providers, and will only award contracts to those who can prove they will deliver reductions in reoffending, and keep the public safe. We need to bring in expertise from the private and voluntary sectors to drive up the quality and performance of community punishments. (NOMS, 2005)

As Rumgay (2007) has noted, the vision provides a further challenge to the Probation Service's traditional ability to protect its professional territory in core work of providing advice to sentencers in the form of Pre-Sentence Reports, and the supervision of offenders in the community and after release from prison. Its relations with the voluntary sector and private industry may over time become less about complementary practice and harmonious professional relations than about relationships based on competitiveness and increasing its own market share by securing contracts in the corrections industry. This extension of contestability to probation's traditional professional terrain, the management of the court order, has alarmed Rumgay (2005) and other academic commentators and the professional association of probation officers (NAPO).

The government's blueprint for the market in probation – *Restructuring Probation to Reduce Offending* (NOMS, 2005) – outlines how NOMS and regional directors of offender management will commission services across Probation Area boundaries and across the custodial and community divide from any organisation in the statutory, private or third sectors. Probation Boards would become Probation Trusts in readiness for competition with a range of other providers, and would not seek to exist if new business is not secured. As Rumgay (2007) has witnessed, the discourse around multi-agency working has shifted from the language of complementary practice and mutual cooperation to contestability and competition, where old colleagues and partners could now become competitors.

Key themes in multi-agency working in corrections

As a way of responding to crime and disorder, multi-agency working has developed in a somewhat technical sense. The idea that combining the respective talents and resources of a variety of organisations must be more effective than leaving increasingly complex tasks to a single organisation is a somewhat taken-for-granted position. Rarely in the criminal justice system have multi-agency approaches to offending behaviour been scrutinised. Leaving aside the present volume, there have been few attempts to unpick the difficulties inherent in joining up statutory, voluntary and private sector bodies and indeed the debate has foundered on the technicalities of constructing 'duties to comply', 'contestability arrangements' and the development of a contract culture. Few have asked the question: what is the impact of engaging the charitable and business sector in the explicit punishment of offenders? Fewer still have asked: what will the 'penal voluntary sector' actually look like when contestability and the marketplace in corrections is in full swing (Corcoran, 2009)? There remain key issues in multi-agency working that require academic and research attention.

Multi-agency working and effectiveness

While much has been written about the importance of multi-agency working in probation and the human services more generally, there is currently a dearth of academic research or political interest into the effectiveness of multi-agency arrangements in probation work (Rumgay, 2003, 2007). There remains an embryonic literature and research base as to effective multi-agency working arrangements in the crime and disorder field (Crawford, 1999); however, in probation work there is little research evidence as to whether the co-option of the voluntary and private sector adds value to the arrangements provided by the statutory sector. Moreover, we know very little as to what constitutes the key ingredients from which effective multi-agency arrangements are made. What we do hear in the media's reporting of the correctional field, is the contribution of poor inter-agency arrangements to several failings in the system's ability to protect society from dangerous criminals. Furthermore, multi-agency arrangements are seen to contribute to the absence of shared understandings of roles and duties, quality communication between agencies and swift multi-agency action to remedy the dangerous situation (Clift, this volume; Nash and Williams, 2008). Thus far, we have heard more about the failings of multi-agency working than about its effectiveness.

Some commentators such as Nellis (2002) have posited that the hegemonic status of multi-agency arrangements arises more from political doctrine and 'third way' politics than empirical evidence to suggest it as the best way forward. As such, it is unchallenged and yet remains untested in its ability to improve quality in corrections (Nellis, 2002). In terms of quality, Rumgay (2007) notes that a frenzy of partnership activity in recent years has resulted in tensions and short-termism rather than a profound change to the quality of interventions delivered to offenders. Furthermore, the Probation Service has had to build capacity to develop a whole new layer of bureaucracy in order to manage the multitude of multi-agency processes in arrangements such as Supporting People, Local Area Safeguarding Children Boards, and Crime and Disorder Reduction Partnerships.

Moves to reshape multi-agency working and incorporate elements of competition between organisations from the government's reshaping probation agenda arise not from a pilot study into such a move or an abundance of evidence, but from a glance across at the prison privatisation strategy and an unflinching confidence in the powers of the market in social provision. Fifteen years after partnership was first adopted in a formal sense, questions remain about whether policy makers and practitioners are able to ascertain the successful elements or conditions that make healthy and successful partnerships, or those which create disastrous ones. Multi-agency working is often taken for granted as being a universally good thing.

So when multi-agency arrangements are being created in the field of probation, we need to question whether issues such as building of consensus on achieving realistic outcomes, sharing agendas, information and knowledge, sharing accountability and outlining key values are fully considered. Or is consideration reduced to a process of securing best value and efficiencies from a limited group of competitors and the signing of contracts?

Multi-agency working, values and ethics

The increasing presence of both the voluntary and private sectors in the probation function may bring improved efficiency and innovation. What may be less apparent is the importance of a new range of values and ethics in the work with offenders. The government has placed great emphasis on the third sector's ability to innovate and develop reflexive interventions for service users. Indeed, as Pycroft (2006) has charted, the strength of the third sector remains a considerable challenge for the newly created Probation Trusts. In some sense, Probation Areas already appear to be playing catch-up in their ability to reflect service user views and demands in shaping their services. In addition, the 'penal voluntary sector' (Corcoran, 2009) may have to adapt its own traditional value base and ethical stances away from service user perspectives, should it successfully participate in a criminal justice system riddled with political considerations and where service user (offender) rights are a poor second to the rights and wishes of victims and the public. In a conference entitled 'Partners or prisoners? Voluntary sector independence in the world of commissioning and contestability', the NOMS third sector head, Tina Jenkins, concluded that successful charities would be those who could turn their attention to these new 'clients' or central players in the criminal justice system much like the reconfigured Probation Service has done over the last decade (Garland, 1997).

Furthermore, the voluntary sector's involvement with offenders has traditionally maintained a strong rehabilitative and welfarist stance (Garside, 2004; Corner, 2006). It may be a misnomer to talk about the third sector's ability to bring innovation and creativity to what is essentially punishment. Questions could be asked about the third sector's ability to bring innovation and uniqueness to punishments that are increasingly exclusionary and punitivism. For example, how would the penal voluntary sector (Corcoran, 2009) feel about administering a pilot that withdrew state benefits from offenders who were non-compliant with their community order?

The greater role afforded to the private sector has even greater value and ethical considerations. There has been significant concern and controversy regarding the increasing marketisation and privatisation of sections of the criminal justice system and the world of probation work has been no exception. Commercial interests in administering punishment challenge existing ethics of punishment. Malcolm Feeley's (2002) analysis of the effects of private sector entrepreneurs outlines how innovation and attempts to increase market share create demand for, and then supply of, new forms of control or punishment from a commercial standpoint. In terms of community corrections, Feeley (2002) asserts that the involvement of private sector business ethics can radically change the nature of what community punishment can be. He charts the rise and growth of private sector security firms with surveillance technologies to monitor the movements of individuals and how such companies have seen the community punishment field as a growth area. Of note is Feeley's concern that the private sector or 'entrepreneurs of punishment' do not merely replace existing forms of punishments with more effective ones but rather can actually change the nature of the punishment itself. For Feeley (2002) and Nellis (2007), electronic monitoring, voice recognition and the use of the polygraph can replace the subtle care and control value base that has traditionally characterised the human relationship between offender and state probation officer. As such technological surveillance and control become core parts of punishment and human supervisory relationships based on trust, motivational work and challenge move to being a distance second. Indeed, a replacement of people by technology is what Nellis has coined 'techno corrections' (Nellis, 2006). Such a move is not as implausible as it may seem. In 2004, the then Minister for Correctional Services, Paul Goggins, heralded the future of community sentences as characterised by 'geo-fencing to enforce exclusion zones' with an assertion that 'we have to open the possibility of tagging to all adult offenders' in a community, which could resemble a 'prison without the bars' (Nellis, 2006: 60). Such a move is mirrored by Ethnie Wallis's career move from director of the National Probation Service to senior partner with Fujitsu Siemens with a brief to increase the amount of technology in the criminal justice system.

Despite continual protestations, to consider outcomes rather than ideology, values and ethics about who delivers does really matter in criminal justice. The incorporation of commercial interests into the punishment of offenders is not value free. Feeley's (2002) and Nellis's (2006) work encourages us to see how efficiency saving can be coupled with a desire to increase market share of the probation function. As a result, new techniques can be developed in order to grow and capture more of the market, which may have significant results for the character of punishment as we know it. Perhaps the worst case of commercial interests affecting the practices of punishment is in the case of Pennsylvania Judges Mark Ciavarella and Michael Conahan, who are said to have received $2.6 million for ensuring that juvenile suspects were jailed in prisons operated by private sector prison companies. Some of the youths were jailed despite the objections of their probation officers and most had no legal representations. Incredibly, some of the young people had committed no crime. An estimated 2,000 juveniles have been sentenced by Ciavarella since the scheme started in 2002 where both judges would have received financial incentives to maximise their use of private sector custodial facilities (Monbiot, 2009).

Harnessing diversity or replicating the state?

The third sector's creativity, its independence from government and its involvement of thousands of volunteers (including offenders and ex-offenders and mentors) can break down barriers, change attitudes and build the motivation necessary to bring about positive and lasting change. The stress on the third sector's difference is inherent in policy discussions. 'The third sector has unique and positive attributes which are different from the public and private sector' (Hanson, 2008: Foreword). It has 'specialist knowledge' and with its independence comes innovation and reflexivity. Indeed, some commentators have gone so far as to say that the entire £1 billion NOMS project will actually be changed by the tidal wave of change unleashed by the voluntary sector (Sutcliffe, 2006). The strengths of the sector, it is argued, lie in its diversity, its capacity for innovation and dissent as well as in its local roots.

It is clear that by transforming the number and complexity of approaches to interventions with offenders the third sector's diversity and difference is highly valued. Of significant pride is the development of service user designed and led interventions, which the third sector has a unique track record of undertaking. In addition, voluntary and community organisations are seen as gatekeepers to mainstream services for offenders with a multitude of problems that impact directly on their ability to move away from criminal behaviour. This is particularly pertinent for substance misuse services, where offenders on licence or a community order will need to continue the work undertaken as part of their punishment after it ends. Similarly, Helen Mills' (2009) work discusses how the voluntary and community sector could be an important provider of culturally responsive interventions delivered to black and minority ethnic offenders who have been traditionally hard to reach by mainstream statutory criminal justice agencies (Mills, 2009; Hilder, this volume).

How this 'innovative' approach to working with offenders by voluntary and community sector agencies will be applied to punishment is an important consideration. There is much to admire and keep in the third sector's ability to deliver interventions to disenfranchised and vulnerable individuals in society from 'outside' of the criminal justice system. By presenting their services as client-led, non-compulsory, non-punitive and engaging, traditional interventions from voluntary organisations have more chance of reaching those hard to reach than the coercive and punitive state. The third sector remains largely wedded to a welfarist, helping and humanistic approach to working with people when it exists outside the criminal justice system. The key challenge and concern is when it operates as a fully fledged member of the state's network of punishment. Will voluntary organisations be able to resist the mission creep towards public protection and risk-based interventions, the termination of interventions and services based on technical 'breaches' of court orders? Recent talk of 'non-negotiable support' in the third sector (by the Youth Justice Board) may be evidence of a new term of engagement with citizens who happen to be part of the criminal justice caseload.

What is an important consideration here is that by co-opting the third sector in a commercialised probation function, thereby involving voluntary organisations in the central function of punishing offenders, what one can risk is the erosion of the independence, creativity and flexibility of intervention that the third sector can offer and which were sought in the first place. Rather than bringing the sector's strengths of innovation, advocacy and creativity of ideas to the table, the possibility is that by competing with the state, voluntary organisations will not have the room to manoeuvre in delivering community punishments such as unpaid work or drug treatment requirements. As a result of the state's presence, increased managerialism, the narrowness of the contract culture, National Standards and the politics of punishment, the third sector in probation may result in conformity, control and a reconfiguration of the voluntary sector in the image of the state. Squeezed out will be the sector's traditional independence to campaign and challenge penal policy and the service user or client-centred nature of its work.

These are important considerations as only with independence and freedom can the third sector offer offenders anything different from the traditional statutory criminal justice agencies. At its worst, the punishment of citizens becomes everyone's responsibility. Without freedom to advocate for offenders, the third sector merely adds to an ever-thicker mesh of organisations in society who effectively punish and control citizens by being a service provider of punishment. By incorporating the voluntary sector to undertake the state's work, the criminal justice system merely builds capacity rather than innovates and progresses. With growing and securing contracts in the penal system comes a price to pay with compromised values and loss of independence for voluntary sector organisations.

The threat to the third sector of closer relationships with the state has led to differences of opinion within the charitable sector itself. The debate between whether the voluntary sector needs to reshape and mould probation work away from the current punitive agenda or whether it should draw a line in the sand that should never be crossed, still has some way to go before it can be resolved (Benson and Hedge, 2009; Silvestri, 2009).

Summary of key points

- Multi-agency working under the NOMS framework will be characterised by greater complexity, fluidity and the erosion of traditional notions of complementary arrangements.
- The impact of contestability and the opening up of probation work to the private and third sectors will result in new understandings of the way in which state punishment in the community will be organised and governed. The future will undoubtedly have ethical dilemmas with commercial interests sitting alongside public protection, rehabilitation and security. For example, there is the distinct possibility that in the future, a private sector security company, which has previously successfully bid to run a prison may also be competing to win probation work in the community.
- Will such an arrangement make end-to-end offender management more of a reality as the same company will stretch across the custodial and community divide, or will strict enforcement action effectively increase the company's profits through more offenders being placed into its custodial operation?
- On the contrary, should NOMS allow both the third and private sectors to be rewarded for offering something innovative, different, advocatory and more efficient with clear roles as to how these organisations can add value when partnering the Probation Service, then there is an opportunity for multi-agency working to significantly impact on the quality of the supervision and interventions that offenders receive in a diverse community.

Points for further consideration

- Consider a voluntary organisation or partnership you work with and reflect on the 'added value' this multi-agency arrangement makes to your organisation and the interventions offenders receive. What is different or creative about this work with offenders?

References

Benson, A. and Hedge, J. (2009) 'Criminal justice and the voluntary sector: a policy that does not compute', *Criminal Justice Matters*, 77, 34-6.

Carter, P. (2003) *Managing Offenders, Reducing Crime: A New Approach*. London: Prime Minister's Strategy Unit.

Corcoran, M. (2009) 'Bringing the penal voluntary sector to market', *Criminal Justice Matters*, 77, 32-3.

Corner, J. (2006) 'Just another service provider? The voluntary sector's place in the National Offender Management Service', in Tarry, N. (ed) *Returning to its Roots? A New Role for the Third Sector in Probation*. London: Social Market Foundation.

Crawford, A. (1999) *The Local Governance of Crime: Appeals to Community and Partnerships*. Oxford: Oxford University Press.

Feeley, M. (2002) 'Entrepreneurs of punishment: the legacy of privatization', *Punishment and Society*, 4(3), 321-44.

Garland, D. (1997) 'Probation and the reconfigurement of crime control' in Burnett, R. (ed) *The Probation Service: Responding to Change*. Proceedings of the Probation Studies Unit First Colloquium, Probation Studies Unit Report No 3. Oxford: University of Oxford Centre for Criminological Research.

Garland, D. (2001) *The Culture of Control, Crime and Social Order in Contemporary Society*. Oxford: Oxford University Press.

Garside, R. (2004) 'Who delivers and why it matters', *Safer Society*, 21, 7-9.

Hanson, D. (2008) 'Foreword', in Ministry of Justice, *Working with the Third Sector to Reduce Re-offending*. London: Home Office.

Home Office (1990) *Partnership in Dealing with Offenders in the Community*. London: Home Office.

Home Office (1993) *Partnership in Dealing with Offenders in the Community: Submission of Partnership Plans*. Probation Circular 17/1993. London: Home Office.

McGuire, J. (ed) (1995) *What Works with Offenders*. Chichester: Wiley.

McLaughlin, E., Muncie, J. and Hughes, G. (2001) 'The permanent revolution: New Labour, new public management and the modernization of criminal justice', *Criminology and Criminal Justice*, 1(3), 301-18.

Mills, H. (2009) *Policy, Purpose and Pragmatism: Dilemmas for Voluntary and Community Organisations Working with Black Young People Affected by Crime*. London: Centre for Crime and Justice.

Monbiot, G. (2009) 'This revolting trade in human lives is an incentive to lock people up', *The Guardian*, 3 March. Available at www.guardian.co.uk/commentisfree/2009/mar/03/prison-population-titan-jails

Nash, M. and Williams, A. (2008) *The Anatomy of Serious Further Offending*. Oxford: Oxford University Press.

Nellis, M. (2002) 'Probation, partnership and civil society', in Ward, D., Scott, J. and Lacey, M. (eds) *Probation: Working for Justice*. London: Whiting and Birch.

Nellis, M. (2007) 'NOMS, contestability and the process of technocorrectional innovation', in Hough, M., Allen, R. and Padel, U. (eds) *Reshaping Probation and Prisons*. Bristol: The Policy Press.

NOMS (National Offender Management Service) (2005) *Restructuring Probation to Reduce Offending*. London: Home Office.

NPS (National Probation Service) (2001) *The New Choreography: An Integrated Strategy for the National Probation Service for England and Wales*. London: Home Office.

Pycroft, A. (2006) 'Too little, too late? Service user involvement and the Probation Service', *Community Justice Matters*, 64(1), 36-7.

Rumgay, J. (2003) 'Partnerships in the Probation Service', in Chui, W.H. and Nellis, M. (ed) *Moving Probation Forward*. Harlow: Longman Pearson.

Rumgay, J. (2004) 'The barking dog? Partnership and effective practice', in Mair, G. (ed) *What Matters in Probation*. Cullompton: Willan Publishing.

Rumgay, J. (2005) 'NOMS bombs', *Howard Journal*, 44(2), 206–8.

Rumgay, J. (2007) 'Partnerships in probation', in Gelthorpe, L. and Morgan, R. (eds) *Handbook of Probation*. Cullompton: Willan Publishing.

Silvestri, A. (2009) *Partners or Prisoners? Voluntary Sector Independence in the World of Commissioning and Contestability*. London: Centre for Crime and Justice.

Sutcliffe, G. (2006) 'Foreword' to Tarry, N. (ed) (2006) *Returning to its Roots? A New Role for the Third Sector in Probation*. London: Social Market Foundation.

Tarry, N. (ed) (2006) *Returning to its Roots? A New Role for the Third Sector in Probation*. London: Social Market Foundation.

CHAPTER 3

Clients or offenders?
The case for clarity of purpose in
multi-agency working

Carrie Skinner

Aims of the chapter

■ To explore the development and role of punishment in the work of the Probation Service.

■ To review the development of multi-agency working within the National Offender Management Model to deliver interventions to offenders.

■ To consider the impact of partnership working for practitioners from the probation setting and voluntary sector.

■ To consider the user experience of interventions delivered by partnerships.

■ To offer suggestions for enhancing the effectiveness of partnerships.

The rise and rise of punishment

What does the Probation Service stand for in the 21st century? Its official purpose is defined as protecting the public, reducing reoffending, ensuring the proper punishment of offenders in the community, ensuring offenders' awareness of the effects of crime on the victims of crime and the public, and the rehabilitation of offenders (NPS, 2001). These aims mark a significant change from the 'advise, assist and befriend' objectives of the previous century embodied in the 1907 Probation of Offenders Act. The Secretary of State for Justice, speaking at a conference for trainee probation officers in February 2009, stated that probation was 'no longer a social service – it is about punishment and reform' (Straw, 2009). Contemporaneous crime policy falls clearly within a correctionalist paradigm so that disadvantage, misfortune and exclusion have become reframed as matters of personal choice and individual inadequacy. Organisations working with offenders have seen their practice reconstructed as punishment, risk management and treatment regardless of the individual's rights or interests (McNeill, 2004).

Yet practitioners, whether new or seasoned, continue to cite the humanitarian nature of the Probation Service in helping individuals to reform, expressed through care, help and support, as the principal reason for the work and where most job satisfaction is gained. Despite restructurings, government directives and managerial practices, the traditional ethos of the Probation Service remains stubbornly evident among its frontline practitioners (Farrow, 2004; Robinson and Burnett, 2007; Annison et al, 2008; Skinner, 2008). Traditional values that have informed probation practice understood offending to be located within a social and environmental context, arising from poverty, social exclusion, inadequate socialisation and/or maladjustment. It followed from this rationale that by treating offenders with decency and humanity, supporting their efforts to secure goods and services through addressing disadvantage and problem solving, individual offenders would stop offending, disadvantages could be addressed and problems overcome. Whitehead and Statham (2006) also identify how deeply held beliefs about the intrinsic moral worth of individuals regardless of their deeds continue to inform practice despite the ascendancy of correctionalism.

If there is disagreement within the ranks about the purpose and methods of working with offenders, there will inevitably be confusion for others, notably those partner agencies who work alongside the Probation Service and the offenders themselves. An exploration of the ascendancy of punishment is therefore justified in order to understand the ways that interventions for offenders have been newly designed and delivered.

> Why did you choose to work within the criminal justice system? What ideas about crime, punishment and justice influenced your decision? Divide your reasons between the two categories of 'reform' and 'retribution'. Have these changed or strengthened over time?

As just one small organisation operating within the criminal justice system, the Probation Service is not immune from wider social, economic and political events (see Pycroft, this volume). Changes in the way that crime, punishment and rehabilitation are understood will have a profound and longlasting effect. A neoconservative understanding of crime and a loss of belief in rehabilitation have contributed to the Probation Service reforming as an agency for corrections, administering punishment in the community as an alternative to custody. The 1990s saw the incumbent Conservative government and New Labour in opposition both embrace 'new populism' (Garland, 2001), resulting in an extraordinary amount of legislation aimed at offender populations deemed to be the most capable of causing serious harm.

Within this developing legislative framework, the Probation Service has been obliged to focus on the supervision of high-risk offenders, with risk management rather than client support becoming the organising principle of probation practice (Kemshall, 2002). The Effective Practice Initiative launched in 1998 required all offenders deemed at risk of reoffending to have their cognitive deficits treated through attendance at accredited programmes while financial incentives and performance measurements ensured managerial compliance with the government agenda.

The transformation of the Probation Service from offender support to coercive control (Burnett et al, 2007) has not been easy. Moving the service away from its traditional values and cultures has been attempted through centralised control and standardisation of practice. Over the space of a decade, the service has endured significant attempts to remodel it so that it is better able to deliver government policy on crime, fundamentally changing its purpose and requiring it to deliver punishment through 'community incapacitation and exclusion' (Gough, 2005:95).

The 2003 Criminal Justice Act introduced a new sentencing framework, replacing the different community sentences with the generic Community Order, which provides the court with a list of requirements to attach. In a further diminution of the professional relationship, formerly the bedrock of traditional probation practice, individual supervision between the practitioner and offender is now just one of 12 requirements. The Act also required that 'punishment, in some degree or another, would be a part of every sentence' (NOMS, 2006).

Yet despite the Secretary of State's summation of a new orientation, probation officers continue to espouse traditional values and their persistence can be evidenced through the presence of a sustained critique. Each twist and turn of policy development aimed at reforming the service into a correctional agency through the jettison of core values has been subject to scrutiny and challenge (Oldfield, 1994; Chui and Nellis, 2003; NAPO, 2006; and others).

For example, probation officer training has received a sustained critique from commentators anxious that the professional knowledge base for working with disadvantaged and damaged individuals remains (Littlechild, 1996; Pillay and McQuillan, 2000; Nellis, 2001, 2003; Knight, 2002; Treadwell, 2006). Concerns have been aired over attempts to standardise practice resulting in the loss of professional discretion over assessment, intervention and enforcement decisions (Eadie and Winwin Sein, 2005/06). Challenges have been made over role boundary erosion as differently qualified staff, Probation Service officers and offender supervisors, are given responsibility for complex cases without sufficient knowledge or supervisory oversight (Bailey et al, 2007). The implementation of the Effective Practice Initiative has been heavily criticised for prioritising attendance at accredited programmes over other interventions (Gorman, 2001; Mair, 2004). The linking of Area funding to performance targets has resulted in high numbers of offenders being channelled through programmes, many of whom were unsuitable or unready for such a commitment. Yet at the same time as attrition rates have grown, new research is showing the importance of the supervisory relationship in decisions to desist from crime (Rex, 1999; McNeill, 2004a; Partridge, 2004; and others); without support and motivational encouragement, without the sense that someone is listening to their story and cares about what happens, individuals simply will not attend programmes or receive treatment. As a result, official recognition of the importance of the supervisory relationship for the reduction of crime has slowly been revived and has been given some impetus via the introduction of the National Offender Management Model (NOMM).

Introduced in 2005, the NOMM explicitly identified the need for an 'offender-focused human service approach', with offenders being managed in a consistent, coherent and constructive way throughout their entire sentence, whether in prison or in the community. Each offender should be allocated an offender manager responsible for their assessment, for the design of an individualised sentence plan and for ensuring that the plan is implemented. This person is also the main point of contact for partner organisations working with the offender. The 'One Sentence; One Manager' structure is supported by the four Cs of supervision – consistency, commitment, consolidation and continuity – that are 'derived from studies of how offenders themselves experience their relationship with the correctional services and thus provide a valuable user perspective within the model' (NOMS, 2006: 17). Other relational factors that are recognised as important in promoting desistance from crime have been identified, such as the showing of mutual respect and liking; open, warm and enthusiastic communication; humour; and a general interest in the individual as a person (Dowden and Andrews, 2004). Practitioners might be forgiven for thinking that these show more than a passing similarity to social work values that have imbued the service's work for many years.

However, the NOMM still stops short of advocating inclusionary practice. Its language and descriptions reveal a belief about offenders as essentially self-serving and uncooperative with the aims of supervision. They are frequently referred to as 'projects' and 'cases' and it is assumed that 'Most offenders will not cooperate with their Sentence Plan simply because one exists' (NOMS, 2005: 8). Depersonalised descriptions of functions and tasks rely on coercive rather than negotiated methods, so that staff must strive 'to reconcile its traditional rehabilitative mission with the contemporary political imperatives of implementing "proper punishment" and protecting the public' (Canton, 2007: 239). The NOMM introduced four tiers of intervention – punish, help, change and control (NOMS, 2006) – to which offenders are allocated on the basis of assessed risk. The four tiers are layered so that the more complex the case, the more interventions and resources are required for its management. Thus, an individual assessed as being a tier 4 case will be required to be punished, helped, changed and controlled, with punishment being a common factor for all tiers.

> What have your experiences of the NOMM been? Is it operational in your Area? Thinking of the individuals you work with, how accurately does the NOMM describe their experience of supervision? How do you reconcile the need to both rehabilitate and punish?

Where the NOMM appears to validate responsive, individualised practice designed to support desistance from crime, there is evidence that practitioners have welcomed it along with anticipated improvements for information exchange and continuity of care (PA Consultancy and MORI, 2005). The person-centred approach to working with offenders is identified as more rewarding and effective (McNeill, 2004; Annison et al, 2008). There is, however, evidence that practitioners believe that the continuing priority given to public protection and punishment means that the professional relationship remains undervalued (Robinson and

Burnett, 2007; Annison et al, 2008; Skinner, 2008). High caseloads combined with budget cuts and the need to meet targets have seen resource-hungry rehabilitative support demoted in favour of systems and outcomes that 'manage' offenders. Officer accountability for the management of the sentence is clearly ascribed in the NOMM, and where fear, blame and censure dominate organisational culture, practitioners may favour punitive controls over rehabilitative interventions (Kemshall, 2008). The tiering system requires qualified staff to manage large caseloads made up exclusively of high-risk individuals with complex needs. In a resource-deficient and over-bureaucratised environment, probation officers complain of isolation and unrelenting pressure, juggling competing priorities with little support or advice as numbers of qualified colleagues or managers decrease (Skinner, 2008). Unsurprisingly and perhaps not unconnected, the Probation Service has been found to have the highest rate of staff sickness in the public sector (NAO, 2006). The NOMM has encouraged Areas to adopt a project management style of supervision whereby a team will deliver a range of interventions to one offender. This model requires the project manager to be responsible for the work of the team, supervising the quality of input from others. However, some probation officers have voiced unease at what they see as 'buck-passing' from management to staff. If a serious further offence is committed, then it is likely that the project manager will be held accountable rather than those who manage the organisation.

A key rationale for the creation of the National Offender Management Service (NOMS) was to improve the service offered to short-term prisoners. A number of reports criticised the neglect of those sentenced to under 12 months and released without supervision who became caught in a revolving door of reoffending and custody. The 2003 Criminal Justice Act introduced a new sentence – Custody Plus – that combined a short period of imprisonment with a licence period of at least six months' duration. The sentencing court could attach the same range of conditions as available for Community Orders, solving the anachronism of high-risk individuals being released from custody unsupported. Necessarily, better coordination between the Probation and Prison Services would be required for such a sentence to work. However, Custody Plus has been deferred indefinitely as the difficulty in resourcing such a penalty became apparent. Its popularity with the sentencing court could have placed unacceptably high demands on both the Prison and Probation Services, further inflating prison numbers and probation caseloads. Without it, though, the rationale for the development of NOMS is weakened and those individuals who present a high-risk of reoffending upon release continue to remain unsupported.

Multi-agency working – the practitioner perspective

For staff in the Probation Service, restructuring and change have been a constant theme over recent years. The 'permanent revolution' (McLaughlin et al, 2001) of modernisation that aims to achieve a seamless criminal justice system has left many practitioners feeling unclear about the need for more radical change (Robinson and Burnett, 2007). They have seen the notion of rehabilitating offenders academically and morally challenged; their professional qualifying route altered to remove any connection with social work; and their professional value base tainted with the requirement to punish. Considerable uncertainty surrounds the purpose of the supervisory process, with many practitioners expressing belief that the goal of rehabilitation is awarded little organisational value (Farrow, 2004; Skinner, 2008). Practitioners have identified a growing trend among managers to ascribe the goal of rehabilitation as a legacy of the social work era, an optional extra that detracts from the real business of enforcement, deadlines and record keeping. As Areas increasingly employ staff without probation officer training who have neither an understanding of nor a commitment to its venerable traditions, it will become easier for the focus to move to the more punitive aspects of the job, surveillance, control, enforcement, and so on, leaving the task of rehabilitation to the third sector.

With the expectation that increasing numbers of partner agencies will become involved in the delivery of interventions with offenders, probation staff require a working knowledge of how a range of different services support the goal of reduced reoffending. Their risk assessment will provide the basis on which decisions are made about which interventions will be most effective in meeting the needs of a particular offender. The sentence plan will identify how, when and by whom interventions will be provided in order to meet the requirements within the resources available. It will specify who will do what and when in order to achieve all the objectives that have been set. For the plan to be implemented, the individual must have access to identified interventions. This involves brokerage – the process of securing and deploying the right interventions – and the complexity of this task varies depending on the interventions the offender needs.

The Probation Service in fact has a long history of working with the voluntary sector and community groups to address the social needs of offenders. Understanding crime as a consequence of social deprivation (Robinson, 2007), the service worked with individuals to enhance both their human and social capital. Many Probation Areas developed local partnerships to tackle specific issues that were affecting their communities. Significantly, these local arrangements were characterised by cooperation rather than competition, utilising the specialist skills and experience of a wide range of groups, benefiting from collaborative working to address the needs of offenders in order to deliver offender reform and safer communities. For example, the Probation Service where the author was employed worked jointly with the police to promote responsible road use where drink driving and joy riding had been identified as problems for the community; had partnerships with family centres designed to support parents subject to probation supervision, had an actively managed volunteer group to support and mentor individuals and organised surgery days in the office with the local mental health, drug and alcohol teams present. Formal agreements, negotiated at management level with statutory partners to deal with child protection, accommodation and court matters, were brokered and the probation hostel that housed a mixture of bailees and individuals on licence and orders worked closely with its neighbours to promote integration, having open days, fundraising events and regular volunteering projects. The 'mixed economy' of provision was already in existence yet it differed from the contestability and commissioning vision evolving from practitioner innovation rather than centrally imposed missive, with a commitment to local rather than national innovation (see Gough, this volume).

Misunderstanding about roles and responsibilities of different agency workers is repeatedly found in the partnership literature (Burnett and Appleton, 2004; Sheffield Hallam University, 2005, cited in Burke, 2005; Rumgay, 2007) yet time spent on getting to know agency personnel would largely overcome such difficulties. Knowledge, interpretation and judgement about suitable interventions require both 'thinking' and 'doing' time but government ministers and civil servants who are responsible for designing and awarding contracts and local managers within the service appear to have limited understanding of the skilful work that is required for successful multi-agency working. NAPO (2006) warns that the continued denigration of the knowledge base required for effective practice with offenders by those in charge of awarding contracts is likely to result in inaccurate referrals and inadequate supervision, having the potential to increase risk to the public. Raynor and Maguire (2006) agree and argue that organisational change on the scale that has transpired may actually lessen effectiveness and see the Probation Service and the wider criminal justice system lose further credibility as organisational failures surface. The money that has been spent on restructuring and reorganising the service over and over again could have been invested in staff training and development that would have raised both the performance of the service and the morale of those working on the frontline.

> Make a list of all the voluntary or not-for-profit organisations that support offenders in your area of work. How familiar are you with what they do? Have you visited their premises, met their workers, clarified your understanding of what they do? If not, identify the obstacles that prevent you from doing this.

Voluntary sector involvement in multi-agency work

The voluntary sector has proved its capability for innovation, flexibility and responsiveness to diversity, which makes it an appropriate partner to work with criminal justice agencies in reducing crime (Lowit, 2006). The offender population has typically experienced exclusion, alienation and punishment from the main state institutions and the successful track record of voluntary agencies engaging with hard-to-reach groups may be due to their separateness from statutory organisations. Unquestionably too, the voluntary sector has the experience to deliver local services to meet local need and, in some cases, social justice. For example, organisations like the Prison Reform Trust have highlighted the way that prisons are used as repositories for groups of individuals whose personal circumstances are too complex for the usual self-help quick fix preferred by the state agencies, and more recently the Howard League for Penal Reform (2009) has attacked conditions for children in custody as 'seriously unsafe'. With a focus on the social exclusionary experience of the individual, the voluntary sector has presented a challenge to the monocultured view of evidence-based penal policy, preferring voluntarism over coercion, inclusiveness over exclusion and humanitarianism over business effectiveness (Corner, 2006: 55).

From the government's point of view, the introduction of competition in the delivery of criminal justice services is a key driver to improvement but what does this opportunity mean for those voluntary agencies already offering a service to this client group? Corner (2006) argues that there is a fine line between increased business and compromised values, of secure funding and loss of independence. The voluntary sector's strength lies in the fact that it innovates specialist, dynamic, flexible and confidential services that reach some of the most marginalised individuals and groups in society. Organisations thinking of becoming a partner of NOMS risk being viewed as part of the state apparatus and may lose connection and legitimacy with their local communities and service users. If voluntary organisations accept the invitation to work more closely with NOMS, they may find that their services are shaped and determined to the specification of the larger organisation rather than their own vision. In effect, they risk becoming just another provider of offender services in the same mould as the statutory sector.

Most voluntary partnership agencies are either national or very local; few if any are regional. Many local agencies will have evolved from grassroots initiatives and are likely to be staffed with enthusiastic, like-minded people who have 'grown' with their organisation. Services will have developed to meet a gap and will be informed by the needs of those who use them. Decisions to work more formally with the statutory services could instigate wholesale change to ethos and practice and as such require careful handling. Volunteers may be replaced with paid staff, limits may be placed on client confidentiality and systems may be introduced that focus on accountability rather than effectiveness of outcome.

If complex problems that have led to the offending behaviour are not understood, it is also unlikely that they will be addressed. Some partnership agencies are unsuitable for the level of risk an offender poses yet fail to recognise their limitations with profound consequences (HMI Probation, 2006). Some work to different understandings of crime using methods that may be oppositional to those delivered by the Probation Service; many will have differing beliefs on the benefits of coercive versus voluntary treatments. Others may have undergone rapid expansion but are subsequently unable to meet contractual obligations due to system overload and staff shortages.

When punishment is brought into the equation, new challenges emerge. Research on voluntary and community involvement in two Probation Areas found the issue of enforcement problematic; probation staff had a responsibility to promote enforcement whereas community organisations had evolved from a framework of voluntarism and consensual engagement. Enforcement was identified as a key challenge to successful partnership working with staff unwilling to disclose information that might threaten the engagement of the client and potentially disrupt progress (Sheffield Hallam University, 2005, cited in Burke, 2005).

The current economic crisis is likely to impinge significantly on the voluntary sector. Insecurity and unpredictability in funding already hamper the efforts of this sector to invest in staff and service development. Nellis (2006) warns that the more organisations have to engage in competition for government contracts, the more likely it becomes that they will adopt the perspectives and values of the private sector and lose their own distinctive character. Although winning a contract can provide short-term financial stability, the fact that contracts tend to be time-limited can have a negative impact on service planning and recruiting and retaining staff. Smaller organisations have complained of additional costs being incurred due to the complicated negotiations and procedures involved in applying for government contracts that large organisations will be able to assimilate (Women's Aid, 2005). Currently, commissioning does appear to have favoured a few large service providers rather than specialist or locally based organisations.

The service user perspective

There appears to be political consensus on the need to make services more user-focused, with most areas of social policy recognising the benefits that client contributions can make (Pycroft, 2005). National Service Frameworks require organisations to consult with service users in order that developments are made in line with need. Their involvement is a prerequisite for funding and demonstrates the organisation's credentials for giving a voice to users in designing and delivering services that make a difference. Yet when the services are for offenders, the direction of travel appears to be at odds with the prevailing view.

Penal policy of the last few decades has been motivated by the need to reduce crime rather than to assist the offender to reform. Rehabilitation has been redefined and embedded in the new culture of crime control, 'carefully targeted, rationed and subjected to evaluative scrutiny; offence-centred rather than offender-centred, targeting criminogenic need rather than social need' (McNeill, 2004b: 422). When offenders are seen as 'different from us' or as 'alien others', it is easier to be sceptical about the merits of rehabilitation and accepting of the justification for punishment. It is also easy to ignore the contribution they might make to improving interventions designed to address reoffending.

Unsurprisingly then, few surveys have bothered to ask offenders for their views on the service they have received and even fewer have been invited to contribute to service development. Yet what this small amount of research does show is that overwhelmingly the single most important approach to changing offending behaviour is the presence of a trusting, empathic relationship between the offender and the worker (Holt, 2002; Dowden and Andrews, 2004; Partridge,

2004; Burnett and McNeill, 2005; Ward and Maruna, 2007). This discovery has profound implications for NOMS and challenges the view of offenders as rational actors requiring punishment and offered only conditional opportunities to address their offending behaviour. Instead, it invites a way of working that prioritises building professional relationships while assessing risk, needs and strengths that can be incorporated into a jointly developed plan that supports change. The use of partnership agencies requires careful coordination so that 'fragmentation' does not result whereby the individual being supervised is passed around to a number of different providers unable to form a meaningful relationship or understanding of the purpose of the interventions. Clarity about the role, responsibility and purpose of the intervention is therefore essential for all concerned, suggesting that practitioners will need to demonstrate personal commitment to their cases as well as to organisational targets.

In 2006, a Probation Circular was issued that asked Areas to 'identify and promote best practice in the engagement of offenders in the delivery and development of services provided by local probation areas' (PC10/2006). Following on from this, PC 10/2007 requested that Areas develop their own strategies for obtaining and using feedback from service users as well as encouraging offender engagement in Probation Boards' activities. There appears to be some recognition that offender engagement is necessary if targets on crime reduction are to be met. A national stakeholder feedback group has been set up to collate information from the Areas on their user involvement and a questionnaire for offenders to give feedback on their experiences of supervision is currently being piloted and is intended to be rolled out for national use. Additionally, a full performance measure will shortly be introduced on engagement with offenders as part of service delivery.

> Are you aware of user involvement in service development in your place of employment? Do you encourage service user feedback on your practice? Is this something you could instigate on a regular basis?

Conclusion

Throughout this book, it is acknowledged that the legal and policy frameworks for multi-agency working are now embedded in the different organisations providing services for offenders. This chapter has explored the elevation of punishment within the Probation Service and its impact on effective multi-agency working. It has argued that confusion exists for both practitioners and users about the purpose of partnership intervention now that the Probation Service has been rebranded as an 'agency of corrections'. Budget constraints, high caseloads and the widespread use of non-probation qualified staff within a competitive performance culture have led the service into promoting technical rather than individualised assessments that ignore the social and economic context of offending. Such weakening of the 'professional relationship' between worker and client will inevitably lessen the chance of uncovering the individual's unique pathway into offending so that punishment and the treatment of cognitive deficits ascribed to all members of the same offending group becomes the purpose of intervention. Within this rationale, partnership involvement becomes further punishment, undermining the goal of inclusion and reducing the overall effectiveness of the criminal justice system.

It has been suggested that those with responsibility for contracting out services in NOMS have little knowledge or understanding of working with offender populations and that different cultural practices and knowledge bases will conflict if organisational aims are not harmonised. Complex tendering processes, short-term contracts and the uncertainty that a competitive environment brings can also damage an organisation's integrity with users and staff. For those third sector organisations that have won contracts to work with non-voluntary clients, the problems will have become apparent. Reporting requirements will have challenged the value of voluntarism and service provision may have been 'modified' to meet contract specification.

User involvement in developing service provision has been a late addition where offenders are concerned. Perhaps the threat of contestability has been the catalyst for change, exposing just how far the criminal justice system is lagging behind other organisations in employing user expertise to plan and shape services (Pycroft, 2006). If the Probation Service is to compete with others to deliver interventions, it will need to demonstrate that it has developed mechanisms that involve and invite critical feedback from its offender service users. This will not be achieved easily; at every opportunity, government has sought to establish its credentials as the party of law and order through harsher penalties, legislating on selected groups identified as risks to the law-abiding majority. This image will be hard to dislodge and quite how those groups who have been so vilified are to be involved in service provision will be an interesting development. Just how far will the inclusion agenda reach out to offenders?

Finally, some thoughts on how best to maximise partnership services to offenders while enhancing overall effectiveness in reducing reoffending:

- Honest and open acknowledgement of the social and economic context of most offending is necessary so that punishment can be separated from interventions to reform. This will facilitate clarity of purpose for both practitioners and service users and enable partnership agencies the freedom to create specific and individualised services that can support those at the margins.
- A shift in organisational culture is needed to recognise the importance of successful relationships to facilitating offender engagement. Understanding the narratives that offenders give for their lives and behaviours takes time and can only be accomplished once trust has been established.
- Partnerships also require time to establish; new contracts will often mean that agencies coalesce around different identities and working conditions and will need space to develop service protocols. Practitioners will need to feel their way in newly constituted services, otherwise delivery will suffer.

- It remains essential that users are fully involved in the development and evaluation of services in order to ensure relevance and accessibility.

Points for further consideration

■ What scope is there for developing an inclusive 'client'-focused perspective in your organisation?

■ What practical ways can you devise that will enable more successful partnership referrals?

■ Identify the different forms that punishment may take and consider your role in delivering this.

Further reading

Carnwell, R. and Buchanan, J. (2009) *Effective Practice in Health, Social Care and Criminal Justice* (2nd edition). Maidenhead: Open University Press.

McNeill, F., Batchelor, S., Burnett, R. and Knox, J. (2005) *21st Century Social Work: Reducing Re-offending: Key Practice Skills*. Edinburgh: Scottish Executive.

Ward, T. and Maruna, S. (2007) *Rehabilitation*. London: Routledge.

References

Annison, J., Eadie, T. and Knight, C. (2008) 'People first: Probation Officer perspectives on probation work, *Probation Journal*, 55(3), 259-71.

Bailey, R., Knight, C. and Williams, B. (2007) 'The Probation Service as part of NOMS in England and Wales: fit for purpose?', in Gelsthorpe, L. and Morgan, R. (eds) *Handbook of Probation*. Cullompton: Willan Publishing.

Burke, L. (2005) *From Probation to the National Offender Management Service: Issues of Contestability, Culture and Community Involvement.* Issues in Community and Criminal Justice Monograph 6. London: Napo Publications.

Burnett, R. and Appleton, C. (2004) *Joined-up Youth Justice: Tackling Youth Crime in Partnership.* Lyme Regis: Russell House Publishing.

Burnett, R. and McNeill, F. (2005) 'The place of the officer–offender relationship in assisting offenders to desist from crime', *The Probation Journal*, 52(3), 221-42.

Burnett, R., Baker, K. and Roberts, C. (2007) 'Assessment, supervision and intervention: fundamental practice in probation', in Gelsthorpe, L. and Morgan, R. (eds) *Handbook of Probation*. Cullompton: Willan Publishing.

Canton, R. (2007) 'Probation and the tragedy of punishment', *The Howard Journal*, 46(3), 236-54.

Chui, W.H. and Nellis, M. (eds) (2003) *Moving Probation Forward: Evidence, Arguments and Practice.* London: Pearson Longman.

Corner, J. (2006) 'Just another service provider? The voluntary sector's place in the National Offender Management Service', in N. Tarry (ed) *Returning to its Roots? A New Role for the Third Sector in Probation*. London: Social Market Foundation.

Dowden, C. and Andrews, D.A. (2004) 'The importance of staff practice in delivering effective correctional treatment: a meta analysis', *International Journal of Offender Therapy and Comparative Criminology*, 48(2), 203–14.

Eadie, T. and Winwin, S, (2005/06) 'When the going gets tough will the tough get going? Retaining staff in challenging times', *VISTA*, 10(3), 171–9.

Farrow, K. (2004) 'Still committed after all these years? Morale in the modern-day Probation Service', *Probation Journal*, 51(3), 206–20.

Garland, D. (2001) *The Culture of Control: Crime and Social Order in Contemporary Society*. Oxford: Oxford University Press.

Gorman, K. (2001) 'Cognitive behaviouralism and the Holy Grail: the quest for a universal means of managing offender risk', *Probation Journal*, 48(1), 3–9.

Gough, D. (2005) '"Tough on probation": probation practice under the National Offender Management Service', in Winstone, J. and Pakes, F. (eds) *Community Justice: Issues for Probation and Criminal Justice*. Cullompton: Willan Publishing.

HMI Probation (2006) *Offender Management Inspection Programme* (electronic version). Available at http://inspectorates.homeoffice.gov.uk/hmiprobation/inspection-programmes.html/offender-inspection.html/?version=1

Holt, P. (2002) 'Case management evaluation: pathways to progress', VISTA, 7(1), 16–25.

Howard League for Penal Reform (2009) *Analysis of the Inspectorate of Prisons Reports on Young Offender Institutions Holding Children in Custody*. London: Howard League for Penal Reform. Available at www.howardleague.org/fileadmin/howard_league/user/pdf/YOI_Inspections.pdf

Kemshall, H. (2002) 'Risk, public protection and justice', in Ward, D., Scott, J. and Lacey, M. (eds) *Probation: Working for Justice*. Oxford: Oxford University Press.

Kemshall, H. (2008) *Understanding the Community Management of High Risk Offenders*. Milton Keynes: Open University Press.

Knight, C. (2002) 'Training for a modern service', in Ward, D., Scott, J. and Lacey, M. (eds) *Probation: Working for Justice*. Oxford: Oxford University Press.

Littlechild, B. (1996) 'Future shock: education and training in the Probation Service', *Issues in Social Work Education*, 16(2), 86–100.

Lowit, N. (2006) 'The National Offender Management Service – the case for change', in Tarry, N. (ed) *Returning to its Roots? A New Role for the Third Sector in Probation*. London: The Social Market Foundation.

McLaughlin, E., Muncie, J. and Hughes, G. (2001) 'The permanent revolution: New Labour, public management and the modernization of criminal justice', *Criminology and Criminal Justice*, 3(1), 301–18.

McNeill, F. (2004a) 'Supporting desistance in probation practice', *Probation Journal*, 51(3), 241–7.

McNeill, F. (2004b) 'Desistance, rehabilitation and correctionalism: developments and prospects in Scotland', *The Howard Journal* 43(4), 420–36.

Mair, G. (2004) *What Matters in Probation?* Cullompton: Willan Publishing.

NAO (National Audit Office) (2006) *The Management of Staff Sickness in the Probation Service*. London: The Stationery Office.

NAPO (2006) 'A history of NOMS – three years of costly bureaucracy and chaos' (electronic version). Briefing Paper for the JUPG. Available at www. napo.org.uk/cgi-bin/dbman/db.cgi?db=defaultanduid=defaultandID=153an dview_records=1andww=

Nellis, M. (2001) 'Community values and community justice', *Probation Journal*, 48(3), 34-8.

Nellis, M. (2003) 'Probation training and the community justice curriculum', *British Journal of Social Work*, 33, 943-59.

Nellis, M. (2006) 'NOMS, contestability and the process of technocorrectional innovation', in Hough, M., Allen, R. and Padel, U. (eds) *Reshaping Probation and Prisons: The New Offender Management Framework*. London: Centre for Crime and Justice Studies.

NOMS (National Offender Management Service) (2005) *The National Offender Management Service Offender Management Model, Version 1*. London: Home Office.

NOMS (2006) *The NOMS Offender Management Model*. London: Home Office.

NPS (National Probation Service) (2001) *The New Choreography: An Integrated Strategy for the National Probation Service for England and Wales*. London: Home Office.

Oldfield, M. (1994) 'Talking quality, meaning control: McDonalds, the market and the Probation Service', *Probation Journal*, 41(4), 186-92.

PA Consultancy and MORI (2005) *Action Research Study of the Implementation of the National Offender Management Model in the North West Pathfinder*, Home Office Online Report 32/05. London: Home Office.

Partridge, S. (2004) *Examining Case Management Models for Community Sentences*, Home Office Online Report 17/04. London: Home Office.

Pillay, C. and McQuillan, T. (2000) *Building the Future: The Creation of the Diploma in Probation Studies*. London: NAPO.

Pycroft, A. (2005) 'A new chance for rehabilitation: multi-agency provision and potential under NOMS', in Winstone, J. and Pakes, F. (eds) *Community Justice: Issues for Probation and Criminal Justice*. Cullompton: Willan Publishing.

Pycroft, A. (2006) 'Too little, too late?', *Criminal Justice Matters*, 64(1), 36-7.

Raynor, P. and Maguire, M. (2006) 'End-to-end or end in tears? Prospects for the effectiveness of the National Offender Management Model', in Hough, M., Allen, R. and Padel, U. (ed) *Reshaping Probation and Prisons: The New Offender Management Framework*. Bristol: The Policy Press.

Rex, S. (1999) 'Desistance from offending: experiences of probation', *Howard Journal*, 38(4), 366-83.

Robinson, G. (2007) 'Rehabilitation', in Canton, R. and Hancock, D. (eds) *Dictionary of Probation and Offender Management*. Cullompton: Willan Publishing.

Robinson, G. and Burnett, R. (2007) 'Experiencing modernization: frontline probation perspectives on the transition to a National Offender Management Service', *Probation Journal*, 54(4), 318-37.

Rumgay, J. (2007) 'Partnerships in probation', in Gelsthorpe, L. and Morgan, R. (eds) *Handbook of Probation*. Cullompton: Willan Publishing.

Skinner, C. (2008) 'Probation in the 21st century: an ethnographic study in identifying the values, knowledge and skills used to deliver rehabilitation'. Unpublished Masters dissertation. Institute of Criminal Justice Studies, University of Portsmouth.

Straw, J. (2009) 'No soft options left for criminals'. Speech at the University of Portsmouth Study School, Portsmouth, UK, February.

Treadwell, J. (2006) 'Some personal reflections on probation training', *The Howard Journal*, 45(1), 1-13.

Ward, T. and Maruna, S. (2007) *Rehabilitation*. London: Routledge, Taylor and Francis Group.

Whitehead, P. and Statham, R. (2006) *The History of Probation: Politics, Power and Cultural Change 1876–2005*. Dartford: Shaw and Sons Limited.

Williams, B. (1996) *Counselling in Criminal Justice*. Buckingham: Open University Press.

Women's Aid (2005) *Consultation Response: Managing Offenders, Reducing Crime – Role of the Voluntary and Community Sector in the National Offender Management Service* (electronic version). Available at www.womensaid.org.uk/domestic-violence-articles.asp?section=00010001002200180001anditemid=1164

CHAPTER 4

Diversity and the policy agenda in criminal justice

Mark Mitchell

Aims of the chapter
- To outline the history of the concept of diversity.
- To review the impact of diversity policies within the criminal justice system in England and Wales.
- To discuss the conceptual and practical difficulties inherent in any attempt to implement diversity plans.
- To assess whether at a policy level a shared commitment to diversity facilitates partnership working across the 'correctional' agencies.

Introduction

Rather like a wet bar of soap, 'diversity' is a slippery concept – one that is almost impossible to grasp. Yet in recent years it has become one of those words that, like 'democracy' and 'freedom', are cheered every time they get a mention. How did diversity achieve such high prominence across the public policy terrain; what has been its impact within the criminal justice sector in particular; what difficulties face organisations that seek to devise and implement diversity plans; and has diversity been a help or a hindrance in furthering the kind of multi-agency partnership working that is essential if rates of reoffending are to be reduced and more offenders are to be rehabilitated? These questions provide the core concerns that will be addressed in this chapter.

Diversity – a brief history

For anyone with a longstanding interest in policies designed to combat discrimination in the UK, the recent rise and rise of the concept of 'diversity' must have come as a surprise. The standard literature on equality of opportunity from the 1970s and 1980s makes hardly any mention of the term (see, for example, EOC, 1985; Gregory, 1987); and the reawakening of interest in the issue of human rights, associated with rising levels of migration and asylum across the European Union (EU), was not accompanied by any significant discussions of diversity, choosing rather to focus on the issue of multiculturalism as a possible basis for a new form of citizenship. (Mitchell and Russell, 1998; Sassen, 1999). Yet over the past 10 years, diversity policies have become standard fare across most of the public sector and many public sector organisations have appointed diversity advisors to oversee the implementation of these policies. So how did this happen? How did a term that was not widely used in discussions and debates about how to increase fairness and equality in society rise to the predominant position it now occupies?

To answer this question, we need to recognise that for well over 30 years, from the early 1960s onwards, the campaign for legislation to support the attainment of equality of opportunity in the UK drew much of its inspiration and most of its key ideas from the US, particularly from the US 1963 Equal Pay Act and the US 1964 Civil Rights Act. It was these pioneering pieces of legislation that became the inspiration for equal opportunity campaigners in the UK. Thus, the somewhat timid efforts to combat race discrimination through the 1965 and 1968 Race Relations Acts and the much more radical attempts to address more structural causes of inequality by tackling direct and indirect discrimination in the 1975 Sex Discrimination Act and the 1976 Race Relations Act all drew their inspiration from across the Atlantic.

Diversity as a policy driver in the UK owes its origins to two interrelated developments that began to shape public policy in the late 1990s. The first of these was the response by the Labour government to the publication of the Macpherson report into the murder of Stephen Lawrence (Macpherson, 1999). This will be discussed in more detail in the next section of this chapter. But the second development took place at the level of the EU. For the first time, the European Commission and the individual member states began to recognise that, in addition to sex discrimination, other forms of discrimination were having an adverse impact on the operation of the European labour market. In retrospect, we can see that the UK's longstanding, relatively progressive and US-influenced anti-discrimination legislation had a significant impact in shaping the development of European initiatives in this field. At the same time, the way in which the EU's anti-discrimination directives were rolled out as part of a broader ideological framework of 'valuing difference' helped to shape the way in which these directives were implemented in the UK.

Following the signing of the Amsterdam Treaty in 1997, EU member states began to take the issue of discrimination much more seriously, particularly in relation to the operation of the labour market. The Treaty committed the EU to issue appropriate directives to ensure that member states introduced national legislation to combat discrimination in five new areas of social life and at the same time to strengthen the previous directives relating to equal pay and sex discrimination. As a result, new laws to protect people against discrimination on the grounds of racial or ethnic origin, religion or belief, disability, age and sexual orientation were agreed by all EU countries in 2000 and were harmonised with a new directive covering sex discrimination.

> Anti-discrimination laws to protect people against being discriminated against on the grounds of racial or ethnic origin, religion or belief, disability, age and sexual orientations were agreed by all EU countries in 2000. This means that all 27 countries in the EU today are required to incorporate these rules into their national laws. As well as making sure that these laws are respected, the European Commission works to inform citizens of their rights and responsibilities, to raise awareness of discrimination, and to promote the benefits of diversity. (www. stop-discrimination.info/27.0.html)

It is clear that the development of these European directives was strongly influenced by countries like the UK, which had had considerable experience of the operation of anti-discriminatory legislation. The distinction between direct and indirect discrimination and the provision for positive action, for example, were strikingly similar principles that had shaped the laws in the UK since the mid-1970s, as can be seen in the following:

> The directives recognise explicitly that outlawing discrimination will not necessarily be enough by itself to ensure genuine equality of opportunity for everyone in society. Specific measures might be called for to compensate for disadvantages arising from a person's racial or ethnic origin, age or other characteristics which might lead to them being treated unfairly.
>
> For example, ethnic minorities may need special training and specific help to have a reasonable chance of finding a job. Putting on training courses or making different arrangements especially for them are ways of improving their chances. The directives allow positive action of this kind to be undertaken and do not regard it as infringing the principle of equal treatment. (www.stop-discrimination.info/84.0.html)

One of the principal ways in which the Commission has promoted diversity is through the 'For Diversity, Against Discrimination' campaign, which commenced in 2003. The campaign strap line demonstrates clearly the thinking behind the campaign and the concern that an over-emphasis on 'banning discrimination' is likely to be perceived as portraying what the EU is against rather than what it stands for. The European directives outlawing discrimination on the grounds of sex, race/ethnicity, disability, age, religion and sexual orientation are seen as a means by which member states can foster and encourage greater levels of tolerance and mutual self-respect between individuals who are 'different'. Valuing difference is the goal and anti-discrimination legislation is a prerequisite for achieving this. In contrast to the 1960s and 1970s, the link between discrimination and the denial of civil/human rights has been decoupled and the emphasis on rights has been downplayed in favour of diversity.

Diversity and criminal justice in England and Wales

The impact within the UK of this shift in emphasis towards valuing difference and diversity can be traced through a number of important initiatives that took place from the late 1990s onwards. Most importantly, the publication in 1999 of the report of the Macpherson Inquiry into the murder of Stephen Lawrence promoted a degree of soul searching within criminal justice agencies. Macpherson had concluded that the Metropolitan Police Service (MPS) was institutionally racist because its organisational culture was characterised by 'processes, attitudes and behaviour which amount to discrimination through unwitting prejudice, ignorance, thoughtlessness and racist stereotyping which disadvantage minority ethnic people' (Macpherson, 1999: para 6.34). Because of institutional racism, the service provided by the MPS to London's black and minority ethnic communities was unprofessional and ineffective. The multiple failures that occurred during the investigation of the Stephen Lawrence murder were not just a consequence of the incompetence of individual police officers. Rather, because of common sense racist assumptions and attitudes that were deeply embedded in the organisation, the murder had been investigated less competently than if a white teenager had been unlawfully killed. This of course implied that other criminal justice organisations might also be infested with routine, taken-for-granted ways of operating that disadvantaged individuals from the black and minority ethnic communities, whether as employees or as service users of these organisations.

The Labour government's response to the Macpherson Inquiry was to introduce the first significant modifications to the 1976 Race Relations Act for 25 years. The most important change was the requirement for public sector organisations to introduce race equality schemes designed to eliminate race discrimination, foster harmonious race relations and actively promote race equality. Under the 1976 Act, employers had been permitted to introduce a range of positive action measures to promote more equal access to scarce goods and services in society. But there was no duty to take positive action and it was only permitted if an organisation could demonstrate that there was existing under-representation of individuals from the black and minority ethnic communities in terms of access to recruitment, training and development, promotion and/or service provision. Following the passage of the 2000 Race Relations (Amendment) Act, positive action became a mandatory obligation for nearly all major public sector organisations.

Additional equalities legislation has been needed to implement the EU directives and ensure that the UK's anti-discrimination laws and employment regulations are fully aligned with the new European requirements. This has presented the Labour government with an opportunity to extend the principles enshrined in the 2000 Race Relations (Amendment) Act to other areas. Consequently, because of the 2005 Disability Discrimination Act and the 2006 Equality Act, major public organisations in the UK are now required to develop disability equality and gender equality schemes in addition to their existing race equality schemes. However, no such duties apply to the other areas covered by the European directives and, as a result, we now have in effect a two-tier system of legislation in the UK. On the one hand, most of the public sector, together with private sector organisations that deliver services that have been 'contracted out' by the public sector, are required actively to promote race, gender and disability equality through positive action measures. On the other hand, in the areas of religion/faith, age and sexual orientation, no such public duties to secure greater equality apply. While it is now unlawful to discriminate directly or indirectly in terms of employment or in the provision of goods and services on the basis of an individual's religion, age or sexual orientation, there is no requirement on the public sector to develop equality schemes in these areas.

The response of all the major criminal justice agencies to these legislative changes has, on the surface, been exemplary and it is no exaggeration to say that diversity came to occupy a centre-stage position in the strategic plans of most of these agencies in the early years of the new millennium. However, analysis of the ways in which these diversity policies have evolved over the last 10 years shows two clear trends. First, there has been growing focus on equality at the expense of diversity in strategic and business planning, exemplified by the emergence of what is known as the 'single equality policy'. This shift in emphasis from diversity to equality reflects both the implementation of the European directives and the merger of the Commission for Racial Equality, the Disability Rights Commission and the Equal Opportunities Commission to form the Equality and Human Rights Commission in October 2007. Second, there has been a growing trend to prioritise action planning – as well as the allocation of the resources to achieve targets – on those areas where agencies have a statutory duty to promote equality. As a result, across the criminal justice system we have witnessed the emergence of a two-tier distinction between the areas of race, sex/gender and disability where this statutory duty exists and the areas of sexual orientation, age and religion where no such statutory duties apply. These trends will be illustrated by reference to the published plans of the MPS, the Crown Prosecution Service (CPS) and the Prison and Probation Services.

Perhaps unsurprisingly given the fact that the Macpherson report had labelled it an institutionally racist organisation, the MPS was first to grasp the diversity nettle. In November 1998, just as the Macpherson Inquiry was concluding its hearings, the MPS adopted its *Protect and Respect* diversity strategy (see Grieve and French, 2000: 15). As the Metropolitan Police Authority resported in 2000 (MPA, 2000), this strategy was updated following the Inspector of Constabulary's report *Policing London: Winning Consent* (HMIC, 2000) and was subsequently replaced with a new *Diversity Strategy* in 2005 to reflect the changing legal terrain that has been outlined above (MPS, 2005). A Diversity Directorate (now the Diversity and Citizen Focus Directorate) was established to oversee a massive programme of training and development, internal performance monitoring and external community engagement. The current *Equalities Scheme 2006–10*, which was updated in 2008, sets out equality targets for each of the six areas now covered by anti-discrimination laws as a result of the European directives (MPS, 2008a).

In 2003, the Crown Prosecution Service (CPS) was aspiring to become 'a beacon organisation in terms of equality and diversity both as employer and prosecutor' (CPS, 2003: 19). The same document refers explicitly to the CPS race equality scheme and to its work with the Commission for Racial Equality (see, for example, 2003: 6) and the Disability Rights Commission (see, for example, 2003: 19). In 2006, the CPS published a comprehensive *Single Equality Scheme* (CPS, 2006), which was updated in 2008. This document also sets out equality action plans for all six areas that are now covered by legislation, although it is noticeable that the plans for disability, gender and race are far more comprehensive than those for sexuality, religion and age. The same difference of emphasis in relation to race, sex and disability equality can be found in the *Equalities Scheme* of the MPS, where the monitoring of actual performance against the targets set out in the MPS *Equalities Scheme* appears to be well established (see, for example, MPS, 2007, 2008b).

In 2001, the new National Probation Service made 'valuing and achieving diversity' one of the nine 'stretch objectives' that were at the core of its first corporate plan (NPS, 2001: 33-7). Likewise, the corporate and business plans of the Prison Service make similar commitments, with statements like: 'The Prison Service remains determined to promote diversity, eliminate racism and improve the representation of minority ethnic staff in its workforce' (HM Prison Service, 2003: 26).

Today, both the Probation and Prison Services' commitments to diversity are subsumed under the National Offender Management Service's (NOMS) *Single Equality Scheme* (Ministry of Justice, 2009b). However, the scheme is almost entirely devoted to the work of the Prison Service, both in the monitoring of past performance and in the setting of future targets as 'each of the 42 probation areas is separately responsible for developing an equality scheme which covers service delivery and employment functions across the range of equality issues' (Ministry of Justice, 2009b: 3).

The NOMS *Single Equality Scheme* also makes explicit reference to the 'business case' for diversity (Ministry of Justice, 2009b: iii), in line with the way that both the European Commission and the UK's Department for Trade and Industry have attempted to 'sell' diversity by emphasising its potential economic benefits in recent years (see, for example, DTI, 2005; European Commission, 2008). However, this business case is not reflected in the NOMS business plan itself (Ministry of Justice, 2009a). Here, diversity and equality are mentioned only briefly and in ways that restate in the most general way the values that should be expected of any organisation, public or private, that is responsible for delivering services to the public. For example, is anyone surprised that NOMS is committed to deliver its services 'with decency, valuing diversity and promoting equality' (Ministry of Justice, 2009a: 11)?

Implementing diversity: conceptual and practical difficulties

The public sector's love affair with the concept of diversity began to cool after the publication of the report by the Community Cohesion Review Team into the riots that took place in Bradford, Burnley and Oldham in the summer of 2001 (Home Office, 2001). The report raised some disturbing questions about the extent to which black and minority ethnic communities in some parts of the UK were increasingly leading lives that were almost entirely separate from other communities.

> Whilst the physical segregation of housing estates and inner city areas came as no surprise, the team was particularly struck by the depth of polarisation of our towns and cities. The extent to which these physical divisions were compounded by so many other aspects of our daily lives was very evident. Separate educational arrangements, community and voluntary bodies, employment, places of worship, language, social and cultural networks, means that many communities operate on the basis of a series of parallel lives. These lives often do not seem to touch at any point, let alone overlap and promote any meaningful interchanges. (Home Office, 2001: 9)

The text of the report is replete with positive references to the importance of diversity and makes an impassioned plea for everyone to recognise that the days of a 'monoculturalist view of nationality' are no longer relevant to Britain in an increasingly globalised world (Home Office, 2001: 18). At the same time, the support for diversity is subject to an important caveat, namely that it should be underpinned by a shared commitment to citizenship, comprising common values, moral principles and codes of behaviour, together with support for political institutions and participation in politics (Home Office, 2001: 13).

> This needs a determined effort to gain consensus on the fundamental issue of 'cultural pluralism'. In other words, an acceptance, and even a celebration, of our diversity and that within the concept of citizenship, different cultures can thrive, adding to the richness and experience of our nationality. (Home Office, 2001: 18)

The report appears to be saying that a commitment to valuing and achieving diversity will not in itself provide the 'glue' required to secure community cohesion. In other words, valuing diversity is a necessary rather than a sufficient condition for any society characterised by a wide range of sociocultural differences. Consequently, it follows that 'valuing difference' can never be unconditional. The extent to which we are able to feel at ease with, actively participate in and even enjoy life in a diverse society is dependent on deeper values and moral principles that comprise the basis of our civic culture and that sustain the mutual respect that is a prerequisite for, at the very least, the toleration of difference.

It is clear from the above discussion that no society or organisation can respect and value all differences unconditionally. Rather, there must be limits to difference and diversity. The problem is that there is nothing inherent in these concepts themselves to enable organisations or individuals to determine what these limits should be. Neither are these merely philosophical conundrums, of interest only to those who inhabit academic ivory towers. Professionals from across the public sector continue to face serious dilemmas over their approaches to certain cultural practices that many find abhorrent but that are deeply rooted in some of our minority communities, for example female circumcision, polygamy and the ritual slaughter of animals (see Parekh, 2000, especially chapters 8 and 9, for an interesting discussion of some of the dilemmas raised by these cultural differences). Most would agree that cultural relativism, the belief that white middle-class professionals should never act in ways that impose 'alien' Western values on minority ethnic communities or act in ways that undermine or marginalise their alternative cultural beliefs and practices, cannot provide a coherent basis for professional intervention. An unquestioning commitment to 'multiculturalism', where the traditions and practices of minority communities are always respected, is wrong in principle and unsustainable in practice. This is why social workers are generally agreed that there must be limits to multiculturalism in relation to childcare/protection practice (see Cheetham, 1982: 143-6; Watson, this volume). The problem today is that a 'relativism of difference' threatens to replace cultural relativism because of the unquestioning acceptance of the principle of diversity. This in turn is disempowering for professionals since it provides no guidance on where to draw the line when it comes to valuing and respecting differences.

> Imagine you are the manager of a hostel. A male offender wishes to display white supremacist posters and other far Right material in his room. When challenged by staff, he claims that he has the right to display this material because the local Probation Trust has a policy of valuing diversity. What is your decision on this matter and how will you justify this decision to your line manager?

However, the problems with diversity are not solely conceptual; they are also practical, and raise significant issues for practitioners who work in a multi-agency context and particularly in relation to the community sector. All organisations have to make hard choices over the use of scarce resources and must therefore prioritise between competing interests when implementing their diversity policies. A broad commitment to valuing difference does not help when deciding precisely how the resources available to implement this commitment should be allocated. In view of this, it is perhaps unsurprising that most organisations prioritise those areas that have been legally designated as more important than others. Thus, as we have seen above, policies designed to address disadvantage and discrimination in the areas of race, sex/gender and disability tend to figure more prominently in action plans than those that focus on age, religion and sexual orientation because of the statutory disability, gender and race equality duties that recent legislation has imposed on many public sector organisations.

This should not be taken to mean that diversity/equality policies are a waste of time. Some of the plans and policies of criminal justice agencies that were discussed in the previous section should, if implemented fully, begin to address some of the deep-rooted institutional disadvantages within these agencies. The Accelerate programme, a two-year management development programme offered to middle managers with a disability and/or who are from one of the black and minority ethnic communities and who work in probation or youth justice, is a good example of how these agencies can translate fine words into actions. (For details of the Accelerate programme, see YJB, 2009.) But this and similar programmes across the public sector represent the specific ways in which these agencies have responded to meet what are now legal requirements, namely to take action to promote disability, gender and race equality in an active manner. The contribution that such programmes make to addressing institutional discrimination and disadvantage in these areas have come about as a result of legislative changes and not as a result of any general commitment to valuing and achieving diversity.

Of course, the six areas of difference now subject to legal regulation represent only a tiny fraction of those that can and sometimes do result in disadvantage. Take, for example, left-handedness. The writer of this chapter is often struck when lecturing to large groups of students in one of the many new and well-equipped lecture theatres across the campus where he works that many of the lecture theatres are very poorly equipped for those who write with their left hand. This is because the seats have retractable tables, all of which are designed for people who write with their right hand. The same is true of many of the computer rooms around the campus, where each computer is fitted with a right-handed mouse. This is a clear case of institutional discrimination against left-handed people and one which, in an ideal world, should be addressed by ensuring that at least 10% of the tables and computers are designed for those who are left-handed. But to rectify this disadvantage would require the commitment of additional resources involving hard choices between competing priorities. In the circumstances, it is not surprising that most organisations give greater weight to meeting their legal responsibilities and downplay other areas of institutional discrimination.

> Think about the organisational context where you work and/or study. Can you identify areas of institutional discrimination that, while not unlawful, are disadvantageous and unfair to particular groups?

Diversity and partnership working

This section will address the question: is diversity a help or a hindrance to multi-agency working? At first glance, the common commitment to valuing difference and respecting the diversity of people's lifestyles and choices might appear to provide a solid foundation for the partnership work that is essential if rates of offending and reoffending are to be reduced. Furthermore, the legislation that now applies to all the major criminal justice agencies requiring them to take positive action measures to meet their disability, gender and race equality duties, should in theory provide a common basis for the development of training and development programmes that, at the very least, are founded on a common approach to equal opportunity in employment and promotion. At a policy level, the information given above about the Accelerate programme provides an example of a positive action management development programme run for middle managers from both probation and youth justice designed to address the under-representation of staff at senior management level who have a disability and/or who are from one of the black and minority ethnic communities. For practitioners there are good examples of interventions developed by partnerships between relevant agencies, and which seek to develop an empowerment approach by utilising relevant community resources (see Hilder and also Goldhill, this volume).

However, the lack of definitional clarity over the concept of diversity inevitably makes it more complicated for staff from different agencies to work seamlessly together, particularly on practice-related matters. The conceptual/definitional muddle is further complicated by the use of alternative, perhaps complementary concepts, such as equality, which as we have seen is increasingly coupled together with diversity in the strategic and business plans of criminal justice agencies. Further, the continuing use of the term 'anti-discriminatory practice' across the probation service, which has its origins in attempts to reconceptualise social work theory and practice in the late 1970s and early 1980s, represents another complicating factor (see Thompson, 2006). This is an issue that the writer has experienced as a barrier to group learning in the training and development of multi-agency youth offending teams, where what was a core professional value to anyone from a professional social work background was a source of incomprehension and confusion to some of the police officers and health professionals present (see Pamment, this volume).

The previous paragraph makes reference to the following concepts:

■ equality;
■ diversity;
■ anti-discriminatory practice.

What do you understand by these terms? Are they linked or do they refer to different things?

On a more practical level, there is another reason why diversity cannot provide a secure value. The message that has come across loud and clear to the writer, who has been responsible for delivering diversity training to trainee probation officers for the last six years, is one of suspicion and lack of receptivity to diversity training. Many of them complain of being in effect 'diversified to death', since diversity issues are continuously raised in every part of their training programme. At the same time, the trainees are acutely aware of the enormous gap between the rhetoric of diversity policy on the one hand and the reality of implementing this in ways that respect and value the vast array of offenders' individual differences on the other. The dissonance created complicates and muddies the link between the strategic commitment to diversity and day-to-day probation practice. In part, this 'implementation gap' can be blamed on the lack of resources deployed to manage offenders in the community in ways that take full account of their individual differences and diverse needs. As we have seen in the previous section, faced with hard choices over how scarce resources are to be used, most agencies have taken the decision to prioritise those areas of difference that are covered under the UK's existing equalities legislation.

However, the difficulties encountered in transposing diversity policy to everyday professional practice cannot be explained entirely by reference to a lack of resources. It is important to recognise that many of the 'diversity dilemmas' that professionals across the criminal justice system face cannot be resolved or answered by appealing to the diversity policies of their agencies. Practice cannot be 'read off' from policy in this way. As a result of years of experience of anti-racist community work, the writer of this chapter has come to appreciate that anti-racist practice can rarely if ever be deduced logically from a more general commitment to anti-racism. In the same way, taking the right 'diversity' decision, one that gives concrete expression to an agency's policy of valuing and achieving diversity, is rarely an easy or straightforward matter for practitioners.

> Can you identify any 'diversity dilemmas' that have arisen in the organisation where you work and/or study? How might such dilemmas be resolved in ways that are compatible with the equality/diversity policies of your organisation?

Such practice dilemmas are normally best resolved through informal discussion among team members, especially when those members are drawn from a variety of agencies with different professional/organisational cultures and values. But here, too, concerns about 'saying the wrong thing' in relation to diversity may undermine confidence in discussing and debating practice dilemmas that have a diversity dimension to them. To this extent, there may be a grain of truth in the popular myth that 'diversity disempowers' if practitioners are worried about what their colleagues will say or do should they express uncertainty about how to resolve a difficulty that has a diversity dimension to it. Successful multi-agency collaboration is bound to be undermined when there are residual concerns over issues related to 'political correctness' and a worry that using an 'inappropriate' phrase may be seen by some as problematic.

Conclusion

This chapter has focused on the challenging problems relating to diversity policy and practice in the criminal justice system and more widely across the public sector. We have seen that shifting political and legislative sands in both the UK and the EU have had a direct impact on the rise – and perhaps partial demise – of diversity across the public sector. Most public sector agencies still make ritual obeisance towards diversity in the most general sense but today this is frequently located within a broader commitment to 'achieving equality' and/or 'promoting community cohesion'. The chapter has tried to show that, in spite of the fine words contained in strategic plans committing agencies to valuing difference and achieving diversity, in practice most of the diversity/equality action planning of these agencies focuses on differences that are covered by the UK's equality and anti-discrimination legislation, namely sex/gender, race, disability, age, religion and sexual orientation. Further, and again in line with the laws relating to equality duties, we have seen that agencies have tended to prioritise differences related to sex/gender, race and disability in their action plans and in the deployment of resources to achieve the targets set. Finally, it has been argued that the conceptual confusion that surrounds the concept of diversity, the unwillingness to focus on practice where the diversity issues are frequently complex and fractured, and an over-emphasis on the rhetorical appeal of the call to respect and value difference at the expense of a more hard-nosed discussion of issues related to priority and practice, have left frontline criminal justice professionals in a state of confusion over how to square the diversity circle.

Summary of key points

- Recent legislation in the UK has been shaped by the EU anti-discrimination directives and the Macpherson Inquiry into the murder of Stephen Lawrence.
- The response to these twin pressures has seen criminal justice agencies and the public sector generally embrace diversity over the subsequent 10 years.
- The evolving equalities legislation has resulted in diversity policies becoming subsumed within more general equality/community cohesion policies.
- These agency policies give expression to little more than the statutory duty to foster greater equality in the areas of sex/gender, race and disability.
- There are serious doubts over whether a general commitment to valuing and achieving diversity is either morally defensible or practically attainable.
- Many criminal justice practitioners feel confused and concerned over how to translate their agency's diversity policy into effective practice interventions.
- A general commitment to 'valuing and achieving diversity' is not particularly helpful to resolving the practice dilemmas that face practitioners.
- Because of the above, there is a danger that a shared commitment to diversity will offer little to facilitate partnership working between practitioners from different agencies.

Further reading

Clements, P. and Jones, J. (2006) *The Diversity Training Handbook: A Practical Guide to Understanding and Changing Attitudes.* London: Kogan Page.

Gelsthorpe, L. and McIvor, G. (2007) 'Difference and diversity in probation', in Gelsthorpe, L. and Morgan, R. (eds) *Handbook of Probation.* Cullompton: Willan Publishing.

Hudson, B. (2007) 'Diversity, crime and criminal justice', in Maguire, M., Morgan, R. and Reiner, R. (eds) *The Oxford Handbook of Criminology.* Oxford: Oxford University Press.

References

Cheetham, J. (1982) 'Some thoughts on practice', in Cheetham, J. (ed) *Social Work and Ethnicity.* London: Allen and Unwin.

CPS (Crown Prosecution Service) (2006) *Single Equality Scheme 2006–10.* London: CPS. Available at www.cps.gov.uk/publications/docs/ses_2006_2010.pdf

DTI (Department for Trade and Industry) (2005) *Women in the IT Industry: Towards a Business Case for Diversity.* London: DTI. Available at www.berr.gov.uk/files/file9334.pdf

EOC (Equal Opportunities Commission) (1985) *Code of Practice: Equal Opportunity Policies, Practices and Procedures in Employment.* London: HMSO.

European Commission (2008) *Continuing the Diversity Journey: Business Practices, Perspectives and Benefits.* Luxembourg: Office for Official Publications of the European Communities.

Gregory, J. (1987) *Sex, Race and the Law: Legislating for Equality.* London: Sage Publications.

Grieve, J. and French, J. (2000) 'Does institution racism exist in the Metropolitan Police Service?', in Green, D. (ed) *Institutional Racism and the Police: Fact or Fiction?* Trowbridge: Civitas.

HMIC (Her Majesty's Inspector of Constabulary) (2000) *Policing London: Winning Consent.* Available at www.nationalarchives.gov.uk/ERORecords/HO/421/2/hmic/pollondn.pdf

HM Prison Service (2003) *Corporate Plan 2003–2004 to 2005–2006: Business Plan 2003–2004.* London: HM Prison Service. Available at www.hmprisonservice.gov.uk/assets/documents/10000153corporateplan2003-2006businessplan03-04.pdf

Home Office (2001) *Community Cohesion: A Report of the Independent Review Team Chaired by Ted Cantle* (Cantle Report). London: Home Office.

Macpherson, W. (1999) *The Stephen Lawrence Inquiry: Report of an Inquiry by Sir William Macpherson.* Cm 4262-1. London: The Stationery Office.

Ministry of Justice (2009a) *NOMS Strategic and Business Plans: 2009–10 and 2010–11.* London: Ministry of Justice. Available at www.justice.gov.uk/publications/docs/noms-strategic-and-business-plans-2009-2011.pdf

Ministry of Justice (2009b) *Promoting Equality in Prisons and Probation: The National Offender Management Service Single Equality Scheme 2009–2012.* London: Ministry of Justice. Available at www.justice.gov.uk/publications/docs/noms-single-equality-scheme.pdf

Mitchell, M. and Russell, D. (1998) 'Fortress Europe, national identity and citizenship', in Carr, F. (ed) *Europe: The Cold Divide*. Basingstoke: Macmillan.

MPA (Metropolitan Police Authority) *HMIC Report 'Winning Consent': Recommendations relating to Consultation and Diversity*. Available at www.mpa.gov. uk/committees/x-cdo/2000/000728/08/#appendix01

MPS (Metropolitan Police Service) (2005) *Diversity Strategy 2005 Consultation*. London: MPS. Available at http://cms.MPS.police.uk/news/policy_ organisational_news_and_general_information/diversity/diversity_ strategy_2005_consultation

MPS (2007) *Disability Annual Report*. London: MPS. Available at www.MPS.police. uk/dcf/equality_stm.htm

MPS (2008a) *Equalities Scheme 2006–10* (updated version). London: MPS. Available at www.MPS.police.uk/dcf/files/equality_stm/MPSEqualitiesScheme_full_3. pdf

MPS (2008b) *Gender Annual Report*. London: MPS. Available at www.MPS.police. uk/dcf/index.htm

NPS (National Probation Service) (2001) *A New Choreography: Strategic Framework 2001–2004*. London: Home Office.

Parekh, B. (2000) *Rethinking Multiculturalism: Cultural Diversity and Political Theory*. Basingstoke: Palgrave Macmillan.

Sassen, S. (1999) *Guests and Aliens*. New York: New Press.

Thompson, N. (2006) *Anti-Discriminatory Practice* (4th edn). Basingstoke: Palgrave Macmillan.

YJB (Youth Justice Board) (2009) *Workforce Development: Accelerate*. London: YJB. Available at www.yjb.gov.uk/en-gb/practitioners/WorkforceDevelopment/ HRandLearning/Accelerate

CHAPTER 5

Multi-agency working with black and minority ethnic offenders

Sarah Hilder

Aims of the chapter

- To explore the contextual issues of discrimination experienced by black and minority ethnic offenders within the criminal justice system and the lack of confidence and credibility this triggers when seeking to engage with the black voluntary and community sector.
- To consider the impact of racism and other influences on personal identity and different models of offending behaviour interventions, including the empowerment model.
- To look at how cultural transference in multi-agency working may impact on black and minority ethnic offenders' experience of community supervision.
- To explore the role of the black voluntary and community sector in reducing reoffending.

This chapter explores some of the changing philosophies and methods that have been applied to multi-agency partnerships working with adult black and minority ethnic offenders. While there are references to developments within the Prison Service, the discussion centres on the supervision of offenders in the community, reflecting the author's own professional practitioner background. Clearly, the transitional and resettlement needs of black and minority ethnic offenders upon their release from prison are also a significant consideration. While the tensions inherent within the partnership arrangements for resettlement work and their fit with the current offender management model (Grapes, 2005) are discussed elsewhere in this volume (see Parkinson), some observations from Sharp et al's (2006) study of resettlement and the more specific experiences of black and minority ethnic prisoners are included here.

Language and terminology

The term 'black and minority ethnic' is used in this chapter in an inclusive manner. At times the term 'Black and Asian' and other terminology may also be adopted when mirroring the words used in the professional and research literature. It is accepted that this all-encompassing approach to the use of language is contested and presents some clear limitations. Therefore, while the limited scope of this chapter necessitates the use of generalised references such as this, it is essential to recognise the diversity of experience within and between the communities that may fall under these collective nouns (Farrow et al, 2007). Use of the term 'black and minority ethnic' is also often underpinned by an assumption that it only refers to non-white groups but it is important not to obscure the experiences of certain white ethnic minorities such as Eastern European migrant groups (Williams et al, 2007). Individual identities are also clearly multifaceted and are not restricted to concepts of race and ethnicity alone. Unsurprisingly, studies (eg Calverley et al, 2004) have highlighted a range of understandings and experiences within the categories of black, Asian and mixed heritage offenders, emphasising that race and ethnic status should not be considered as a singular identity from which all other issues and needs can be determined.

Black and minority ethnic experiences of the criminal justice system

A significant amount of literature and research has accumulated over recent times exploring black and minority ethnic groups' experience of justice, focusing primarily on issues of racism within the criminal justice process and highlighting discrimination at all key stages. Media and political debate continues to perpetuate an intolerance and fear of 'difference', exacerbating beliefs in the deviant behaviours of new migrant groups, with ever-changing trends in social hierarchies of exclusion and discrimination (Newburn, 2007). In 2007/08, black people were still nearly eight times more likely than white people to be stopped and searched by the police under the 1984 Police and Criminal Evidence Act and Asian people were twice as likely to be stopped (Home Office, 2009). This disproportionate representation continues throughout the system. Of British Nationals in June 2008, there were over five times more black people in prison relative to the population than white people (Home Office, 2009). Statistics highlight that black and minority ethnic offenders are more likely than white offenders to be serving a sentence in excess of four years (Williams et al, 2007). Under the 1974 Rehabilitation of Offenders Act, where convictions have attracted a sentence of 30 months or more they will never become spent, which can make rehabilitation and the acquiring of employment far more problematic.

While the main focus of this chapter is on issues of race and ethnicity, increasingly public and political perceptions intertwine this with negative conceptions of particular religions. Islamophobia and the negative stereotyping of Muslims have an enduring history within Western society (Spalek, 2004). However, the events of September 11th 2001 in the US and 7th July 2005 in London resulted in a surge of hate crime against Muslim communities and brought the significance of faith into clear focus when considering crime and victimisation (Spalek, 2004) (see Clift, this volume). Subsequent changes to the policing of young Asian men have been noted as they have become subject to stereotypes of religious extremism and a rigid patriarchal culture (Britton, 2004). Police searches under the 2000 Terrorism Act have increased by 215% from 37,197 in 2006/07 to 117,278 in 2007/08 (Home Office, 2009).

Following the recommendations of the Macpherson Inquiry into the racist murder of Stephen Lawrence in 1993 (Macpherson, 1999), there is clear evidence of developments in policy and training practice pertaining to race and diversity issues for all criminal justice agencies (see Mitchell, this volume). However, as Webster (2007) suggests, the realities for many black and minority ethnic communities are that a more benevolent approach to policing has yet to emerge. With experiences and observations such as this, the expectations of black, Asian and minority ethnic people that they are more likely to be treated by the police as a potential perpetrator of crime, rather than being appropriately supported by the criminal justice system as a victim, are clearly likely to persist.

For the Prison Service Mr Justice Keith's (House of Commons, 2006) report into the death of Zahid Mubarek at the Feltham Young Offender Institute in 2000 at the hands of the racist offender Robert Stewart was highly influential. The report made 88 recommendations for changes to improve practice in relation to race and diversity issues in prisons. Key issues were highlighted pertaining to institutionalised methods of working and in particular the treatment of black and minority ethnic prisoners, the poor execution of the complaints system and unequal access to goods and services. While white staff generally considered many processes within the service to be fair, this was not the perspective of black and minority ethnic staff. Significantly, only 3.5% of the prison staff population identified as black and minority ethnic in comparison with a black and minority ethnic prisoner population of 18% (NOMS, 2008a).

In 2008, the five-year race review published by the National Offender Management Service (NOMS) highlighted the significant progress made by the Prison Service in implementing systems to effectively manage race equality. However, despite these policy and procedural changes, the report acknowledged that the experiences of discrimination by black and minority ethnic prisoners and staff had not been transformed. Significantly, for black and minority ethnic prison staff racial discrimination and harassment was more likely to occur from white colleagues than from white prisoners (NOMS, 2008a).

Some study, albeit limited, has also been made of probation practice with black and minority ethnic offenders. The Home Office Thematic Inspection in 2000 (HM Inspectorate of Probation, 2000) – and the follow-up inspection in 2004 (HM Inspectorate of Probation, 2004) – highlighted concerns relating to an observed subjectivity and bias in the report writing on black and minority ethnic offenders. Observations by Knight and Bailey (2003) also highlighted that the Probation Service should not become complacent, acknowledging the concerns of the National Probation Directorate that the interests of black and minority ethnic offenders were not as well served by the National Probation Service as those of their white counterparts.

A more extensive research study was conducted by Calverley et al (2004) examining the experiences of Black and Asian male offenders supervised by the Probation Service from 2001 to 2003. Reported experiences of community supervision by the Probation Service were favourable. However, early disadvantage was seen by many probationers to be exacerbated by involvement in the criminal justice system and many participants reported experiences of what they often considered to be racist treatment from the police, courts and prison staff (Calverley et al, 2006). Far more tentative steps have been made in terms of any exploration of the specific experiences of women offenders from black and minority ethnic groups and despite many advances in criminological thinking, a gendered, race focus remains undeveloped (Gelsthorpe, 2006).

> What is your understanding of the concept of 'institutionalised racism and discrimination'?
>
> Consider the implications this raises for multi-agency working within the criminal justice sector and how such concerns might be addressed.

Race, ethnicity and offending – approaches to intervention

Criminological debates drawing on experiences of social exclusion and inequality by black and minority ethnic groups, coupled with disproportionate targeting from the police and negative stereotypes of black criminality, are relatively well rehearsed. It has been argued that material deprivation, unemployment, overly zealous policing and racism may all impact on the offending behaviours of some people from black and minority ethnic communities. However, Bowling and Phillips (2002) highlight that no attempt to develop a convincing theoretical account of the offending of black and minority ethnic groups in Britain would be complete without an account of discriminatory experiences within the criminal justice process.

There has been no conclusive evidence to suggest that black and minority ethnic offenders have different criminogenic needs to their white counterparts. However, Calverley et al (2004) observed that frequently the criminogenic needs of black and minority ethnic offenders occurred at lower levels than white offenders who had committed similar offences, again highlighting that black and minority ethnic offenders were sentenced more punitively. Such experiences of racism may have an impact on the compliance and progress of a black and minority offender through the prison and probation systems. Farrow et al (2007) acknowledge that, like any other offenders, black and minority ethnic offenders may be resistant to change. However, it is important that practitioners do not fall into stereotypical assumptions about such behaviour, but understand the many various internal and external factors that may have contributed to such resistance (Vanstone, 2006; Farrow et al, 2007).

Most of the development work by the Probation Service for black and minority ethnic offenders has been driven by staff in larger metropolitan areas and there has been very little national direction (Williams, 2006). A Home Office research study (Powis and Walmsley, 2002) identified 13 programmes that had been developed across 10 Probation Areas, five of which were running at the time of the study in London, Manchester and the West Midlands. While some of these five approaches did use cognitive behavioural methods, many also focused on an empowerment approach.

Empowerment models still endeavour to examine the cognitive processes that result in the choices being made by individuals. However, they also strive to recognise the impact of inequality and discrimination on those choices and examine how a more positive self-conceptualisation and self-identity may better equip an individual to make different choices (Williams, 2006). This is achieved through a variety of methods, including an exploration of cultural history and mentoring providing opportunities for positive role modelling and imitation. The purpose of examining issues of racism and discrimination is not to be seen to legitimise the offending behaviour, rather it establishes a fuller understanding of the context within which choices are made. It encourages individuals to realise a more positive sense of responsibility and investment both to themselves and the community (Williams, 2006).

Although the Powis and Walmsley (2002) study was unable to draw any firm conclusions on the success of the various different models of intervention examined, the pathfinder project that followed took a very specific line, which only saw empowerment work as a preparatory option that was conducted prior to the commencement of an accredited cognitive behavioural programme. Other options pursued included a Think First offending behaviour programme run specifically for Black and Asian participants, a Drink Impaired Drivers Course for Asian offenders as well as an accredited programme run with an ethnically mixed group. Narrowing the scope of the pathfinders in this way curtailed some of the other innovative and creative work, albeit patchy, which had been driven by enthusiastic and committed practitioners prior to that point (Durrance and Williams, 2003). (For a fuller discussion of these issues, see Walmsley and Stephens, 2006.)

In considering an alternative empowerment-based model further, it is important to recognise that the impact of racism will vary in terms of its resonance with individual black and minority ethnic offenders. Apena's (2007) study of young black male offenders highlighted how young black men may internalise negative racial stereotypes, and that while there is no causal link between racial identity and criminal behaviour, racist experiences may impact on an offender's self-talk. While clearly this will not apply to all offenders from black and minority ethnic groups, positive racial identities can be established. Apena (2007) argues strongly that the social context and construction of self should not be ignored when seeking to facilitate changes in offending behaviour. However, such an endorsement needs to be wary of a one-dimensional analysis that focuses only on racism and discrimination. As argued by Macey (2002), strategies that ignore cultural and religious influences and the interaction of gender, age and social class, assume that black and minority ethnic offenders only define themselves in relation to the majority white establishment. A wider concept of personal narrative should therefore be pursued acknowledging the multifaceted and complex realities of people's experience within both their local communities and wider society.

One example would be the need for further research to be undertaken to capture the diverse issues experienced by female offenders from different black and minority ethnic communities. Stigma and shame have been cited as a barrier to some black and minority ethnic women's engagement with support services (Fawcett Society, 2005; Goldhill, this volume). It is therefore vital to recognise that interactions within cultural and community groups may be just as significant as an understanding of external sources of discrimination and exclusion.

The discussion of empowerment leads us to some interesting parallels with models of desistance. McCulloch and McNeill (2008) highlight the three main theoretical components of desistance as maturation, social bonds theory and narrative. The latter two elements have obvious connections with the concept of empowerment, emphasising that in order to facilitate change a practitioner needs to engage with the social context within which an individual's offending behaviour occurs, their ties, investment and positive sense of attachment to their community. The concept of narrative in this sense does not simply recognise that key events and changes are important, but that how an individual manages and responds to these changes is equally significant. An individual's narrative is subjective and influenced by a concept of self-identity of which racial identity and the impact of racism may be a key component.

While an understanding of the specific intervention methods that may follow on from a desistance perspective remains somewhat in its infancy, advocates cite the need for more direct action, with a move away from the current intervention focus, which rests almost entirely on human capital, to one which equally considers the importance of social capital (McCulloch and Farrell, 2008). In this sense, both the informal and formal support mechanisms and assistance that are available to an individual are seen to be as vital as any developments in their cognitive skills. Approaches where criminal justice practitioners proactively engage in partnership with the communities they serve are seen as an essential starting point to establishing a framework to assist in the cessation from crime. Although an understanding of desistance is emerging (see Farrell and Calverley, 2006), this use of language has yet to fully permeate daily probation practice, which remains preoccupied by issues of individual responsibilisation. As a result, there may be ongoing tendencies to view any contributions from the black voluntary and community sector as fulfilling a subsidiary-support, welfare-orientated role rather than being perceived as an active element of a desistance pathway.

'Responsivity' (McGuire, 2002) is the focal point around which current practitioner debates on best practice with black and minority ethnic offenders congregate. Responsivity in community supervision refers to the development, planning and implementation of offender interventions that are compatible to each offender's criminogenic needs, individual characteristics and learning styles and which are delivered in an environment that will support these needs (Cole, 2008). The probation approach to responsivity for black and minority ethnic offenders has subsequently centred on how an offender receives a service and what can be done to facilitate maximum engagement and compliance rather than the consideration of any fundamental variants to programme and supervision content.

> Can empowerment and desistance models of intervention that incorporate partnerships with the black voluntary and community sector be considered as working to address offending behaviour? Give reasons for your answer.

Multi-agency, collaboration and collusion

Nash (this volume) explores the concepts of 'cultural transference' and 'merger' between agencies working in partnership. It is worth reflecting on these concepts in relation to black and minority ethnic offenders' experiences of utilising multi-agency provisions. It is argued that during the process of partnership working the individual identities of the agencies concerned may start to blur and the individual practitioner's adherence to the core values and underpinning philosophies of their host organisation may start to shift and merge. Some smaller black voluntary sector agencies have observed that they have felt under pressure to conform to the dominant ideology of the larger funding organisations. Black and minority ethnic groups are unequal partners and the contract may primarily be a vehicle for performance targets, which may lead to a direct conflict with the values of the black community organisation (Bhui, 2006). Cole (2008) agrees that this is a strategic barrier and that commissioned organisations may become tolerant of or subservient to the larger organisation's culture.

Sharp et al (2006) reported that voluntary agencies were often perceived to be far more responsive and less judgemental by black and minority ethnic prisoners than statutory organisations such as the Probation Service. This was attributed to the use of language and cultural difference and a mistrust of authority stemming from wider experiences of the criminal justice process overall (Sharp et al, 2006, as cited by Williams et al, 2007). However, the result of cultural transference as part of a statutory partnership contract can mean that for the black and minority ethnic offender the unique characteristics of the smaller voluntary, community-based agency that made the service appear more appropriate and accessible in the first place may start to fade.

There is clear evidence that people from black and minority ethnic communities are discriminated against in all of the areas covered in this book. This can be either by way of perpetuating a social construction of black criminality associated with stereotypical images of drug use, mental health and dangerousness, or through a process of marginalisation, exclusion and unequal access to opportunities such as education and training (Race for Justice, 2008). The challenge for criminal justice partnership delivery, then, is to address and resolve rather than compound these issues.

The black voluntary and community sector

As discussed in other chapters, the government's commitment to the involvement of the voluntary sector in public services is well established, as is the statutory agency duty towards race equality as stipulated by the 2000 Race Relations (Amendment) Act (see Mitchell, this volume). The publication of the Home Office Compact in 1998 covered the relationship between the government and the voluntary and community sector by providing a framework to clarify issues of funding, confidentiality, accountability and best practice. Although not legally binding, it was a new and difficult process for black voluntary and community sector agencies to engage with (Race for Justice, 2008). Implemented in 2001, the Compact contained five codes, one of which applied specifically to black voluntary and community organisations that struggled with a lack of experience in negotiating contracts. However, Howson (2007), as cited by Mills (2009), states that this perception of a lack of ability to manage budgets effectively is an unjust yet enduring legacy from the governmental management of financial injections into the black voluntary and community sector in the 1980s. Howson argues that funding at that time set black voluntary and community agencies up against each other as a divisive strategy to undermine the black political movement (Mills, 2009).

The passing of the 2007 Offender Management Act gave rise to a further increase in the commitment to contracted-out services within the Prison and Probation Services. *Working with the Third Sector to Reduce Re-offending: Securing Effective Partnerships* (NOMs, 2008b) is part of the National Offender Management strategic plan for 2008-11. Increasingly, community cohesion and strategies to address inter-faith and intra-faith tensions have been placed on the partnership working agenda (Home Office, 2003). The Faith and Voluntary and Community Sector Alliances were launched in 2005, seeking to widen the scope of voluntary, community and faith-based organisation involvement in the reduction of offending. The alliances promote practical support, pastoral advice and mentoring provided by members of diverse local communities (see Parkinson, this volume).

Boeck et al (2009: 49) cite Chapman and Lowndes (2008), who highlight that the term 'faith community' is increasingly being confused and used as a replacement for the term 'black and ethnic communities'. Clear distinctions should be made. A particular driver for governmental faith-based initiatives has been the concern following the US and London terrorist attacks that disaffected, socially excluded young Muslims may join extremist organisations (Spalek, 2004). An attention to other concerns of social injustice relating to race and ethnicity issues has, it would appear, become diluted under the cohesion agenda.

Observations made by Mills (2009), in her study of voluntary and community organisations working with black young people affected by crime, support this contention. She found that the majority of the voluntary and community providers interviewed did not embrace a definition of their work in terms of race and ethnicity. Concerns were raised by providers that such definitions would stigmatise the young people they worked with. However, those practitioners who had been working in the voluntary and community sector for much longer also suggested that this shift towards to an ethnicity-neutral identity for organisations occurred in the 1990s to 2000s and was influenced by the emerging community cohesion framework. Prior to that it was felt that for many of these smaller agencies there was a strong underpinning ethos of political and social justice, which challenged the mainstream and promoted a positive black identity to assist black young people in coping with issues of disadvantage. It was argued, however, that such an ethnicity-specific focus was seen to subvert the government's agenda and many organisations had to adopt a generic identity in order to secure ongoing funding. The drive to address specific experiences of marginalisation and discrimination may therefore become concealed by some of these agencies within a presentation of generic services open to all (Mills, 2009).

Those voluntary and community sector agencies working predominantly with black and minority ethnic groups include a number of larger organisations such as the National Body of Black Prisoners Support Groups (NBBPSG), Race for Justice and Race on the Agenda (ROTA) who offer national and regional support and guidance for black and minority ethnic individuals and the black voluntary and community sector. They also campaign and seek to influence wider social policy and criminal justice debates. At a local level, black voluntary and community groups fulfil a variety of functions, but tend to have emerged as self-help groups, run by community members themselves rather than the more traditional philanthropic voluntary pursuit of assisting those seen to be disadvantaged (NBBPSG, nd).

The range of partnership services provided by the black voluntary and community sector includes advocacy and human rights work, translation and interpretation services, counselling, mental health services, cultural awareness training for statutory sector staff, black empowerment work, parenting skills, faith-based mentoring, and women-only services (NBBPSG, nd). Many adopt a resource, drop-in centre approach to service provision, where a number of different types of service may be accessed. The Pakistani Resource Centre partnership with Greater Manchester Probation Service, for example, has been well documented over the years, as has the Lancashire Probation Area Asian Offenders Project.

Other black voluntary and community sector projects have examined particular 'crime problems'. An example of this is the Makeda Weaver project to assist young men involved with gangs and gun-related violence to be supported out of crime, run by the Shain Housing Association in Hackney, which accepts referrals from probation, the police and other statutory sector agencies (Race for Justice, 2008). Similar initiatives run in the West Midlands and London Probation Areas. ROTA, a London-based National Lottery funded policy 'think tank', is part of a restorative justice partnership with statutory sector agencies seeking to find reintegrative methods of addressing hate crime. Their Building Bridges project also explores gangs, the use of weapons and youth violence, with a current project focusing on the female voice of violence (Race on the Agenda, 2009).

Britton (2004) provides us with a word of caution before fully endorsing an offence-specific approach such as this, as there is a danger if handled inappropriately that such initiatives may serve to further reinforce social constructions of black criminality. Britton continues that black and minority ethnic people's lack of confidence in the criminal justice system is also exacerbated by what appears to be a general disinterest in the issues of crime and victimisation that impact directly on black and minority ethnic communities themselves and that certain issues only become a general public concern when they are perceived to pose a threat to the majority white population (Britton, 2004).

The enthusiasm for developments in provisions for female offenders is discussed elsewhere in this book (see Goldhill, Chapter 6) but the provision of services for black and minority ethnic women warrants some attention here. In April 2009, the government announced a £15.6 million investment in strategies to prevent and reduce offending by women. This includes grant funding to extend the provision of 'one-stop shops' as a method of providing a range of services to vulnerable women.

Positive examples include the Calderdale Women's Centre in Halifax, the Minority Ethnic Community Support Service in Fenham and the Asha Centre in Worcester (Fawcett Society, 2005). The last of these originated from women-centred work undertaken by the Probation Service, but which due to a lack of accreditation became a voluntary charity-funded project in 2002. Agencies such as Southall Black Sisters provide support for Asian, African and Caribbean female victims of violence and have also been commended for their efforts to engage with women from hard-to-reach minority ethnic groups. Formally funded partnerships for black and minority ethnic female offenders are harder to find, although other funded specialist services such as alcohol and drug counselling and housing support often employ female outreach workers from different minority ethnic backgrounds to encourage participation from hard-to-reach client groups. Problems of confidentiality can lead to a lack of confidence in services, particularly when people from the local minority ethnic community are members of the staff team (Fawcett Society, 2005).

Opportunities and challenges

A key consideration for statutory, voluntary and community organisations entering into a process of multi-agency working with black and minority ethnic offenders is whether the intervention proposed is considered to be a method of reducing the risk of reoffending, or a way of facilitating other perceived welfare-orientated needs, or indeed does it seek to do both? It is difficult to capture the nature of some voluntary sector approaches to working with black and minority ethnic groups as strategies are often developed in an informal and individual basis, but providers such as those described in Mills' (2009) study often express their desired outcomes in terms of changing self-perceptions and beliefs, retaining links with both the empowerment- and cognitive-behavioural-based models discussed earlier. However, Mills (2009) concludes that current governmental expectations remain unclear and that while there is a strong rhetorical emphasis on the role the voluntary sector should play in the reduction of the disproportionate representation of young black and minority ethnic people in the criminal justice system, there is no clarification as to how such agencies are being asked to contribute and how they will be supported. Where partnerships with statutory agencies were in place a sense of tokenism was ascribed.

A survey exercise published by the Joseph Rowntree Foundation (Chouhan and Lusane, 2004) found that some black voluntary and community sector agencies felt unfairly treated by their funding agencies and thought that the level of scrutiny applied to their practice was unacceptable. It was also contended by some that the very important role that the black voluntary and community sector played in civic engagement and social inclusion was often not fully understood.

The Fawcett Society (2005) found that a lack of data was one of the most critical barriers to effective partnership and service delivery for black and minority ethnic women. Agencies often have no clear process of monitoring and evaluation and an informality of approach that may be one of the reasons why their services are seen to be more accessible by service users in the first place. However, it makes it difficult to assess the value of the different approaches undertaken. This may inhibit any critical evaluation, development and improvement to services as well as restricting access to some of the potential sources of funding.

The NBBPSG (nd) advocate a number of good practice benchmarks for statutory agencies engaging in partnership with the black voluntary and community sector. This includes ensuring that joint forums are established and that members of the smaller partnership group sit on diversity advisory panels for Probation and Prison Service establishments. Diversity awareness training for statutory sector staff is also recommended. Similarly, Sharp et al (2006) highlight that there are often significant discrepancies between the stated aims of statutory sector race equality policies and the realities of daily practice and that further staff training is required.

Britton (2000) offers similar observations in her study of a 'Help on Arrest Scheme', a small black voluntary sector organisation offering 24-hour support and advice to black people who had been arrested. The project was met by opposition from police officers who did not accept that the police custody process is racialised. Britton (2000) argues that until strategies to tackle institutionalised racism and discrimination such as this are placed at the heart of statutory agency policy agendas, it is questionable as to whether a genuine partnership with the black voluntary and community sector can ever be achieved.

In relation to the issue of voluntary and community sector organisations being able to compete in a tendering process, NOMS has responded to such concerns via the development of a capacity-building project. CLINKs, Action for Prisoner Families and the Development Trusts Association have all been awarded government funding to establish a national third sector infrastructure to assist small organisations in putting together effective bids for criminal justice sector work. However, general responses to this commissioning process state that larger charities are already 'scaling up' to meet such demands and to what extent smaller black voluntary sector groups will be able and willing to engage in this process is currently unknown.

> Do partnership agencies always need to have a common shared philosophy of approach to working with black and minority offenders and other offender groups in order to be effective?

Conclusions

The following conclusions may be drawn:

- Multi-agency working with offenders from black and minority ethnic communities needs to be considered within the context of the systemic discrimination of such groups at every stage of the criminal justice process and how this echoes wider structural inequalities within society.
- Some voluntary sector organisations are reluctant to explicitly identify ethnicity as part of their organisational remit, for fear of further stigmatising and perpetuating stereotypes of black criminality. However, under more organisational generic labels, concerns are that the particular issues of social injustice experienced by such groups are underestimated.
- Empowerment and desistance models offer a wider perspective that considers the impact of discrimination on an individual's self-identity, their engagement with the community and the context within which choices are made.
- However, an individualised cognitive behavioural approach to 'offence-focused' work currently continues to dominate the statutory approach to community supervision.
- As a result, the main focus of partnership working between statutory and voluntary sector agencies in relation to black and minority ethnic offenders tends to relate primarily to issues of practical support and endeavours to facilitate equal opportunity to mainstream service provisions and requirements.
- What has been fundamentally missing from this discussion is any clear sense of black and minority ethnic offenders' voices. As many have already endorsed (Britton, 2004; Williams et al, 2007; Cole, 2008), a commitment to placing black and minority ethnic offenders' narratives at the heart of any future research is an essential next step.
- In the meantime, any attempts to 'mainstream' the black voluntary and community sector may be missing the point. It suggests an incomplete understanding of the value of small-scale local community provision and triggers connotations of cultural transference and subservient tolerance.
- The black voluntary and community sector's very strength is its capacity to prompt reflection and critique of mainstream criminal justice approaches. There are some exciting, innovative projects where statutory sector agencies

such as probation have embraced such an engagement, but they remain quite isolated examples. Centralisation has thwarted some of this creativity and there are concerns that the additional layer of competitive tendering may continue to airbrush other potential developments out of the picture.

Points for further consideration

- How can a continuous culture of learning, creativity and development in working with black and minority ethnic communities be sustained within statutory sector criminal justice agencies?
- Consider the different strategic priorities that may be in place at national, regional and local levels when answering this question. Are they compatible?

Further reading

Cole, B. (2008) 'Working with ethnic diversity', in Green, S., Lancaster, E. and Feasey, S. (eds) *Addressing Offending Behaviour: Context, Practice and Values*. Cullompton: Willan Publishing.

Macpherson, W. (1999) *The Stephen Lawrence Inquiry: Report of an Inquiry by Sir William Macpherson of Cluny*, Cm 4262-2. London: Home Office.

Williams, K., Atherton, S. and Sharp, D. (2007) 'The resettlement of black and minority ethnic offenders', in Huckelsby, A. and Hagley-Dickinson, L. (eds) *Prisoner Resettlement: Policy and Practice*. Cullompton: Willan Publishing.

References

Apena, F. (2007) 'Being black and in trouble: the role of self perception in the offending behaviour of black youth', *Youth Justice*, 7, 211-28.

Beock, T., Fleming, J., Smith, R. and Thorp, L. (2009) *Volunteering and Faith Communities in England: A Modernising Volunteering Workstream Report*. London: Volunteering England.

Bhui, H.S. (2006) 'Anti racist practice in NOMS: reconciling managerialist and professional realities', *Howard Journal*, 45(2), 171-90.

Bowling, B. and Phillips, C. (2002) *Racism, Crime and Justice*. Harlow: Pearson.

Britton, N.J. (2000) *Black Justice? Race, Criminal Justice and Identity*. Stoke-on-Trent: Trentham Books.

Britton, N.J. (2004) 'Minorities, crime and criminal justice', in Muncie, J. and Wilson, D. (eds) *Student Handbook of Criminal Justice and Criminology* (pp 81-93). London: Cavendish.

Calverley, A., Cole, B., Kaur, G., Lewis, S., Raynor, P., Sadeghi, S., Smith, D., Vanstone, M. and Wardak, A. (2004) *Black and Asian Offenders on Probation*, Home Office Research Study 277. London: Home Office.

Calverley, A., Cole, B., Kaur, G., Lewis, S., Raynor, P., Soheila, S., Smith, D., Vanstone, M. and Wardak, A. (2006) 'Black and Asian probationers: implications of the Home Office study', *Probation Journal*, 53(11), 24–37.

Chouhan, K. and Lusane, C. (2004) *Black Voluntary and Community Sector Funding: Its Impact on Civic Engagement and Capacity Building*. York: Joseph Rowntree Foundation.

Cole, B. (2008) 'Working with ethnic diversity', in Green, S., Lancaster, E. and Feasey, S. (eds) *Addressing Offending Behaviour: Context, Practice and Values* (pp 402-26). Cullompton: Willan Publishing.

Durrance, P. and Williams, P. (2003) 'Broadening the agenda around what works for Black and Asian offenders', *Probation Journal*, 50(3), 211-24.

Farrell, S. and Calverley, A. (2006) *Understanding Desistance from Crime: Theoretical Directions in Resettlement and Rehabilitation*. Milton Keynes: Open University Press.

Farrow, K., Kelly, G. and Wilkinson, B. (2007) *Offenders in Focus: Risk, Responsivity and Diversity*. London: The Policy Press.

Fawcett Society (2005) *Black and Minority Ethnic Women in the UK*. London: The Fawcett Society.

Gelsthorpe, L. (2006) 'The experiences of female minority ethnic offenders: the other "other"', in Lewis, S., Raynor, P., Smith, D. and Wardak, A. (eds) *Race and Probation* (pp 100-21). Cullompton: Willan Publishing.

Grapes, T (2005) *NOMS Offender Management Model*. London: NOMS.

HM Inspectorate of Probation (2000) *Towards Race Equality: Thematic Inspection Report*. London: HMIP.

HM Inspectorate of Probation (2004) *Towards Race Equality: Follow up Thematic Inspection Report*. London: Home Office.

Home Office (2003) *Community Cohesion Pathfinder Programme: The First Six Months*. London: Home Office.

Home Office (2009) *Statistics on Race and the Criminal Justice System 2007/08: A Ministry of Justice Publication under Section 95 of the Criminal Justice Act 1991*. London: Home Office.

House of Commons (2006) *The Report of the Zahid Mubarek Inquiry*. London: HMSO.

Knight, V. and Bailey, R. (2003) 'An investigation into minority ethnic prisoners' perceptions and knowledge of the Probation and Prison Service in the East of England'. Unpublished report for the National Probation Service (East of England).

McCulloch, T. and McNeill, F. (2008) 'Desistance-focused approaches' in Green, S., Lancaster, E. and Feasey, S. (eds), *Addressing Offending Behaviour: Context, Practice and Values*. Cullompton: Willan Publishing.

Macey, M. (2002) 'Interpreting Islam: young Muslim men's involvement in criminal activity in Bradford', in Spalek, B. (ed) *Islam, Crime and Criminal Justice* (pp 19-49). Cullompton: Willan Publishing.

McGuire, J. (2002) *Offender Rehabilitation and Treatment: Effective Programmes and Policies to Reduce Re-offending*. Chichester: John Wiley.

Macpherson, W. (1999) *The Stephen Lawrence Inquiry: Report of an Inquiry by Sir William Macpherson of Cluny*, Cm 4262-2. London: Home Office.

Mills, H. (2009) *Policy, Purpose and Pragmatism: Dilemmas for Voluntary and Community Organisations Working with Black Young People Affected by Crime.* London: Centre for Crime and Justice Studies, King's College London.

NBBPSG (National Body of Black Prisoners Support Groups) (nd) *Good Practice Guide: A Practical Guide for Practitioners Working with BME Communities within the Criminal Justice System.* Available at www.nbbpsg.co.uk/links.php

Newburn, T. (2007) *Criminology.* Cullompton: Willan Publishing.

NOMS (National Offender Management Service) (2008a) *Race Review: Implementing Race Equality in Prisons, Five Years On.* Race and Equalities Action Group. London: NOMS.

NOMS (2008b) *Working with the Third Sector to Reduce Re-offending: Securing Effective Partnerships.* London: NOMS.

Powis, B. and Walmsley, R.K. (2002) *Programmes for Black and Asian Offenders on Probation: Lessons for Developing Practice*, Home Office Research Study 250. London: HMSO.

Race for Justice (2008) *Less Equal than Others: Ethnic Minorities and the Criminal Justice System.* York: CLINKS.

Race on the Agenda (2009) *Transformation Justice Project.* London: Race on the Agenda. Accessed at www.rota.org.uk/pages/default.aspx

Sharp, D., Atherton, S. and Williams, K. (2006) *Everyone's Business: Investigating the Resettlement Needs of Black and Minority Ethnic Groups in the West Midlands.* Birmingham: Government Office West Midlands.

Spalek, D. (2004) 'Islam and criminal justice', in Muncie, J. and Wilson, D. (eds) *Student Handbook of Criminal Justice and Criminology* (pp 123-33). London: Cavendish.

Vanstone, M. (2006) 'Room for improvement: a history of the Probation Service's response to race' in Lewis, S., Raynor, P., Smith, D. and Wardak, A. (eds) *Race and Probation* (pp 13-24). Cullompton: Willan Publishing.

Walmsley, R. and Stephens, K. (2006) 'What works with black and minority ethnic offenders: solutions in search of a problem?', in Lewis, S., Raynor, P., Smith, D. and Wardak, A. (eds) *Race and Probation* (pp 164-81). Cullompton: Willan Publishing.

Webster, C. (2007) *Understanding Race and Crime.* Milton Keynes: Open University Press.

Williams, K., Atherton, S. and Sharp, D. (2007) 'The resettlement of black and minority ethnic offenders', in Huckelsby, A. and Hagley-Dickinson, L. (eds) *Prisoner Resettlement: Policy and Practice* (pp 224-44). Cullompton: Willan Publishing.

Williams, P. (2006) 'Designing and delivering programmes for minority ethnic offenders', in Lewis, S., Raynor, P., Smith, D. and Wardak, A. (eds) *Race and Probation* (pp 145-64). Cullompton: Willan Publishing.

CHAPTER 6

From pillar to post: multi-agency working with women offenders

Rachel Goldhill

Aims of the chapter

■ To demonstrate the importance of considering women as a separate group with specific unmet needs in the criminal justice system.

■ To explore the advantages of partnerships.

■ To discuss how funding and resource issues get in the way of productive strategies.

■ To show what positive steps are required to improve the situation.

This chapter explores the benefits and drawbacks to multi-agency working with women offenders and from the different perspectives of the Probation Service, voluntary agencies and service users. It examines what has been accomplished to date and argues that only with a proper resourcing strategy, a coordinated approach and shared goals will effective community support be facilitated to prevent the increased use of prison sentences for women.

Unmet needs

In recent years, women have suffered progressively harsher treatment in the criminal justice system. In 1996, 4,179 women were sentenced to immediate custody whereas by 2006 the number stood at 7,391, an increase of 77% (Patel and Stanley, 2008: 11). This has not been due to a rise in the seriousness of female offending (Gelsthorpe et al, 2007) but to a doubling of the use of prison for less serious summary offences. In 2006, 75% of women prisoners received sentences of less than 12 months, so with no licence period for short-term prisoners this meant limited opportunities for support or supervision (Patel and Stanley, 2008: 11, citing Ministry of Justice, 2007).

Women offenders are far from being a homogenous category, yet because of the gendered nature of all aspects of society, including crime, they constitute a distinct group within the criminal justice system. Both research studies (eg Carlen and Worrall, 2004; Gelsthorpe et al, 2007) and the government-sponsored Corston Report (2007) conclude that most women offenders have complex, multiple problems (Corston, 2007: 15). Some problems replicate those of men, for example poverty and drug misuse, but Offender Assessment System (OASys)[1] data (cited in Gelsthorpe et al, 2007: 7) show that housing, sex work, lack of education/ training skills, and mental health are especially problematic areas for women, as they represent a lack of opportunities, which perpetuates exclusion.

Additionally, qualitative differences between women's and men's experiences in the criminal justice system have been identified (Corston, 2007: 17), specifically emotional aspects relating to reproductive, biological difference (such as menstruation, pregnancy and giving birth). Most significantly, the majority of women offenders are also victims who have undergone prolonged sexual and other physical violence and come from multiply disadvantaged backgrounds (Rumgay, 2004b: 8-9). Hedderman et al (2008: 9) found that female motivation to commit crime was based on desperation, unlike male motivation, which was characterised by rebellion. Lack of self-worth inhibited change because women offenders felt that their situation was hopeless. Blanchette (2002, cited in Hedderman et al, 2008: 7) explored criminogenic needs (dynamic risk factors that can be influenced through interventions to prevent offending), suggesting that there are women-specific criminogenic needs as well as those for both males and females. She went further to explain that 'even when men and women appear to have similar needs, the ways these intersect with offending may still differ' (2002, cited in Hedderman et al, 2008: 7). Having suffered physical and/or sexual abuse may not be considered a criminogenic need in itself but, combined with other psychological and social processes, greater risk of offending is predicted. Social aspects also impact on women offenders, as it is they who take the main responsibility for parenting and care of older people while simultaneously dealing with their own problems as outlined above (Carlen and Worrall, 2004: 42). It is often this accumulation of factors that is significant for female offenders.

Prison is more serious for women too, as when released they can find themselves caught in a vicious cycle. For those who already experience social exclusion prior to custody then the evidence suggests that the situation deteriorates even further upon release (Corston, 2007: 3). Single mothers with substance misuse problems discover the virtual impossibility of being reunited with their children following custody (Chigwada-Bailey, 2003: 134). As Housing Benefit is removed from prisoners serving more than 13 weeks, ensuing homelessness means that social services are unable to return their children to them. Fifty-nine per cent of women held on remand do not go on to receive custody as their sentence yet still experience these repercussions (Home Office, 2004, cited in Goldhill, 2009). Askwith (2008) argues that accommodation is frequently the most crucial area because it underpins women's emotional and physical security as well as their relationships, in contrast to men who tend to prioritise employment. When links are made between accommodation and the welfare of the children, there are broader repercussions. Alongside the financial demands made on the public sector to provide alternative residences for these children, there is the emotional cost of separation from the mother, leading to social problems arising from changes in the children's behaviour at school and on the streets (Matrix Knowledge Group, 2007).

Despite presenting as a heterogeneous group, women offenders do share certain significant characteristics. Very few have just one single need (Hedderman et al, 2008) and with generally complex and interlinked issues they often lie outside the parameters of the statutory agency whose focus is predominantly on punishment and fulfilling the sentence of the court (Gelsthorpe et al, 2007: 51). Research has shown that women respond best within a supportive, women-only, holistic, caring environment that allows them the time to 'open up' to the same worker while also being offered practical assistance (Patel and Stanley, 2008: 13). It has been suggested by Gelsthorpe et al (2007: 27) that there should be an emphasis on empowerment, developing an awareness of the choices open to them, and asking women offenders themselves about their preferences; one such preference is the wish to blend in with 'normal' women, those who have not offended (Corston, 2007: 61). Such opportunities are not available within the sole confines of the criminal justice system, as the women will mix only with other offenders.

Recent legislation has started to address these considerations and has been closely followed by reviews and policy documents detailing how implementation could take place. The 2006 Gender Equality Act made explicit that criminal justice agencies must ensure equal outcomes in the treatment of men and women. Under this legislation, public bodies now have a legal duty to show that they are recognising and dealing with the specific needs of women (see Mitchell, this volume). Gelsthorpe et al (2007: 12) explain that equal outcomes do not amount to treating everybody in the same way. Corston (2007: 3) argues that vulnerable women, already disadvantaged, are further stigmatised and discriminated against once they come into contact with the criminal justice system. She makes the point that the experience of prison revictimises individuals who have been subjected to abuse as children and adults (2007: 5). Also recommended is urgent action for the large numbers of women with mental health problems; that the seven pathways to resettlement (set up by the government in 2004 to ensure that each area has an action plan to reduce reoffending) should not be separated from each other but integrated to meet the women's multiple and overlapping needs; and that there should be two further distinct pathways for women offenders – to support those who have been abused and those involved in prostitution (Corston, 2007: 46). Shortly after the publication of the Corston Review, the Fawcett Society set out its assessment of provision for women offenders in the community (Gelsthorpe et al, 2007). Both reports arrived at the same conclusion: that for the majority of women offenders, management in the community was preferable to that in custody, and within community management the voluntary sector, in particular locally based women's centres, should play a much larger role (Corston, 2007: 63; Gelsthorpe et al, 2007: 32).

Which interventions with women offenders would draw out and resolve their difficulties as described above?

Why partnership working?

Partnership working is a multifaceted phenomenon relating to interactions between statutory agencies, between statutory and voluntary organisations and between these agencies and the service users and their families. Mills and Codd (2008: 11) state that offenders' relatives provide valuable sources of social capital (the opportunities for individuals to advance themselves through social networks) in attempts to minimise social exclusion and maximise desistance. Development of partnerships has been promoted by the government as the 'solution to many social ills' (Rumgay, 2007: 551), insisting that solitary organisations, however well intentioned, cannot properly counteract serious social problems and the reality of multiple disadvantage on their own. Partnerships are considered the way forward since they appear to open up dramatic and creative opportunities for stopping offending.

The partnership approach in criminal justice is based on the notion that offenders' difficulties resemble those of other socially disadvantaged groups. Access to wider local resources is only available through multi-agency working and in particular the voluntary sector (Rumgay, 2004a: 134). Voluntary organisations are seen as having a commitment to focusing outwards to the community and so are in a better position to understand local needs (Malloch et al, 2008: 394). Change, variation and combining forces is expected as an integral part of their remit and these are factors to be welcomed, not avoided (Rumgay, 2004a: 131).

> What difficulties could arise in implementing partnership interventions for female offenders?
>
> What strategies and resources do you have to deal with these issues?

Women-only centres

Voluntary sector agencies seem to offer more attractive inducements, defined by flexibility and availability towards women offenders. They exist without the restraints commonly associated with statutory public services, focusing on social circumstances instead of pathologising, labelling or monitoring the individual and placing greater emphasis on rehabilitation through support and therapy as opposed to punishment. In particular, community women's centres are most favoured, by practitioners at grassroots level (Roberts, 2002), by government directives – the Women's Offending Reduction Programme (WORP) (2004) (see below) and the Corston Report (2007) – and by academics (Carlen and Worrall, 2004; Gelsthorpe and Sharpe, 2007; Gelsthorpe et al 2007), as offering the best prospects for preventing and stopping offending.

The Asha Centre in Worcester, set up in the early 1990s, with close links to the Hereford and Worcester Probation Service and incorporating the West Mercia programme for women offenders, came to be seen as the flagship of good practice (Roberts, 2002). The Asha Centre was held up for praise in WORP (2004), which aimed to reduce custodial sentences for women through enlarging and improving community facilities. As part of the WORP directive, a one-off government grant of £9.15 million was provided to fund the Together Women Programme (TWP), which consisted of three 'one-stop shop' women's centres in Yorkshire and Humberside, Leeds, and Doncaster and Bradford, and two others in the North West – Liverpool and Greater Manchester (Gelsthorpe et al, 2007: 10-11). Similar innovations have been established at two centres in Scotland – Corton Vale and the 218 Centre.

The most fundamental traits of women's centres are that staff should be 'dedicated, caring, qualified, ex-addicts/ex-offenders, female role models' (Carlen and Worrall, 2004: 118). Preventive interventions, as well as statutory work, can be undertaken with a stronger focus on the development of collaborative opportunities so that female offenders can be given a voice. The focus is on a shared value system where there is an all-woman staff group, some of whom are in the process of overcoming personal difficulties themselves (Malloch et al, 2008: 389). At the New Bridge Project in Liverpool, women prisoners are trained by National Association for the Care and Resettlement of Offenders (NACRO) and prison/probation staff to be housing advisors at HMP Low Newton. Constraints of time are not as stringent as in a statutory agency so if a woman arrives in a distressed or agitated state, sufficient space is allowed for expression of feelings. As one client at the 218 Centre explained (cited by Hedderman et al, 2008: 15), 'They don't talk down to me; they don't tell me what to do … they always gave me alternatives'. (See Pycroft, this volume, on the policy background to concepts of service user participation and Skinner, this volume, for how this might inform offender management models.)

A common thread running through the centres is the commitment to improve women's health – through prescribing medication, psychological and psychiatric services, counselling and alternative therapies. At the 218 Centre, women are guided through a programme incorporating three phases. The first phase – called SAFE – focuses on offending, substance misuse and stabilisation, where the key provision is a one-to-one worker who arranges the prescription of drugs, suitable accommodation and the establishment of benefits claims. Women then move on to the next phase – CONNECTIONS – which aims to reduce substance misuse, and involves programme work and the development of relationships to increase support networks and re-establish social bonds in order to prepare for a life free from substance misuse. The final stage – LOSS – moves the women towards independence through contact with Employment, Training and Education and therapeutic input (Malloch et al, 2008: 386).

The Together Women Projects, which were set up in 2006 in five probation areas in the North West, Yorkshire and Humberside, are based on best practice from the smaller-scale initiatives such as the Asha Centre and the 218 Centre and place importance on a 'tailored response to individual needs' in contrast to the 'one size fits all' associated with the 'What Works' agenda and the offender management model (Hedderman et al, 2008: 1). Engagement and compliance are encouraged initially through home visits set up to encourage a strong worker–offender relationship prior to attendance at the Together Women Centre. Available services, such as debt assistance, benefit claims and counselling are explained in familiar surroundings, at the woman's home, and afterwards telephone calls reinforce work aimed at collaboration and trust. Emerging from these projects is the central message that there are no quick fixes, only the slow building or rebuilding of social, economic and emotional networks.

Resourcing and funding

One of Corston's (2007: 46) assertions is that drugs, housing, welfare and childcare services should interconnect but that currently 'artificial divisions' between agencies drain the small voluntary organisations and create confusion and alienation. Although not negating the intrinsic value of many voluntary sector contributions, awareness of these difficulties raises questions as to whether there is sufficient coordination, at ministerial as well as at ground level, for there to be a widespread national response. The chapter therefore continues with an exploration and assessment of the main factors restricting progress in partnership working.

In 1990, Carlen (cited in Malloch et al, 2008: 393) was arguing that community rehabilitation schemes tended to be fragmented rather than holistic and affected by separate legislation and policy in the spheres of housing, work and education. The lack of joined-up planning at senior level with minimal consultation in the early stages of the programme was also noted when the 218 Project was set up in 2003 (Loucks et al, 2006: 59). Problems remained in the basics for the women, finding suitable accommodation and swift access to help with drugs. Clarke (2004: 26), in her analysis of women service users, argues that one-off projects will not bring about major changes while there is a lack of movement at policy level. Contradictory messages have marked the government approach to offenders epitomised by a modicum of humanitarianism alongside the far more dominant punitive stance, which tends to prevail (Goldhill, 2009). The greater propensity for custodial sentencing and more recently for large warehouse-type prisons has depleted resources in the community (Owers, 2004; Owers, cited by Make Justice Work, 2009). Inadequate services are then left to deal with issues such as co-morbidity (the combination of drugs and mental health, or alcohol and drugs) where unhelpful barriers remain between drug and health service agencies (Borrill et al, 2003) (see Winstone and Pakes, and also Rees, this volume).

Underpinning many of the problems is the issue of funding. At first the demonstration projects received generous cash injections, but when the models were rolled out nationally, little, if any, money was made available. Government responses to Corston's recommendation for further 'one-stop shops' exemplify this. It accepted the recommendation 'in principle' but with no further funding and subject to a 'full evaluation … undertaken in 2009' (Ministry of Justice, 2007: 24). Increased media attention and antagonism towards ex-prisoners, single parents and girl gangs has meant that women offenders are politically unpopular when having to compete for funding against less controversial groups (Malin, 2007: 287).

The small numbers of women compared with men in the criminal justice system have contributed to this sidelined position. Gelsthorpe (2006: 114) stresses that black and minority ethnic women are particularly vulnerable due to having very low numbers within which are included a variety of ethnicities (see Hilder, this volume). Data are lacking on what proportion of women on probation caseloads come from black and minority ethnic groups (Gelsthorpe, 2006: 114). Malin's study (2007: 287) on rehousing following custody reveals that while some local authorities are well informed, others possess limited knowledge of the problems, resulting in women offenders' relegation to low priority compared with other vulnerable groups. Her research (2004) examines the Supporting People initiative, which was part of the government's national accommodation strategy in 2003, to provide housing support to vulnerable individuals, including prisoners. Local Supporting People Consortia bring together the principal partners who have an interest in commissioning services of relevance to these groups, which include female offenders; namely Primary Care Trusts, local authority housing, social services and the Probation Service. Probation Areas, having pooled all of their supported housing funds into this approach, are key players in determining strategy. Malin (2007: 296) found that with no available formal channels for information exchange between Supporting People-funded voluntary sector projects, the process of securing financial backing became immensely complex, and paralysed the process. With both the Probation Service and the voluntary sector struggling 'to carve out a place at the planning stage', Malin (2007: 296) found few advocates for female offenders.

Similar difficulties have occurred in other voluntary sector projects. The criminal justice liaison and diversion schemes in relation to women offenders evaluated by Nacro (Hunter et al, 2008) examined three main areas: the ability to make and retain contact with women offenders with mental health needs; whether women were enabled to stay in the community; and the identification of aids and blocks to providing practical and emotional support to women. In terms of funding, the study concluded that under-resourcing seriously jeopardised the schemes. Proof of need had to come from an administrative infrastructure, which was not yet in existence (Hunter et al, 2008: 10), which in real terms meant that appropriate facilities were not present when demand was greatest – in the evenings and at weekends.

In respect of funding, Clarke (2004: 26) describes a problematic scenario where funding is short term and reviewed annually, thus creating uncertainty and instability. The lack of medium-term financial security leaves staff anxious about their employment prospects and service users anxious about the potential loss of crucial support. Gelsthorpe and Sharpe (2007: 216) outline the central dilemmas of funding constraints as the following: either voluntary organisations have to devote valuable time to fundraising or they are sponsored by the statutory sector with no security that the contract will be renewed; or the contract is conditional on working in a prescribed way in line with the punitive and managerialist ethos embedded within the public sector. Changes at the 218 Centre demonstrate this predicament. Despite the initial, seemingly generous financial input to the project, the complexities of funding arrangements for accessing aftercare resources became very problematic and lacking in strategic oversight (Loucks et al, 2006: 60). As one addiction worker from the 218 Centre put it, 'What good will it do to spend £5,000 on treatment for a woman then put her in a flat surrounded by 25 drug users?' (Loucks et al, 2006: 61). With an increasing emphasis on criminal justice objectives, the 218 Centre was instructed to show cost effectiveness by offering the courts an alternative to custody. In practice this meant a shift from self-referrals to Court Orders; a heightened focus on offending behaviour programmes led by probation; and aftercare provision reduced from 12 months to 12 weeks. Thus, by entering into a closer partnership with statutory agencies, the Centre has been nudged away from its original values, which focused on gender-responsive and gender-sensitive practices.

How have you used the *Offender Management Guide to Working with Women Offenders* (NOMS, 2008)?

What are the barriers (if any) to implementing its proposals?

What would you consider as 'success' in interventions with women offenders?

Would partnership agencies share this viewpoint?

One of the stumbling blocks to partnership working is the confusion surrounding what constitutes 'success' (or in managerial terms, what outcomes are expected). With performance linked to funding, the criteria on which the allocation of resources is decided is a vital factor. However, 'success' is somewhat of a moveable feast, subject to different interpretations at different times (at the start of a project or when it has become more established and dependent on fluctuations in the economy); in different localities; and to different interested parties (politicians, the sentencers, statutory agencies, the voluntary sector and the women themselves). 'Success' may mean less use of custody and greater responsivity to vulnerable women in general; it can be aimed at low- or high-risk offenders; it might involve reductions in or actually stopping offending; and either complete abstinence or controlled use of drugs (Malloch et al, 2008: 392). There are mixed views on whether the goals are to tackle criminogenic needs (those needs that can be influenced through interventions to prevent offending) or welfare needs and, as we have seen, the distinction between these may be slight for many female offenders.

Without adequate information about which interventions have been effective, Siyunyi-Siluwe (2006: 4) identifies the difficulties in breaking down barriers and filling gaps in provision. Rumgay (2004a: 135) describes how the current standardisation approaches to research and policy clash with the observed need for empowerment and the dilemmas this presents to statutory and voluntary agencies. The lack of self-worth and sense of hopelessness commonly experienced by women are not considered as criminogenic needs and so not given value or credence in the statutory accredited programmes. Malloch et al (2008: 385) similarly comment on the political and philosophical tensions in providing a service responsive to women's needs while fulfilling justice-related policy objectives.

Such perspectives are apparent in the report on the Together Women Project (Hedderman et al, 2008: 28). Whereas the Together Women staff thought that the project did prevent custodial sentencing and remands, magistrates and court legal advisors contrastingly believed that women were not being diverted from prison. Referrals to the Together Women Project were not viewed by the magistrates as alternatives to custody because programmes had not been formally accredited by the panel, were unenforceable, less structured and more tailored to the individual than offender management programmes. Nevertheless, the Together Women Project was cited in court as a reason for not imposing custody. The 218 Centre evaluations showed that referrals from criminal justice sources increased with sentencers' awareness of the programme (Loucks et al, 2006: 27) but it was clear that over time there was also a shift to wanting a more structured, justice-related programme, limiting time for other options and concerns, such as health and life skills (Loucks et al, 2006: 21).

With varying beliefs about the goals of partnership work and doubts about the validity and purpose of projects, communication among stakeholders can deteriorate and opportunities be missed. Action research on the Together Women Project revealed that younger female probation officers did not see the need for woman-only holistic centres, and male officers expressed frustration at not being able to work with women offenders, feeling excluded from the women's rehabilitative process (Hedderman et al, 2008: iii). Difficulties also occurred for some criminal justice staff in acknowledging women as victims as well as offenders (Hedderman et al, 2008: 14). The women using multi-agency services have often had poor experiences with statutory 'helping' agencies in the past and they fear becoming fully engaged, in case painful issues are raised. Clarke (2004: 29) contends that women offenders will be more receptive to voluntary sector agencies offering support, contact with others, greater flexibility and a personalised approach.

However, offender managers are well trained and highly skilled in empathic and practical interventions so that women offenders themselves may resist transfer to other organisations if it means separating from an offender manager who has become important to them. Burnett and McNeill (2005: 231-2) have explained the 'interpersonal processes that support change' within the probation setting and draw on Rex's (1999) study, which has described the 'loyalty and trust' in this relationship. The widespread use of links between probation offices and women's resource centres has been proposed by Gelsthorpe et al (2007; Gelshorpe and Sharpe, 2007: 216), but studies have yet to show whether the contact with statutory organisations is welcomed or whether staff there possess the skills and confidence to offer interventions to offenders. Robinson (2005: 314) has warned against greater fragmentation in service delivery, with offenders who can become confused about who is supervising their Order and who to contact in an emergency, and upset at having to repeat their 'stories' to a variety of workers in different agencies.

Despite the limitations of research in partnership working, what is clearly visible in the available studies is the considerable variation in resourcing between local areas. Patel and Stanley (2008: 29-30), concentrating on seven Probation Areas in England and Wales, examined the use of requirements attached to Community Orders and Suspended Sentence Orders, and significant differences were shown. One issue of particular significance for women offenders was that the Community Order mental health requirement had hardly been used since its commencement in April 2005 and divergence between mental health treatment facilities was vast, with only seven out of 42 Probation Areas responsible for 55% of the mental health requirements (Patel et al, 2008: 32). Several reasons for this have been put forward by Solomon and Silvestri (2008: 32), such as the availability of psychiatric consultants, diagnoses of 'a minor or untreatable mental illness', prioritising the more immediate concern of drug misuse and individual women resisting the stigma of the 'mentally ill' label.

Criminal justice liaison and diversion schemes were set up to divert those women offenders exhibiting poor mental health away from the criminal justice system, towards health and social services (Hunter et al, 2008). 'Success' was assessed by seeing whether an appropriate range of community-based health and criminal justice services existed and were being applied to meet the women's needs. Multidisciplinary staff, and in particular access to psychiatrists who could obtain inpatient provision, were considered key to the establishment of good practice (Hunter et al, 2008: 3). Yet none of the schemes were composed of multidisciplinary staff, one scheme had just one paid worker, half the schemes had no input from a psychiatrist and all had major problems in accessing inpatient beds. Where input did exist it was generally sporadic and dependent on the informal goodwill of individual workers rather than formal structures, so if staff moved elsewhere, inter-agency work was abandoned (Hunter et al, 2008: 5).

> To what extent do partnership agencies need to share a common philosophy of approach in order to promote empowerment among women offenders?

What is needed?

The response to the Corston Report has been half-hearted, with Corston's (2007: 78) call for the re-emergence of the 2000 National Health Service (NHS) commitment – to provide women-only day centres for mental health in every authority – rejected by the government, and funding for the extension of the Together Women Project has not been forthcoming (Ministry of Justice, 2007:

28 and 9). Nevertheless, an increasing clarity and recognition about positive ways forward has emerged at an ideological and, to a more limited extent, at a practical level. Some of the aspects have already been acknowledged and put into action. Practice documents such as the *Offender Management Guide to Working with Women Offenders* (NOMS, 2008) now accept that interventions should be women-only, holistic, delivered by caring staff and that female offenders are likely to have multiple problems. However, such moves in themselves are not enough.

In the establishment of accommodation services for NOMS South West, Askwith (2008) has proposed a number of essential elements for work with women offenders. Protocols should be set up from the start to ensure that communication channels are functioning between all identified stakeholders. Coordination of partnership working should be under a named individual and there should be a single point of referral for prison and probation staff and women offenders (Askwith, 2008: 2-4). A crucial move is to have services based in court so as to engage with the magistracy in an effort to avoid custodial sentencing. Askwith (2008: 10) argues that in order for sentencers to be better informed on community resources their participation on the Strategic Planning Group should be encouraged.

Hunter et al (2008: 3) have likewise set out good practice pointers for inter-agency diversion schemes, which emphasise accessing a range of health and social care facilities. Mental health services should be women-specific with training for non-specialist staff to recognise and contribute to treatment of eating disorders and self-harm. A focus on locating provision at not just one but several stages in the criminal justice process is also recommended.

Without exception the main research projects advocate giving service users a voice, to empower, increase engagement and offer valuable feedback (Clarke, 2004; Malin, 2007; Askwith, 2008; Hedderman et al, 2008; Hunter et al, 2008; Malloch et al, 2008; Mills and Codd, 2008; Patel and Stanley, 2008). Siyunyi-Siluwe (2006) has promoted listening to the views of black and minority ethnic women through focus groups, surveys and involvement in management committees. She emphasises the importance of having staff who speak the minority groups' languages, allowing women to mix more freely and diminishing their sense of isolation and exclusion. When asked, women state that their top priority is accommodation and transport (Patel et al, 2008: 13). Flexibility of agencies to fit in with childcare means that outreach work of voluntary agencies is important, as are home visits and developing employment skills that do not restrict women to a '9 to 5' structure. There should be an increased emphasis on signposting to women's services and this has been encouraged within offender management with the recommendation of a digest of the areas' resources (Gelsthorpe et al, 2007; NOMS, 2008: 13).

Conclusions

Both statutory and voluntary agencies have a part to play in working both independently and together to improve women offenders' lives by lowering the risk of offending and of custodial sentencing. This chapter has shown that:

- Partnership work with female offenders, although generally conceived with enthusiasm, will not continue to flourish until it stops being viewed as the cheap alternative with only limited funding set aside for female offenders.
- The emerging pattern in terms of multi-agency working is that there are a handful of demonstration projects in large towns or cities (which are well resourced but only for a finite period) and there are partnerships that are ill-conceived and poorly resourced from the start. The partnerships that work well are flexible enough to listen to and incorporate the voices and experiences of the women themselves and of each other in shaping those services.
- In essence, public policy particularly under New Labour has sought to address social exclusion in the form of multiple and interacting needs and to create National Service Frameworks, but in the case of women offenders this is lagging behind. There is still reliance on individuals who are prepared to champion the cause, which although estimable will ultimately prove inadequate.
- What then is still lacking is proper funding, coordination at senior management planning level and the motivation at government level to implement an infrastructure nationally that will bring the recommendations of Corston and others to fruition.

Further reading

For up-to-date statistics on women offenders, see www.crimlinks.com

For a recent comprehensive review of women in the criminal justice system, see Fawcett Society (2009) *Engendering Justice: From Policy to Practice*. London: Fawcett Society. Available at www.fawcettsociety.org.uk/documents/Commission%20report%20 May%2009.pdf

To gain a better understanding of the implications of a gendered approach, see Walklate, S. (2004) *Gender, Crime and Criminal Justice*. Cullompton: Willan Publishing.

Note

[1] The Offender Assessment System (OASys) is the National Offender Management Service risk assessment tool.

References

Askwith, D. (2008) *Commissioning Accommodation Support Services for Women Offenders Toolkit.* NOMS South West.

Borrill, J., Maden, A., Martin, A., Weaver, T., Stimson, G., Farrell, S. and Barnes, T. (2003) *Differential Substance Misuse Treatment Needs of Women, Ethnic Minorities and Young Offenders in Prison: Prevalence of Substance Misuse and Treatment Needs,* Home Office Online Report 33/03. London: Home Office. Available from www.homeoffice.gov.uk/rds/pdfs2/rdsolr3303.pdf

Burnett, R. and McNeill, F. (2005) 'The place of the officer–offender relationship in assisting offenders to desist from crime', *Probation Journal,* 52(3), 221-42.

Carlen, P. and Worrall, A. (2004) *Analysing Women's Imprisonment.* Cullompton: Willan Publishing.

Chigwada-Bailey, R. (2003) *Black Women's Experiences of Criminal Justice: Race, Gender and Class: A Discourse on Disadvantage.* Winchester: Waterside.

Clarke, R. (2004) *"What Works" for Women Who Offend: A Service User's Perspective.* London: Griffin Society.

Corston, J. (2007) *The Corston Report: A Review of Women with Particular Vulnerabilities in the Criminal Justice System.* London: Home Office.

Gelsthorpe, L. (2006) 'The experiences of female minority ethnic offenders: the other "other"', in Lewis, S., Raynor, P., Smith, D. and Wardak, A. (eds) *Race and Probation* (pp 100-20). Cullompton: Willan Publishing.

Gelsthorpe, L. and Sharpe, G. (2007) 'Women and resettlement', in Hucklesby, A. and Hagley-Dickinson, L. (eds) *Prisoner Resettlement: Policy and Practice* (pp 199-223). Cullompton: Willan Publishing.

Gelsthorpe, L., Sharpe, G. and Roberts, J. (2007) *Provision for Women Offenders in the Community.* London: Fawcett Society.

Goldhill, R. (2009) 'The Corston Report: reading between the lines: towards an understanding of government policy in relation to vulnerable women offenders', *Prison Service Journal,* 184, 13-19.

Hedderman, C., Palmer, E. and Hollin, C. (2008) *Implementing Services for Women Offenders and those 'At Risk' of Offending: Action Research with Together Women.* Ministry of Justice Research Series 12/08. London: Ministry of Justice.

Hunter, G., Boyce, I. and Smith, L. (2008) *Criminal Justice Liaison and Diversion Schemes: A Focus on Women Offenders.* London: Nacro Institute of Criminal Policy Research.

Loucks, N., Malloch, M., McIvor, G. and Gelsthorpe, L. (2006) *Evaluation of the 218 Project.* Edinburgh: Scottish Executive Justice Department.

Make Justice Work (2009) *Make Justice Work Respond to HM Inspector of Prisons for England and Wales Annual Report.* Press Statement. London: Make Justice Work. Available at http://makejusticework.org.uk/tag/anne-owers/

Malin, S. (2004) *Supporting People: Good News for Women Ex-Prisoners?* London: Griffin Society.

Malin, S. (2007) 'Housing and support after prison', in Sheehan, R., McIvor, G. and Trotter, C. (eds) *What Works with Women Offenders.* Cullompton: Willan Publishing.

Malloch, M., McIvor, G. and Loucks, N. (2008) 'Time out' for women: innovation in Scotland in a context of change', *Howard Journal*, 47(4), 383-99.

Matrix Knowledge Group (2007) *The Economic Case For and Against Prison.* London: Matrix Knowledge Group. Available from www.matrixknowledge.co.uk/

Mills, A. and Codd, H. (2008) 'Prisoners' families and offender management: mobilizing social capital', *Probation Journal*, 55(1), 9-24.

Ministry of Justice (2007) *The Government's Response to the Report by Baroness Corston of a Review of Women with Particular Vulnerabilities in the Criminal Justice System.* London: HMSO.

NOMS (National Offender Management Service) (2008) *The Offender Management Guide to Working with Women Offenders.* London: Ministry of Justice.

Owers, A. (2004) 'Rights behind bars: the conditions and treatment of those in detention', International Human Rights Day lecture, London School of Economics. Available at www.lse.ac.uk/collections/humanRights/articlesAndTranscripts/Rights_behind_bars.pdf

Patel, S. and Stanley, S. (2008) *The Use of the Community Order and the Suspended Sentence Order for Women.* London: The Centre for Crime and Justice Studies.

Rex, S. (1999) 'Desistance from offending: experiences of probation', *The Howard Journal*, 38(4), 366-83.

Roberts, J. (2002) 'Women-centred: the West Mercia community-based programme for women offenders'. in Carlen, P. (ed) *Women and Punishment* (pp 110-124). Cullompton: Willan Publishing

Robinson, G. (2005) 'What works in offender management?', *The Howard Journal*, 44(3), 307-18.

Rumgay, J. (2004a) 'The barking dog? Partnership and effective practice', in Mair, G. (ed) *What Matters in Probation* (pp 122-45). Cullompton: Willan Publishing.

Rumgay, J. (2004b) *When Victims Become Offenders: In Search of Coherence in Policy and Practice.* London: Fawcett Society.

Rumgay, J. (2007) 'Partnerships in probation', in Gelsthorpe, L. and Morgan, R. (eds) *The Handbook of Probation* (pp 542-64). Cullompton: Willan Publishing.

Siyunyi-Siluwe, M. (2006) *Good Practice in Meeting the Needs of Ethnic Minority Women Offenders and those At Risk of Offending.* London: Fawcett Society.

Solomon, E. and Silvestri, A. (2008) *Community Sentences Digest.* London: The Centre for Crime and Justice Studies.

CHAPTER 7

Working together to manage risk of serious harm

Suzie Clift

Aims of the chapter

■ To consider the use of risk of serious harm within criminal justice and multi-agency working.

■ To outline current statutory arrangements concerning partnership working in relation to managing risk.

■ To identify common themes within multi-agency working and serious further offences.

■ To identify professional issues for those engaged in the multi-agency management of risk of serious harm.

■ To discuss the contribution of the community in managing risk.

The emergence of a risk society (Beck, 1992), the multiplication of risk (Turner, 2001) and a rise in a risk agenda are well documented, as is their subsequent impact on criminal justice. Gough (this volume) has already considered the role of the corrections policy agenda within current criminological theory, highlighting Garland's theory of responsibilisation and the role of a multiplicity of agencies in governing crime. This chapter builds on this notion, and considers how this works in practice, specifically when managing risk of serious harm within the community through a multi-agency approach. It could be argued that multi-agency working in relation to high-risk offenders in order to protect the public has become the most significant area of multi-agency working within criminal justice. With recent high-profile cases demonstrating failures and tensions within multi-agency working, its role and effectiveness have become subject to intense scrutiny, its role and function gaining even greater prominence in the process. As such, an understanding and ability to work within a multi-agency setting is a fundamental role for all those working within criminal justice, regardless of whether this is in a statutory or non-statutory setting.

This chapter begins by highlighting the dominant role that risk plays within criminal justice and the complexities that exist in assessing and managing it. Following this it considers the management of risk of serious harm through the use of statutory Multi-Agency Public Protection Panels (MAPPPs), leading to the consideration of specific serious further offences, highlighting common, and sadly recurring, themes with regards to 'failures' within multi-agency working. Finally, consideration is given to the role and increasing use of communities in managing risk of serious harm, in particular sex offenders and, more recently, terrorism.

Risk within criminal justice

'Risk' as a concept is not easily defined. Traditionally it has been a neutral term, meaning the chance of gain or the chance of loss (Parton, cited in Kemshall, 2001: 11). However, Douglas (cited in Kemshall, 2001: 11) notes how risk has become increasingly linked with notions of danger and harm (referring to 'dangerization' within society), with risk currently being associated with a probability calculation that a harmful behaviour will occur. In the context of this chapter, risk is taken to mean the likelihood of an event occurring (Nash, 2006: 17) as well as the impact caused, something that Nash (2006: 17) notes requires the consideration of the inherent 'quality' of the behaviour, a point that will be returned to later.

The key criminal agency involved in assessing and determining levels of risk is the National Offender Management Service (NOMS). This is primarily undertaken through the use of the Offender Assessment System (OASys), where risk is considered in terms of risk of reoffending and risk of serious harm. 'Risk of serious harm' is defined as 'an event which is life threatening and/or traumatic, from which recovery, whether physical or psychological, can be expected to be difficult or impossible' (Home Office, 2006, ch 8, p 3). Within OASys, there are four levels of risk of serious harm (Ministry of Justice, 2009):

- *Low:* Current evidence does not indicate likelihood of causing serious harm.
- *Medium:* There are identifiable indicators of risk of serious harm. The offender has the potential to cause harm, but is unlikely to do so unless there is a change in circumstances – for example, failure to take medication, loss of accommodation, relationship breakdown, drug or alcohol misuse.
- *High:* There are identifiable indicators of risk of serious harm. The potential event could happen at any time, and the impact would be serious.
- *Very high:* There is an imminent risk of serious harm. The potential event is likely to happen imminently, and the impact to be serious.

Assessment of risk

The two most common methods used to assess risk within criminal justice are actuarial and clinical assessments. Actuarial assessments use static factors that are largely unchangeable, an example being OGRS (Offender Group Reconviction Scale), which generates a percentage of likelihood of reconviction for a particular offender group (not an individual) by utilising the offender's age, number of convictions and other static facts. Such assessments are used as a means of prediction and do not provide explanations for the causes of the criminal behaviour. Clinical assessments are based on interviews and the observations of skilled practitioners.

While it is acknowledged that these types of assessments can be easily impaired through a lack of knowledge by the practitioner and are open to subjective bias and discriminatory attitudes, they can assist in identifying key personal and situational factors. Unsurprisingly, the clinical assessment is more time consuming and in order for it to be of use in terms of managing high-risk offenders it is vital that a precise, shared definition of risk is worked to; without this the practitioner's assessment will be clouded by differing perceptions of what it is, and therefore what indicators exist, for the detection of future offending behaviour. Clearly, an understanding of the relevance of the information is imperative, bringing us back to Nash's (2006: 102) observation regarding the importance of the quality and context of the behaviour.

While a combination of the two types of assessment is most often advocated (for example OASys), the criminal justice system has, in recent years, seen a greater emphasis being placed on actuarial methods, which utilise facts and offer clearly defined baselines and guidelines for application. However, Nash (2004: 22) notes the tensions of such an approach, highlighting the prominence of actuarial methods of assessment within probation, which are based on studies that examined large groups of offenders, thereby limiting their application from a generalised offender population to individual offender assessments (Kemshall, 2001: vi), by potentially providing overly simplistic outcomes that fail to capture the complexity of the processes involved. Petherick, (2005: 12) reiterates this, stating that while certain levels of accuracy can be achieved with reoffending in general, based on certain demographic and criminological factors, these factors provide poorer predictions for those offenders convicted of rape, murder or indecent assault (in other words those most likely to be assessed as posing a risk of serious harm). Here the overriding factor that proved most effective was previous convictions. As Floud and Young (cited in Nash, 1999: 20) argue, an assessment of the risk that a person presents must not 'rest only on the propensity to cause wilful harm, but the evidence must be specific to him and this precludes the determination of dangerousness by purely actuarial methods'. So already it is clear that for risk assessments to be of use the information that informs them must be complete and current, underpinned by knowledge of their relevance and application.

With increasing emphasis being placed on accountability and adopting a defensible position, a climate of uncertainty exists within the criminal justice agencies. Professionals are working in a culture of fear and blame, where 'failure' on their part can result in disastrous consequences. Therefore, there is a temptation for practitioners to overestimate risk so as to avoid blame. There is also the potential for the increased use of standardised risk assessment across criminal justice agencies, resulting in a 'dilution' of agency difference (expertise) and skills (Nash, 2004: 23), with responsibilities being diffused, a tension that will be returned to later.

Multi-Agency Public Protection Arrangements (MAPPA)

> Since their introduction, other countries around the world view MAPPA as a beacon of best practice in public protection. They are a fundamental part of the way in which the government has reformed the criminal justice system to ensure it is focused on its core aim of protecting the communities it serves. (David Hanson, Minister for Justice, 20 October 2008)

In parallel with recent moves towards longer or indeterminate prison terms for 'dangerous' offenders, increasing attention has been paid to ways of monitoring and controlling their behaviour while in the community. Central to this has been the development of multi-agency cooperation and the introduction of Multi-Agency Public Protection Panels (MAPPPs) through the 2000 Criminal Justice and Court Services Act. In essence, MAPPPs are a statutory requirement that certain agencies cooperate to better protect the public. The underlying assumption being that the assessment and management of certain risks will be more effective when a variety of professional perspectives, knowledge and skills are utilised (Nash, 2006: 160); 'MAPPA is not a statutory body in itself but is a mechanism through which agencies can better discharge their statutory responsibilities and protect the public in a co-ordinated manner' (Ministry of Justice, 2009: 31).

The 2003 Criminal Justice Act extended the responsible authorities of the Probation Service and the police to include the Prison Service and established a reciprocal 'duty to cooperate' between the responsible authorities and a range of other authorities (NPD, 2004: 13), including local authority social services, job centres, local education and housing authorities, Youth Offending Teams and local Primary Care Trusts. In March 2003, national guidance was published, which further clarified MAPPPs' role and identified three categories of offenders to be included within the arrangements: registered sex offenders, violent and other sex offenders receiving a custodial sentence of 12 months or more and any other offenders who are considered to pose a risk of serious harm to the public (NPD, 2004: 13). Offenders subject to a MAPPP are managed at three levels:

- *Level 1: Ordinary Risk Management* – where the risks posed by the offender can be managed by one agency without significantly involving other agencies.
- *Level 2: Local Inter-Agency Risk Management* – where significant involvement from more than one agency is required, but where either the level of risk or the complexity of managing the risk is not so great as to require referral to level 3.
- *Level 3: Multi-Agency Public Protection Panel (MAPPP)* – this relates to the 'critical few' and includes offenders who present risks that can only be managed by a plan that requires close cooperation with a multi-agency approach at a senior level, due to the complexity of the case and/or because of the unusual resource commitments it requires. It can also be used for offenders who are not assessed

as being a high or very high risk but are likely to receive a high level of media scrutiny and/or public interest in the management of the case.

The 'critical few' who require multi-agency cooperation at a senior level (level 3: MAPPP) represent 2.14% of the total (Ministry of Justice, 2008b) and, according to Wood (2006: 310), most closely characterise perceptions of dangerousness. In 2007/08, 50,210 people were subject to MAPPA, 23.37% of which were managed at level 2 (Ministry of Justice, 2008b), the vast majority being subject to level 1.

Cooperation

MAPPP has no authority itself but is a set of administrative arrangements. Instead, authority rests with each of the agencies involved, thus in order for it to be effective, cooperation is essential, at the very least to avoid conflict of authority and at best to achieve coordination of risk management. Indeed, the *MAPPA Guidance* states that agreement between agencies is a goal rather than a requirement (Ministry of Justice, 2009). Despite this, the legislation does not provide a definition of the role of the duty to cooperate (DTC) agencies. Instead, it requires that the 'meaning of "co-operation" is determined in each area through a "memorandum" drawn up by the RA [responsible authority] with the agencies upon which the Duty to Co-operate is imposed' (Ministry of Justice, 2009: 197). Already it is clear that there is the potential for misinterpretation and differences regarding what is clearly a key part and function of the multi-agency framework and perhaps goes some way in explaining why there continue to be tensions and issues regarding responsibilities and communication, as will be discussed later and in the proceeding chapters by Nash and Watson.

The guidance does provide five characteristics of the DTC, which should be 'reflected' within the memorandum, one of which states that 'it requires the DTC agencies to co-operate only in so far as this is compatible with their existing statutory responsibilities' (Ministry of Justice, 2009: 197). The duty does not require that the agencies do anything other than what they are already required to do, emphasising the sharing of information and the need for collaboration. However, in doing so it also emphasises that this collaboration should not 'undermine the discretion of the representative of each agency, nor does it detract from the responsibility each agency has for making its decision and carrying them out' (Ministry of Justice, 2009: 198). It has been shown that within MAPPA the police are often the dominant agency, which can, as a result, inhibit the contributions made by other agencies (Kemshall, 2008: 67). This dominance could be attributed to a hierarchy of power within multi-agency working. Kemshall (2008: 67) also notes the reluctance of certain professionals to challenge the views of those who they perceive as being of a higher status. A potential reflection of this hierarchy is the use of risk assessment tools within MAPPA. The *MAPPA Guidance* notes that while other risk assessment tools are available and used by the other agencies (for example the Common Assessment Framework used by social services), only specific risk assessments tools are actively utilised and referred to, these being OASys and Risk Matrix 2000, the latter being a specific actuarial tool used in the assessment of sexual and violent offenders (Ministry of Justice, 2009: 82). All other forms of risk assessment can be used to 'complement these'. Such an approach could be indicative of how the use of both statutory and non-statutory agencies within a statutory risk management body has led to the imposition of a criminal justice approach and ethos upon all the agencies involved, including the voluntary sector. It could therefore be argued that agencies whose role has traditionally been to work outside of the criminal justice process are being subsumed by a criminal justice culture, potentially compromising the very nature and philosophy of their role. These tensions between the agencies are alluded to within the latest *MAPPA Guidance*, which is aimed at 'promoting trust between agencies', stating that 'trust must be developed and sustained by professional integrity' (Ministry of Justice, 2009: 61).

The lack of cooperation is further exemplified by a historic lack of attendance at MAPPPs. In 2005, Kemshall et al published their review of MAPPPs, following on from that of Maguire et al in 2001. Here it was noted that in some areas other agencies did not send representatives at all, with attendance from health-related organisations and social services being cited as a problem in five national service areas (see Nash's chapter regarding localised research on the state of multi-agency working) (Kemshall et al, 2005: 6). Their absence resulted in key decisions with regards to resources and action plans being postponed due to the required agency not being present in order to give permission. Unsurprisingly, multi-agency working works best when the agencies attend.

Lieb (2007: 212) adds caution to the reliance on MAPPPs by highlighting the ambitiousness of their goals, which are impeded by 'vague descriptions of actions that will be used to accomplish these expansive responsibilities', noting how those subject to MAPPA begin to take on the characteristics of 'A List of People to Worry About' with collaboration thereby resulting in 'joined-up worrying' (Lieb, 2007: 212). This perhaps bring us back to the point made earlier about the increased use of agencies leading to diffusion and dilution of services through the adoption of a single criminal justice ethos (see Nash, this volume).

Wood (2006: 319) notes how MAPPPs are still unproven in terms of their effectiveness, suggesting that they could lead to increased and arguably unrealistic expectations on the Probation Service, and other agencies, to ensure the risks are minimal. Between 2007 and 2008, of those subject to MAPPA, only two offenders managed at level 3 and 30 offenders managed at level 2 went on to be convicted of a serious further offence (Ministry of Justice, 2008b). Nash (2006: 142) comments that it is anticipated that the number of offenders subject to a MAPPP will continue to grow due to ongoing changes in legislation and the amount of time that offenders will remain registered. To illustrate, the number of registered sex offenders on 1 September 1997 was 4,524 and now stands at over 30,000 (Ministry of Justice, 2008b). The number of sex offenders subject to probation supervision rose by 31% from just over 7,000 in 1996 to 10,094 in

2001 (NPD, 2004: 23). This gives credence to concerns that agencies may soon not have the resources or capacity to cope effectively with the numbers of offenders identified as potentially dangerous (Nash, 2006: 7).

Multi-agency working and serious further offences – the lessons yet to be learnt

Inevitably, serious further offences do occur and this is something that all those working within criminal justice sector will be aware of, many having had first-hand experience of it. Risk, after all, can never be eliminated. However, it can be assessed, reviewed and used to inform the ways in which it is managed, but as we have seen this requires a proactive approach by all those involved. What is of concern is that recent high-profile serious further offences have at their core a recurring theme in relation to poor multi-agency risk management – communication.

Damien Hanson and Elliott White

On 29 November 2004, Damien Hanson and Elliott White murdered John Monkton and attempted to murder his wife. Both were under the supervision of London Probation Area at the time. Damien Hanson had been released from prison on parole on 27 August 2004, having been sentenced to 12 years' imprisonment on 1 April 1998 for offences of attempted murder and conspiracy to rob. Elliot White was subject to a six-month Drug Treatment and Testing Order (DTTO), which had been imposed for failure to comply with the conditions of a Community Rehabilitation Order, relating to unlawful possession of 2.8 grams of cocaine (Bridges, 2006a: 7). The Serious Further Offence Review notes that Elliott White's supervision was haphazard and inconsistent with minimal compliance, and as such it is entirely likely that Mr White would have been unaware of the seriousness of his sentence and community supervision (Bridges, 2006a: 20). The drug treatment was provided by an external agency – Munster Road Centre – and, crucially, poor communication between the two is noted, with liaison described as 'inadequate' (Bridges, 2006a: 20). Without this liaison the monitoring and assessing of any risks, be it risk of reoffending or risk of serious harm, would have been impossible, or at the very least inadequate.

With regards to Hanson, the absence of a clear 'lead' is cited as a key issue. As such, there was a lack of communication and formal liaison between probation and the hostel to which Hanson was released, resulting in a 'lack of clear planning about the purpose and boundaries of Hanson's stay in the hostel' (Bridges, 2006a: 35). Several months after his release, Hanson's compliance with the hostel deteriorated and probation informed the police that his lack of rent payment may lead to recall. Police records state that the following information was subsequently given to probation: 'Damien Hanson was at the time of his release considered a category 2 MAPPA subject being managed at level 1 by the Probation Service'. Alarmingly, this exchange of information was not recorded in the probation case file and even more worryingly there is no evidence from the probation records that any decisions regarding MAPPA had been taken earlier (Bridges, 2006a: 36). A MAPPA referral was not made. Here a valuable piece of information has been communicated yet seemingly not acted upon. The reason for this is unclear but could relate to a lack of understanding about its relevance. What is important in terms of the context of this chapter is that the review highlights that in both the cases the case manager was required to manage and liaise with the providers of services (Hestia hostel in the case of Damien Hanson and the Munster Road substance misuse service in the case of Elliot White) and that 'in both cases the liaison was inadequate and the quality of supervision was adversely affected' (Bridges, 2006b: 44). This was further compounded by a lack of MAPPA involvement, which, in principle, would have promoted and facilitated this, leading to a more accurate risk assessment and ultimately risk management.

Anthony Rice

On 17 August 2005, Anthony Rice murdered Naomi Bryant while on a life licence and, as with Hanson and White, a primary factor highlighted within the Serious Further Offence Review (Bridges, 2006b: 8) was the need for a 'lead responsibility' to be designated at the outset. Arguably, this has been addressed by the formation of the Offender Management Model through the creation of NOMS (see Skinner, this volume), but what is important here is that due to the absence of a 'lead', key information was either not obtained or not communicated effectively to those involved. Integral to the mismanagement of Rice's licence was 'flawed resettlement planning and diffused responsibility', with Anthony Rice being released into a hostel that was, with hindsight, assessed as unsuitable. The reason for this was attributed to a lack of assessment prior to the commission of the serious further offence due to 'a series of assumptions and miscommunications' (Bridges, 2006b: 56). Given the nature of Mr Rice's original offence (attempted rape), he was subject to MAPPA, and this was also highlighted as being a contributing factor in the poor management of Mr Rice's licence and the risks that he posed. It identified that MAPPA had 'allowed its attention to the public protection considerations of this case to be undermined by its human rights considerations' (Bridges, 2006b: 6), Rice being in attendance at the meetings (something that is no longer permitted), diverting attention from the role and function of MAPPA – collaboration in managing risks through information sharing.

Dano Sonnex

On 29 June 2008, Dano Sonnex, together with Nigel Farmer, murdered Laurent Bonomo and Gabriel Ferez. At the time of the murders he was subject to licence supervision by London Probation Area having been released at the latest possible date. His licence formed part of an eight-year custodial sentence imposed for assault with intent to resist arrest, having an imitation firearm with intent, attempted robbery, robbery (x4) and wounding with intent, for which he received eight years (Hill, 2009: 6). Throughout his sentence, Sonnex was seen by several mental health teams in various prisons, most notably in May 2004 at HMYOI [Her Majesty's Young Offender Institution] Aylesbury where a diagnosis of conduct disorder was made. Following the diagnosis a medical officer wrote to the Community Mental Health Team, outlining the findings and ending the memo with: 'the forensic dimension is the greatest concern, especially as he admits that his reactions could kill' (Hill, 2009: 8). Shortly after this, Sonnex was moved to HMYOI Portland and it is not clear whether the medical officer's assessment was available or considered upon transfer. At the time of release this information was available in the Inmate Medical Record, but again it is not known whether this information was readily available or used and remarkably there was no reference to it in any subsequent assessment of Sonnex's risk (Hill, 2009: 8). As such, the assessment appears to have been undertaken in isolation. Unsurprisingly, this has led to a key recommendation: that 'HMPS [Her Majesty's Prison Service] should take steps to ensure that information relevant to the risk posed by a prisoner on release, no matter where such information originates from, should be shared with and used by staff responsible for the management of that offender throughout the course of his or her sentence' (Hill, 2009: 9). Given that the prisons are a responsible authority, the communication of this information, especially in a MAPPA forum, could have led to the active involvement of the Community Mental Health Team in managing Sonnex's risks upon release. Having said this, Sonnex's case was not actually managed by MAPPA upon his release. A referral was made; however, an error resulted in the offence details being omitted from the printed form and therefore the referral was not considered and a re-referral was requested. This was completed but not sent (Hill, 2009: 10) and again an opportunity to adopt a multi-agency approach in managing the licence was missed.

Two days after his release, Sonnex was involved in an alleged offence of kidnap involving his pregnant cousin and her partner. The allegations were withdrawn and as such the case did not proceed but, crucially, sufficient information was available from social services, the police and indeed Sonnex himself, to warrant at the very least a revised risk assessment. Instead, a written warning was issued (incorrectly) by the offender manager. The information was not communicated to MAPPA and the Serious Further Offence Review comments that there was a 'failure to react effectively to information from the social services and self reported by DS [Dano Sonnex]' (Hill, 2009: 23).

On 24 April 2008, Sonnex was remanded in custody for an offence of handling stolen goods, with the offender manager being made aware of this on 30 April. Recall was initiated but not progressed and Sonnex was released on bail on 16 May 2008. It is thought that the decision to release him was considered by the court to be a 'technical' one, as they understood him to be a serving prisoner whose licence was in the process of being revoked, an error that culminated from 'communication confusions between the field and court teams' (Hill, 2009: 23).

Further miscommunication occurred following the recall within the supervising team, with no further appointments being made after Sonnex's release on bail on 16 May, the offender manager believing that the recall had been actioned (the paperwork had in fact been delayed by the senior probation officer) (Hill, 2009: 24)).

Professional issues

The report by Andrew Bridges into the case of Anthony Rice identified 'mistakes, misjudgements and miscommunications' (Bridges, 2006b: 6) by professionals involved in the case, factors that can also be attributed to Hanson and White and Sonnex. This encapsulates the fact that the issue is not just about lack of communication or poor information sharing but, as already discussed, also about the quality of information being shared, the meaning that is attributed to it and the assumptions that may be made as a result. In order for these areas to be resolved, professionals must have sufficient knowledge and training. Indeed, part of the recommendation resulting from the Sonnex case was for increased training in relation to mental health. In addition to this, practitioners need to have the capacity to undertake this work within their role, and as such, appropriate allocation and workload priority becomes even more fundamental. The probation officer responsible for supervising Sonnex had recently qualified and had a caseload in excess of a hundred.

Reder and Duncan (2003) argue that good communication is so fundamental to inter-agency working that it should be prioritised as a core skill and adopted as a key part of professional training. The suggestion is that changes to policies, technologies and the practicalities of communication will be irrelevant if professionals do not develop appropriate interpersonal skills. Again, this is not just about how to convey information appropriately but also how to listen, value (see Nash, this volume) and interpret the information provided by others, all within the context of understanding the nature of risk.

It would, however, be naïve and overly simplistic to state that an increase in knowledge and training regarding the quality and relevance of information is all that is required. It does of course go much deeper than that. It needs to be consolidated with an understanding and appreciation of the role and function of the other agencies involved, and the relevance of information to their role. A reluctance to share information stems not only from miscommunication and lack of resources but also from a fundamental lack of understanding and, more importantly, willingness to understand and work in partnership with other agencies. As Andrew Ashworth (1998: 22) notes, many groups working within criminal justice enjoy 'considerable discretion and … are relatively autonomous', something that does not promote multi-agency working. Each of the agencies will have its own agenda, culture and working ethos and these may not always be entirely compatible with those of the other agencies, regardless of a shared end goal – public protection.

Involving the community – moving beyond the 'statutory'

The focus of this chapter has largely been around professionals and agencies working together to manage risk. A key question, however, is whether risk can ever be successfully managed without the involvement of the community. Kemshall and Wood (2007) note the growth in voluntary and faith-based organisations in working to help manage risk, following the ethos of the Public Health Approach. This approach favours more preventive and educative measures involving the community over criminal justice approaches to risk. The point is made that risk needs to be seen as a public health or social problem that should be addressed by the whole community rather than left to statutory agencies, which are more likely to be reactive and punitive, strategies that are regarded as unsuccessful (Kemshall, 2008).

Circles of Support and Accountability (COSA) exemplify how this approach can work in practice. Originating in Canada, COSA was first developed by Reverend Nigh in 1994 when he arranged with members of his congregation to monitor and reintegrate a repeat sexual offender. The goal of COSA is 'to promote successful re-integration of released men into the community by providing support, advocacy and a way to be meaningfully accountable in exchange for living safely in the community. In doing so, safety is enhanced for the community' (Wilson et al, 2007a, cited in Considine and Birch, 2009: 299). Here we see a clear example of the use of a shared goal in managing risk by promoting a model of inclusion, leading Considine and Birch (2009: 299) to highlight an important paradox: that arguably community safety could be maintained by 'finding a place for our potentially dangerous offenders within it'.

Evaluations so far suggest that these schemes have had significant results in both Canada and the UK (Wilson et al, 2007b, 2007c). It is noteworthy that the COSA approach acknowledges the isolation experienced by many sex offenders released into the community, and how this can increase the risk of reoffending, while also emphasising the need for offenders to take responsibility for their behaviour (Kemshall, 2008). Here reintegration is viewed as essential in managing risks, something that is arguably hindered by MAPPA, which imposes restrictive and coercive measures in order to manage and address risks.

A multi-agency approach has also been adopted in relation to working with faith groups in the community. Spalek et al (2009) note that in the aftermath of the 9/11 and 7/7 bombings, the prevention of violent extremism has become one of the most significant issues facing policy makers in the UK, with Muslim communities becoming the focus of a multilayered and multi-agency approach (Home Office, 2008, cited in Spalek et al, 2009). In 2008, Spalek et al undertook research pertaining to engagement and partnerships between the police and the Muslim communities within the context of counterterrorism, publishing their findings in 2009. Within the report the importance of partnership working is made clear, with information gathering actually being viewed as a secondary benefit of the partnership work (2009: 12), with the primary benefit being community empowerment in tackling extremism. The report highlights the need for a *proactive engagement* approach, with engagement from the community sought in tackling issues before they escalate, allowing communities to become more actively involved in the development of initiatives. This is in contrast to a *reactive engagement* approach where communities are expected to respond and provide feedback to initiatives and events that have already occurred (Spalek et al, 2009: 15). Initiatives such as COSA are excellent examples of the benefits of proactive engagement and can increasingly be seen within other initiatives such as those used by the Lucy Faithful Foundation charity, which also advocates a public health approach to working with sex offenders.

There is also an argument for members of the community to have greater involvement in the statutory arrangements that currently exist to manage risk. In June 2002, the Home Office announced that it was to introduce 'lay' representation on a strategic level of MAPPP, in response to concerns regarding the effective management of dangerous offenders in the community. The rationale and perceived benefits of this were that it would include community needs and opinions regarding decisions about the functioning and development of MAPPA as well as allow for public scrutiny of the methods employed, in effect making professionals accountable to the community. Initially, eight areas were involved in the pilot, with predominantly positive feedback from all involved, although it was recommended that clear guidelines be issued as to their exact function and roles. Following the Baby P case (see Watson, this volume), it has also been announced that lay people are to be invited to sit on Local Safeguarding Children Boards (Carvel and Jones, 2009) and this demonstrates the increasing role that the community will play as a key partner in the overall management of procedures that are designed to protect the public.

Conclusion

Partnership working has become increasingly viewed as the most effective means of managing risk, reflected by increased legislation and provisions for statutory partnership arrangements. Nash and Williams (2008: 108) note that it has become the 'default position for good practice'. However, there are number of issues that threaten to undermine the effectiveness of partnership working in managing risk.

Gough (this volume) has highlighted the context to the current emphasis on multi-agency working and it is clear that there is a need for all agencies involved to play a full and active role if they are to be effective. Within multi-agency settings there are different working cultures that could ultimately result in mistrust, culminating in a reluctance to share information and cooperate, as evident between the police and the Crown Prosecution Service when it was established in 1985 (Davies et al, 2005: 18). Nash and Williams (2008: 108) note that for this type of approach to work, trust and understanding must be inherent yet this has clearly been an area associated with recent multi-agency 'failures'. They comment that if multi-agency working is to improve, communication between those involved 'has to overcome cultural ambivalence and occasional hostility' (Nash and Williams, 2008: 108).

Effective working requires clarity with regards to the roles and responsibilities that each individual and agency will undertake (Nash, 2006). However, a key finding of the inquiries into the cases of Hanson and White and Rice was that the notion of shared responsibility can lead to a lack of coordination and a reluctance to take lead responsibility (Bridges 2006a, 2006b). The reviews by Andrew Bridges clearly identify that lack of consistency and lead responsibility led to the cumulative failures that contributed to a breakdown in public protection.

While no one would disagree that the overriding goal and duty of the agencies within criminal justice is the protection of the public, the ways in which this is to be achieved and the process by which this should occur are not so clear cut. With guidance and legislation omitting key details pertaining to roles and responsibilities and a continuing lack of cohesion between those at the centre of public protection, there remains little hope that we shall not see another example of how this system has been undermined through lack of cooperation and communication.

Summary of key points

- Recent high-profile events and legislation have placed multi-agency working on a statutory footing.
- Formalised partnerships are based on the premise of cooperation and a shared ethos.
- Multi-agency working is about managing risk, not eliminating it.
- Professional issues such as good communication and lead responsibility are essential to effective inter-agency working.
- Professionals must have an understanding of the quality and relevance of the information obtained and as such the nature of risk.
- Partnership working extends beyond statutory arrangements and should involve the wider community.

Points for further consideration

- What are the key skills required for effective communication in multi-agency working?
- How might the competing priorities of different agencies adversely affect the management of risk?

Further reading

Bridges, A. (2006) *An Independent Review of a Serious Further Offence Case: Anthony Rice.* London: HMIP.

Hill, L. (2009) *Investigation into the Issues Arising from the Serious Further Offence Review: Dano Sonnex.* London: NOMS.

Kemshall, H. (2008) *Understanding the Community Management of High Risk Offenders.* Maidenhead: Open University Press.

Nash, M. (2006) *Public Protection and the Criminal Justice Process.* Oxford: Oxford University Press.

References

Ashworth, A. (1998) *The Criminal Process: An Evaluative Study* (2nd edn). Oxford: Oxford University Press.

Beck, U. (1992) *Risk Society.* London: Sage Publications.

Bridges, A. (2006a) *An Independent Review of a Serious Further Offence Case: Damien Hanson and Elliot White.* London: HMIP.

Bridges, A. (2006b) *An Independent Review of a Serious Further Offence Case: Anthony Rice.* London: HMIP.

Carvel, J. and Jones, S. (2009) 'Public get child safety role in wake of Baby P', *The Guardian*, 5 May. Available from www.guardian.co.uk/society/2009/may/05/public-child-safety-role-babyp

Considine, T. and Birch, P. (2009) 'Challenges of managing the risk of violent and sexual offenders in the community', in Ireland, J.L., Ireland, C.A. and Birch, P. (eds) *Violent and Sexual Offenders: Assessment, Treatment and Management* (pp 284-302). Cullompton: Willan Publishing.

Davies, M., Croall, H. and Tyrer, J. (2005) *Criminal Justice: An Introduction to the Criminal Justice System in England and Wales.* London: Longman.

Hill, L. (2009) *Investigation into the Issues Arising from the Serious Further Offence Review: Dano Sonnex.* London: NOMS

Home Office (2006) *Revised Chapter 8 OASys – Risk of Serious Harm to the Individual, and Other Risks.* London: HMSO.

Kemshall, H. (2001) *Risk Assessment and Management of Known Sexual and Violent Offenders: A Review of Current Issues – Police Research Series Paper 140.* London: Home Office. Available from www.homeoffice.gov.uk/rds/prgpdfs/prs140.pdf

Kemshall, H. (2008) *Understanding the Community Management of High Risk Offenders.* Maidenhead: Open University Press.

Kemshall, H., Mackenzie, G., Wood, J., Bailey, R. and Yates, J. (2005) *Strengthening Multi-Agency Public Protection Arrangements (MAPPA).* London: Home Office. Available from www.homeoffice.gov.uk/rds/pdf05/dpr45.pdf

Kemshall, H., and Wood, J. (2007) 'High-risk offenders and public protection', in L. Gelsthorpe and R. Morgan (eds) *Handbook of Probation.* Collumpton: Willan

Lieb, R. (2007) 'Joined-up worrying: the Multi-Agency Public Protection Panels', in A. Matravers (ed) *Sex Offenders in the Community: Managing and Reducing the Risks* (pp 207-18). Cullompton: Willan Publishing.

Maguire, M., Kemshall, H., Noaks, L., Wincup, E. and Sharpe, K. (2001) *Risk Management of Sexual and Violent Offenders: The Work of Public Protection Panels.* London: Home Office. Available from www.homeoffice.gov.uk/rds/prgpdfs/pis139.pdf

Ministry of Justice (2008a) 'MAPPA monitors record number of offenders to protect the public'. News Release. 20 October. Available from www.justice.gov.uk/nes/newsrelease201008a.htm

Ministry of Justice (2008b) *National Statistics for Multi-Agency Public Protection Arrangements Annual Reports 07/08*. London: Ministry of Justice. Available from www.justice.gov.uk/news/docs/mappa-national-figures-2008.pdf

Ministry of Justice (2009) *MAPPA Guidance 2009*. London: Ministry of Justice. Available from www.lbhf.gov.uk/Images/MAPPA%20Guidance%20(2009)%20Version%203%200%20_tcm21-120559.pdf

Nash, M. (1999) *Police, Probation and Protecting the Public*. London: Blackstone Press.

Nash, M. (2004) *Dangerousness and Dangerous Offenders*. Portsmouth: Institute of Criminal Justice Studies, University of Portsmouth.

Nash, M. (2006) *Public Protection and the Criminal Justice Process*. Oxford: Oxford University Press.

Nash, M. and Williams, A. (2008) *The Anatomy of Serious Further Offending*. Oxford: Oxford University Press.

NPD (National Probation Directorate) (2004) *Sex Offender Strategy for the National Probation Service*. London: NPD. Available from www.pathway/cms/showdoc.asp?go=36

Petherick, W. (2005) *Predicting the Dangerousness of a Criminal*. Available from www.crimelibrary.com/criminal_mind/profiling/danger/5.html

Reder, P. and Duncan, S. (2003) 'Understanding communication in child protection networks', *Child Abuse Review*, 12, 82-100.

Spalek, B., El Awa, S. and MacDonald, L.Z. (2009) *Police–Muslim Engagement and Partnerships for the Purposes of Counter-Terrorism: An examination*. Birmingham: University of Birmingham. Available from http://muslimsafetyforum.org/docs/summary%20report%20ct%20police%20community%20partnership%20bham.pdf

Turner, B.S. (2001) 'Risk, rights and regulation: an overview', *Health, Risk and Society*, 3(1), 9-18.

Wilson, R.J., McWhinnie, A., Pichea, J.E., Prinzo, M. and Cortoni, F. (2007a) 'Circles of Support and Accountability: engaging community volunteers in the management of high risk sexual offenders', *The Howard Journal*, 46(1), 1-15.

Wilson, R.J., Pichea, J.E. and Prinzo, M. (2007b) 'Evaluating the effectiveness of professionally-facilitated volunteerism in the community-based management of high-risk sexual offenders: part one – effects on participants and stakeholders', *The Howard Journal*, 46(3), 289-302.

Wilson, R.J., Pichea, J.E. and Prinzo, M. (2007c) 'Evaluating the effectiveness of professionally-facilitated volunteerism in the community-based management of high-risk sexual offenders: part two – a comparison of recidivism rates', *The Howard Journal*, 46(4), 327-37.

Wood, J. (2006) 'Profiling high risk offenders: a review of 136 cases', *The Howard Journal*, 45(3), 307-20.

CHAPTER 8

Singing from the same **MAPPA** hymn sheet – but can we hear all the voices?

Mike Nash

Aims of the chapter
- To explore multi-agency working in a public protection context.
- To argue that while a joined-up agenda has almost become a practice orthodoxy there remain significant barriers to more effective collaboration.
- To show that these barriers, although frequently framed in inquiries into tragedies as 'system failures', may have more complex causes underpinning them, which will require more than 'system strengthening' to rectify.

Undeniably, multi-agency working is regarded as a fundamentally good thing. This book bears witness to its extent as a response to a range of contemporary social problems. There is an underlying message that many heads are better than one and that a variety of expertise brought to bear on a given problem has to be good news. From child protection to safeguarding our streets, a multi-agency approach has become the default position, with numerous inquiries into tragedies underlining the importance of this message and suggesting 'system improvement' in almost all cases (Nash and Williams, 2008). Tragedy, then, is often located in a failure of communication (Wilson, 1974) and means are sought to improve this between agencies that may not traditionally, or even contemporaneously, be natural bedfellows. In other words, a 'failure' in multi-agency working is now one of the major reasons cited to explain human tragedies – often investigations do not look much beyond this. Having developed multi-agency arrangements to improve protection, the default position for failure is now that these systems are not working. Their lack of complete operation has been a useful screen to mask other problems. Unfortunately, this process might conveniently enable individual failings (people or agency) to be minimised as they become subsumed beneath the protective multi-agency blanket. This chapter explores the process of cooperation under the Multi-Agency Public Protection Arrangements (MAPPA) with specific examination of the relationships between the core agencies or 'responsible authorities' (the Police, Probation and Prison Services) and those now having a 'duty to cooperate' (for example, health services, Youth Offending Teams, job centres, social services etc). In particular it begs the question: if so many people agree that multi-agency working is essential, why do so many barriers to effectiveness remain? If commonly accepted and prioritised agendas such as child protection or protecting the public from dangerous offenders are signed up to by various agencies, why do communication problems continue to dominate inquiry reports? Although this chapter primarily focuses on inter-agency communication issues, there is also a consideration of the potential downside to ever-closer working together.

Protecting the public from high risk of harm offenders has rapidly risen to a prominent position in all criminal justice agency policies and practice, undoubtedly resulting from its high political and public profile. That profile is of course predominantly framed and shaped by failure rather than success, the former being more newsworthy. Indeed, since MAPPA were established in the 2000 Criminal Justice and Court Services Act, public protection has featured significantly in Probation Service 'mission statements' and has brought the Probation Service into increasingly closer collaboration with the Police Service (Nash, 1999; Mawby and Worrall, 2004; Mawby et al, 2007) in particular, and more recently the Prison Service and other agencies. By the time of the 2003 Criminal Justice Act, the two original 'responsible authorities' – the Police and Probation Services – were joined by the Prison Service as an additional responsible authority, and a number of other agencies became subject to 'duty to cooperate requirements', many of these perhaps not traditionally regarded as a part of the criminal justice process. In other words, a significant public protection family of agencies had been created by 2003. The rationale underwriting this requirement was of course that a multi-agency approach was best practice and that a legal requirement would serve to overcome any reluctance to share information between agencies that may be less than willing to do so. History had already proved that even in such sensitive areas as child protection, agencies continued to be less than willing to collaborate more closely. The question is, of course, is a legal requirement sufficient to ensure meaningful collaboration and in particular to serve to make confidentiality less of an issue?

It is easy to locate the basis of MAPPA in child protection arrangements. For a considerable period of time, child protection conferences were serviced by a range of agencies, but perhaps with social and health services and the police being the key players. Although senior probation officers were core members, the author recalls that their attendance may have been less than convincing. Equally, the presence of the police on panels may have made agencies such as social and health services less than willing to disclose information, preferring instead to suggest that client/patient confidentiality would be compromised. Although undoubtedly improving over time, a residue of mistrust has remained, even in a field where the bottom line (protecting children) is likely to be readily signed up to by all. It is therefore unsurprising that protecting the public from seriously harmful offenders, with its associated political importance, has been written into law as a requirement rather than a choice. Evaluations of public protection arrangements, pre and post 2003, have demonstrated a great deal of progress (Kemshall et al, 2005). Indeed, the British government has even been moved to declare that its system is 'better than ever' (Home Office, 2004) and subsequently ministers have described it as a beacon of best practice around the world and as a world leader. The remainder of this chapter will explore the extent of collaboration in one geographically defined MAPPA area and assess what might both hinder and facilitate greater effectiveness. However, before that, the distinction between multi-agency and inter-agency will be explored, not least as these terms are used almost interchangeably but have quite different meanings and, perhaps more importantly, different outcomes.

Crawford (1999: 120) distinguishes the two concepts as follows:

- multi-agency – the coming together of a variety of agencies in relation to a given problem;
- inter-agency – entails some degree of fusion and melding of relations between agencies.

This distinction is important in that, depending on agency attitudes to melding and fusion, there may be a reluctance to collaborate more closely if it entails a potential loss of identity or a change to established ethos and values. Furthermore, if a degree of fusion does occur, does this inevitably lead to a loss of the individual and distinctive perspectives and witness instead the creation of a mono-agency view, even if a number of agencies are represented? Does, then, greater multi-agency working lead, by default, to a single view of the problem? Even if not, is the agenda so strong and set that challenges to it, or alternative opinions, are not heard? In terms that now appear precipitous, Thomas (1986: 128) warned social workers what closer collaboration with the police might entail. He suggested that there might be more an incorporation into 'police thinking' and that the police might have been 'educating' social workers as much as in the other direction. His prescient words echo some of the feelings in the sample used in this chapter, 'social work practice will have to call on all its reserves of professionalism to hold its ground and achieve true peer-group collaboration' (Thomas, 1986: 128, cited in Garrett, 2004: 80).

This chapter is based on a questionnaire survey of just over 60 practitioners involved in public protection work to a greater or lesser extent. The agencies involved were police, probation, prisons, social work (local authority and health based) and Youth Offending Teams. Although not a statistically significant sample, it is a reasonable number on which to gauge opinions concerning closer or greater collaboration between them. Generally speaking, respondents were asked to score a number of statements in terms of importance (for example, from extremely important to not at all important). There were also opportunities for free text responses. Due to the relatively small sample number, results are reproduced numerically rather than as percentages.

Accepting that failures in communication or information exchange feature highly in inquiries into tragedies, respondents were asked to rate the importance of information exchange as a benefit of multi-agency working. Of the Youth

Offending Team respondents, all (6/6) rated this as extremely or very beneficial. Numbers for other groups were: 11/14 probation, 18/21 police, 5/6 prison and 13/16 social workers. With such widespread support and agreement as to importance, why then do repeated inquiry reports identify information blockages, or a failure to act on information, as a key finding in the occurrence of tragedy? The research set out to explore perceptions of costs and benefits of closer collaboration among respondents in an attempt to establish what might be undermining the good intentions indicated above.

If Crawford's definition of multi-agency working is accepted, then the incorporation of a range of perspectives, expertise and experience should be regarded as a benefit of collaboration – indeed it is the fundamental rationale for it. This is much more than the simple exchange of information between the agencies and closer to recognising the value of that information and then taking appropriate action in connection with it. In essence it is about respecting the information and the people giving it. As Laming (2009: 36) noted, 'children can only be protected effectively when all agencies pool information, expertise and resources so that a full picture of a child's life is better understood'. For example, among our respondents there was a general recognition that 'expertise from other agencies' was very beneficial, with between a half and two thirds of all respondents agreeing. However, there was a notable exception to this, with only 1/14 probation officers scoring this 'benefit' very highly. As a responsible authority under MAPPA, this finding is surprising to say the least. Similarly, valuing a 'different perspective' should be another positive aspect of multi-agency working but here, if anything, the responses were scored lower than those for other agency expertise. The lowest-scoring agencies were probation (4/14), prisons (2/6) and the police (6/21). These three agencies represent the core responsible authorities under MAPPA and, as such, lead and potentially set the public protection agenda. If they value the perspectives of other agencies relatively lowly then what is the message here for the 'duty to cooperate' agencies? It could be that these other agencies have a differing perspective on public protection than that of agencies with a statutory duty to protect. Therefore their contribution, rather than regarded as a positive addition, may instead be regarded as something of a threat to the established order. This is speculative but some of the responses outlined below may well support this notion based on an absence of trust between partners, even though there is general agreement that multi-agency working is inherently a good thing. At the start of this piece of research therefore a fundamental dichotomy emerges: most agencies in multi-agency public protection agree that sharing of information is important and beneficial, yet learning from others and listening to their perspective is not rated as highly. This could well be a case where process compliance wins out over practice.

Findings such as this must continue to cast doubt on the building of ever-greater databases. The government has launched *ContactPoint*, a database that will include the details of every child under 18 in the UK, including their name, age, address, general practitioner, school and details of every professional working with them (Quinn, 2009).Yet already serious concerns have been raised about the ability of others to access the information concerning 55,000 children regarded as 'vulnerable' on the list. As many as 330,000 professionals could access the database.Yet despite this the government intends pressing on, even though any incoming Conservative government has promised to end the project.[1] Aside from the government's alleged inability to securely hold large databases, the fact that the police intend to use it to search for other crimes has also caused concern. This would reflect the tensions felt by the sample respondents caused by fears that other agencies would use information for purposes other than the matter in hand (for example not for child protection purposes in a child protection case conference – see below). That said, as Hebenton and Seddon (2009: 348) citing Agamben (2005) note, exceptional measures have a habit of becoming the norm when framed in terms of saving the next victim. Perhaps databases never die – they simply transform into something bigger.

Only a third of the probation respondents scored 'gaining greater knowledge of offenders' as extremely or very beneficial (compared with over three quarters of Youth Offending Team staff and two thirds of police). Once again, adding to the knowledge base should be a default position for multi-agency working, so the probation response has to be questioned once more. The probation staff also rated 'more readily identifying children at risk and victims' lower than all other respondents; however, only one half of local authority social workers rated this factor in the highest two categories. Surely anything that aids children at risk has to be fundamental to multi-agency working and to the effectiveness of social services in particular. The probation respondents also scored lowest on 'rapid response to risk and deteriorating circumstances'. This may be explained by the fact that they do not see themselves as an emergency service. However, within public protection terms they do have to respond quickly, in partnership with others and the knowledge held by others may be crucial to the speed and nature of the action taken. These findings point to something of a 'belief gap' between agreement that a multi-agency system or process is beneficial or important and what the actual benefits of that process might be. If this is the case it points more to process compliance rather than making best use of the resources (information/ expertise) resulting from collaboration with others.

Implicit in some of these doubts appears to be issues of trust, or more accurately mistrust. From this small-scale piece of research there remained an enduring concern among respondents that some agencies (notably the Police and Probation Services) felt reluctant to share because they were unsure of the use to which the information would be put, or of its eventual destination. In a child protection context, Reder and Duncan (2003: 93) had cited Morrison (1996: 130) as saying: 'working together means contact between different emotional realities, different systems and different types of bias'. They suggested that this led not only to mistrust, but also to a potential withholding of information. The police in this public protection sample felt that probation officers were reluctant to give information if they believed that the police would use the information for 'other purposes' such as an application for a civil order. Social workers and health workers were, according to police respondents, equally reticent to share unless a court application was made. Police officers also indicated that if they divulged confidential information such as surveillance details to social work staff, it would end up being revealed to families and therefore lose its effect.

Thus, even though there appeared to be a common purpose of public protection, there was evidence of agencies viewing some information as 'theirs' and not to be shared with others, especially if the other agency intended to use it for different purposes. Central to some of these communication issues appears to be the nature of reaching an agreed understanding of what risk actually is. It is clear that agencies differ in their perception of and reaction to risk. For example, the Prison Service may well choose to keep a number of matters 'in-house' and deal with them by way of adjudications. This information may or may not reach the outside world in matters such as parole hearings or indeed the ears of those responsible for the day-to-day management of offenders in the community. Or, very poor and worrying prison behaviour may become quickly downgraded by a sharp improvement in the prisoner's persona, a clear and historic risk apparently lowered by a rapid transformation, as in the Sonnex case briefly discussed below (and see Clift, this volume). There are, then, undoubtedly different perspectives on the nature of the harm that might unfold, when it might occur and who might be the potential victim. In these instances, rather than an agreed position, it appears as if at times agencies retreat to the safety of their professional expertise, which is itself jealously guarded rather than positively informing others. By failing to agree on this most basic of information, a major stumbling block to more effective communication occurs.

The sample of practitioners forming the backcloth to this chapter revealed a pattern of 'problematic' relationships with other agencies, but of concern was the fact that every agency had a 'problem' with a different agency. When asked to identify their most problematic agency, the results were as follows (most problematic and % of respondents):

- Youth Offending Teams – police (66% of all)
- Probation – prisons (64%)
- Prisons – probation (87%)
- Social work – job centre (37%)
- Health – housing authorities (87%)
- Police – health (48%).

Significantly, the police, often regarded as the flies in the ointment, were not universally considered as 'most problematic' in the research, only among the youth justice respondents. Identified problems were common among the agencies and centred on finding the name of the relevant contact, getting hold of that person, absence of key personnel (or deputies) from meetings and obtaining the prompt release of key information.

This is probably not helped by the different risk assessment tools used by agencies. In this piece of research it was evident that the Probation and Prison Services make the greatest use of the Offender Assessment System (OASys), while police predominantly use Risk Matrix 2000. More specialist assessment devices such as the Spousal Abuse Risk Assessment (SARA) were fairly common among probation staff but little used by police and not at all by prisons. Considering the level of violence and abuse conducted within domestic settings it is not difficult to see why different perceptions might arise if its seriousness is seemingly under-assessed, or differentially assessed, by two key agencies (see Tapley, this volume). At the same time, different agencies committed greater or lesser time to training practitioners to actually use these assessment tools and this led to feelings about 'superior' expertise – hardly a good base for equitable practice among different agencies. Overarching the use of different tools is the 'precautionary logic' (Hebenton and Seddon, 2009: 243), which shifts interventions with potentially dangerous offenders into a pre-emptive rather than after-the-fact mode. Despite the pervasiveness of this logic around the world, it may still sit uncomfortably with some practitioners working in a multi-agency context that epitomises risk control (Hudson, 2003: 49-50) to this extent. The assessment and management of risk, lying at the heart of MAPPA, may therefore face barriers over and above basic communication problems.

Multi-agency working is clearly viewed by many, from practitioners to inquiry chairs and government ministers, as crucial to effective 'protection work' in the community. As we know, numerous inquiries into tragedy have highlighted what might in effect be called 'systems failures'. These invariably revolve around poor communication, lack of information or a failure to actually follow the process laid down by the system. It is suggested here that while there may be little disagreement with this broad philosophy, a series of minor hurdles could lead to a substantial barrier being erected against more effective working. As noted above, despite broad agreement over the importance of information exchange, what might prevent this developing fully could be based more on perceptions than process, on feelings rather than actuality. In other words, the basic knowledge base between agencies may be thought to differ so much that effective multi-agency working is simply not possible. As a trainer for MAPPA events, the author finds that agency-specific knowledge and attitudes vary considerably and one is often not in sympathy with the other – despite the common purpose of a protection agenda. Clearly, multi-agency training events can impact positively in helping to create a sense of shared purpose, but post-qualifying training has to go a long way to overcome knowledge and attitudes (cultures) instilled in individual agency initial training programmes. For example, when the Certificate of Qualification in Social Work (CQSW) was removed as the professional qualification for probation officers in 1997, much of the input on child protection was lost. It was as if this role was seen to be in someone else's domain despite child abuse being a crime and the long tradition of multi-agency child protection conferences involving the Probation Service. In attempting to focus the Probation Service more firmly on its 'criminal justice' work it was as if child protection was reconfigured as another agency's problem – probably because it appeared to fit under the 'welfare' cap the government of the day was eager to remove from probation. It has taken a good decade to bring this important role back into the probation domain but meanwhile a crucial multi-agency role has been severely curtailed and expertise diluted.

This again takes us back into the troubled waters of what exactly multi-agency working should mean. For example, is it possible to work effectively with another agency if you have little or no perception of what they do? If there is another 'take' on risk, will this be heard and acted on? Referring back to Crawford's (1999) work it is evident that multi-agency working is based on specific agency policy and perspectives, knowledge and skills coming together to consider a given problem. By definition, that problem is one that crosses agency boundaries but should remain the same problem – it is the response to the problem that should be multi-agency based and not a range of different interpretations of the problem. In other words, the response should not be fragmented along agency lines but be the result of the agencies' combined efforts. It should also be noted that the multi-agency perspective may be brought to bear some time after the case has been running and more likely starting out as the responsibility of one agency only. This is important in the light of Munro's (1999) research on social workers' assessments, which suggests that early impressions are not often altered, even in the light of new evidence. Where does this leave the input of one agency into another, or several of them? As suggested above, it is possible that the public protection agenda has created within MAPPA something like an agreed position on risk of harm, especially between Police and Probation Services. However, this means that for a variety of reasons, the Prison Service may be a lesser partner and if that is the case for a responsible authority, what hope is there for the 'duty to cooperate' agencies? Laming (2009: 37) in respect of safeguarding children noted examples of professional disagreements among practitioners where the view of one was not explored in greater detail, again casting doubt on the essence of good multi-agency working. When discussing how information is given and received between professionals, Reder and Duncan (1999: 65) argue that 'There must be sufficient synchrony between the message-giver and the message-receiver so that the intention, content and associated feelings become shared property'. If there is a basic lack of listening this would appear to be a problematic aspect of multi-agency working.

Lieb (2003: 207) has described MAPPA as 'joined-up worrying', an apt term when the costs of cases going wrong are so high (Nash and Williams, 2008). However, Lieb also refers to Povey's (2001) work on new directions in policing as 'public reassurance' and suggests that the arrangements for dealing with high-risk offenders in the community comes into this category, with MAPPA at the forefront of this reassurance and confidence-boosting strategy (Lieb, 2003: 207). Joined-up working is therefore meant to convey a strong message that many minds and different expertise are being brought to bear on a problem that puts the public at risk – it therefore holds out the promise of 'protection' at best and reassurance as a minimum. Yet as Ayre (2001: 891) reminds us when talking about child protection, 'we must recognise that when we choose for a service a title which we cannot live up to, failure is inevitable'. So is the reassurance false? If the assumption behind this claim is that agencies do actually join up, communicate, share what is important and act on it in a coordinated way, then the answer is probably no. The recent and awful case of 'Baby P' puts a new twist on the old adage that many hands might make light work. In this there were so many agencies involved that each appears to have thought another was going to do something or had already done so, practice that was based on assumptions rather than detailed checking – a potential downside of the multi-agency agenda. Multi-agency working could therefore be described as leading to or fostering an 'assumptive' culture, which could act to reduce professional decisiveness and thereby losing precious time when action is required. The Baby P review, details of which were reported in the *Daily Mail* on 17 March 2009, revealed common failings of poor communication, non-attendance at meetings (notably health staff), insufficiently briefed deputies, delays in calling vital meetings and an absence of basic checking and challenge. In all this, rather than a variety of agencies acting to bolster the prospect of protection, it appears to have, indirectly at least, caused it to be reduced. What emerges is a picture of many professionals involved in the case (Baby P was seen at least 60 times) but singularly failing to join up their thinking and actions. It is stunning that these findings can emerge early in the 21st century after so many similar incidents were reported in the decades preceding this report. If we overlay this with the concept of 'distant suffering' (the ability of the media to engage the public in the suffering of other victims) (Boltanski, 1999, cited in Karstedt, 2002: 303) then it is clear that the anxiety context in which professionals work will carry on increasing.

It is difficult of course to locate failure in these tragic cases as it always hinges on a number of personal and system failings (described as active and latent failures by Johnson and Petrie, 2004: 187). It is difficult to establish what needs correcting but undoubtedly poor judgement and assessment often presage a tragedy. Mistakes will happen and in effect professionals can be guilty of poor practice. That said, in this case so many others were involved it is clear that people further along the process did not really challenge the views or the findings of those who preceded them – the investigative and challenging culture so necessary within and between agencies was clearly absent. The cause of that poor practice might also rest much deeper within the organisation. As Johnson and Petrie (2004: 187) suggest, 'Although it is recognised that individual decision-making might be the final act before an incident occurs, it is the events and decisions made within an organisation prior to the onset of the incident that are critical'. When these problems cross agency boundaries it is likely that the problem will be exacerbated. The Baby P inquiry did rightly report on high workloads, stress-induced sickness absences, poor supervision and management and inadequate training but will a systems response seeking to improve multi-agency communication still emerge as a major recommendation? Laming's (2009: 37) report noted that 'cooperative efforts are often the first to suffer when services and individuals are under pressure'; in other words it might appear that agencies retreat back on themselves at these pressure points, suggesting that multi-agency working remains a fragile policy to say the least.

Conclusion

This chapter has noted that, despite widespread support for the benefits of closer collaboration between criminal justice agencies, the philosophy and practice of multi-agency working remain some way apart. Even where it happens, it is fragile. Even where dominant and priority agendas bring professionals together (public and child protection for example), there remain considerable differences and perceptions of risk and a continuing belief that someone else has taken responsibility. Although intended to 'up-skill', there is a real risk that multi-agency working can act in reverse.

The case of Dano Sonnex shows in many respects that the potential problems highlighted in this chapter still persist. This case involved a released prisoner committing two awful murders while on licence (a serious further offence) in June 2008. Having been convicted of murder in June 2009, a number of inquiry and review reports were published focusing on how this tragedy had developed (Ministry of Justice, 2009). The headline was that under-resourced probation staff had made wrong risk assessment judgements and had not initiated recall (or further risk assessment processes) when they could have.

In essence this was an example of a latent failure but real problems arose in professional judgements. That said, many of the time-honoured problems identified in tragedy inquiries arose again, notably: poor transfer of information between agencies, a split between information inside and outside of custodial institutions and its use in risk assessment, a ready acceptance of apparent offender 'change' and the overriding of professional judgement by 'systems'.

As suggested earlier, assessments once made are not reviewed often enough in the light of new developments. In this case, Sonnex and another individual allegedly tied up a relative and her partner and put pillows over their heads two days after release. As no charges were pressed by the victims, no further action, other than a general warning, was taken. At the very least this should have triggered a major review of risk. In other words, this type of situation requires experienced, competent and confident staff. It requires those involved in any agency to feel able to challenge prevailing views, to listen to others and to think outside the box. Multi-agency working does not solve this problem. Indeed, it is very time consuming and resource intensive and may just have a negative impact on occasions. Sonnex was assessed as a tier 2 offender and as such was not under the auspices of MAPPA, was not in a public protection team and was supervised (most unfortunately for her) by a newly qualified probation officer.

The elaboration of public protection processes has led to a concentration of skills in public protection teams at the expense of general offender management – an area where, according to the chief inspector of probation, the majority of serious further offending occurs (Bridges, 2006).

Each new tragedy will, as noted earlier, lead to system strengthening proposals from government; Baby P and Sonnex are but the latest examples to demonstrate this need. Yet systems rely on the people in them to work effectively, to exercise their professional skills as best they can and in association with other colleagues. There may well be an increase in blame attached to a lack of resources as the UK enters a round of significant public expenditure cuts. At the same time, if the government could get to grips with a public protection system growing out of control it might just reduce the pressure on those professionals involved to make their job slightly easier. If professionals were just able to have time to actively communicate and listen to others and not assume that other organisations will undertake work and carry out tasks in order to protect, the world conceivably might just be a safer place.

> ## Points for further discussion
>
> ■ How important is it to maintain individual agency culture and identity within multi-agency frameworks?
> ■ Can you think of ways in which multi-agency working, particularly in public protection, has altered the ways in which individual agencies work – and to what extent is this a good or not so good development?

Note

[1] Since coming to power in May 2010, the coalition government has confirmed that it intends to scrap *Contact Point* although it will remain in use until a new system is found.

References

Ayre, P. (2001) 'Child protection and the media: lessons from the last three decades', *British Journal of Social Work*, 31, 887–901.

Crawford, A. (1999) *The Local Governance of Crime: Appeals to Community and Partnerships*. Oxford: Oxford University Press.

Garrett, P.M. (2004) 'Talking child protection: the police and social workers "working together"', *Journal of Social Work*, 4(1), 77–97.

Hebenton, B. and Seddon, T. (2009) 'From dangerousness to precaution: managing sexual and violent offenders in an insecure and uncertain age', *British Journal of Criminology*, 49(3), 323–62.

Home Office (2004) **'Public protection from dangerous offenders better than ever'**. Press Release. 28 July.

Hudson, B. (2003) *Justice in the Risk Society*. London: Sage Publications.

Johnson, S. and Petrie, S. (2004) 'Child protection and risk management: the death of Victoria Climbié', *Journal of Social Policy*, 33(2), 179-202.

Karstedt, S. (2002) 'Emotions and criminal justice', *Theoretical Criminology*, 6(3), 299-317.

Kemshall, H., Mackenzie, G., Wood, J., Bailey, R. and Yates, J. (2005) *Strengthening Multi-Agency Public Protection Arrangements*. London: Home Office.

Laming, Lord (2009) *The Protection of Children in England: A Progress Report*. London: The Stationery Office.

Lieb, R. (2003) *Joined-up Worrying: The Multi-Agency Public Protection Panels*. WSIPP Working Paper 03-00-1101. Washington, DC: WSIPP. Available from http://wsipp.wa.gov/rptfiles/03-00-1101.pdf

Mawby, R. and Worrall, A. (2004) '"Polibation" revisited: policing, probation and prolific offender projects', *International Journal of Police Science and Management*, 6(2), 63-73.

Mawby, R., Crawley, P. and Wright, A. (2007) 'Beyond "polibation" and towards "prisipolibation"? Joint agency offender management in the context of the Street Crime Initiative', *International Journal of Police Science and Management*, 9(2), 122-34.

Ministry of Justice (2009) A series of reports investigating the case of Dano Sonnex can be found online at www.justice.gov.uk/news/announcement040609a.htm

Munro, E. (1999) *Common Errors of Reasoning in Child Protection Work*. London: LSE Research Articles Online. Available from http://eprints.lse.ac.uk/archive/00000358/

Nash, M. (1999) 'Enter the polibation officer', *International Journal of Police Science and Management*, 1(4), 360-8.

Nash, M. and Williams, A. (2008) *The Anatomy of Serious Further Offending*. Oxford: Oxford University Press.

Quinn, N. (2009) *Criminal Justice Management*, 12(1), 28-9.

Reder, P. and Duncan, S. (2003) 'Understanding communication in child protection networks', *Child Abuse Review*, 12, 82-100.

Wilson, J. (1974) *Language and the Pursuit of Truth*. Cambridge: Cambridge University Press.

CHAPTER 9

Sharing or shifting responsibility? The multi-agency approach to safeguarding children

Aileen Watson

Aims of the chapter

- To consider the role of multi-agency working in safeguarding children.
- To identify current policies and statutory arrangements in relation to multi-agency working.
- To discuss the professional issues that multi-agency working can raise.
- To highlight the aspects of multi-agency working that can enhance or impede the safeguarding of children.

> I am in no doubt that effective support for children and families cannot be achieved by a single agency acting alone.... It is a multi-disciplinary task. (Laming, 2003: 6)

The last 30 years have witnessed a growing emphasis on collaborative working as the most effective means of safeguarding the welfare of children. The death of Maria Colwell at the hands of her stepfather and the subsequent inquiry in 1974 sparked the development of multi-agency arrangements to protect children (Howarth, 2009: 113). In the 1980s, the statutory framework for multi-agency working was established with the implementation of the 1989 Children Act and its requirement that agencies collaborate and work together to help and protect children and young people (Cheminais, 2009). Most recently, Lord Laming's (2003) inquiry into the death of Victoria Climbié sparked an overhaul of child services and a change in emphasis from child protection to the need to safeguard the wellbeing of all children.

The government responded to Lord Laming's report with the publication of the Green Paper *Every Child Matters* (DfES, 2003), which set out a different approach to children and childhood (Parton, 2006). The Green Paper focused on the importance of child development and the need for early intervention to avoid the risk of problems in the future, particularly in relation to issues such as education and employment (Parton, 2006: 139). In terms of child protection,

Every Child Matters built on the ideas already established in *Working Together to Safeguard Children: A Guide to Inter-Agency Working to Safeguard and Promote the Welfare of Children* (DH et al, 1999), in that it focused on the need to safeguard and promote the welfare of children. This was a significant shift from the *Working Together* guidance produced in 1991 (Home Office et al, 1991), where the focus was on protecting children from abuse (Parton, 2006: 103). The 1999 guidance also emphasised the need for agencies to work together to support children and families and that there should be shared responsibility for safeguarding children from harm (DH et al, 1999).

The 2004 Children Act provides the legislative framework for many of the proposals outlined in the Green Paper. Section 10 of the Act requires local authorities to make arrangements to promote cooperation between the local authority and those considered to be relevant partners. Agencies considered to be relevant partners are outlined in Table 9.1.

Section 11 of the 2004 Children Act makes it a requirement that these agencies function in a way that promotes the welfare of children and that their services pay due regard to the need to safeguard children. The Act also replaced Area Child Protection Committees with Local Safeguarding Children Boards. The boards consist of senior managers from different services who determine the local arrangements for safeguarding children. The boards are responsible for determining the nature of the safeguarding arrangements in their local area based on national policies. The move acknowledges the importance of appropriate inter-agency arrangements as a means of ensuring collaborative working and also the need to be responsive to particular area needs (Howarth, 2009: 116). Underpinning the Children Act and central to the *Every Child Matters* Green Paper are five outcomes that are seen as being key to the wellbeing of children and young people:

- being healthy (physical/mental health and emotional wellbeing);
- staying safe (protection from harm and neglect);
- enjoying and achieving (education, training and recreation);
- making a positive contribution (to society);
- achieving economic and social wellbeing (DfES, 2003).

The initiatives put forward by the government in response to the Victoria Climbié inquiry emphasise the need for 'joined-up working' and acknowledge the multifaceted nature of risk in relation children and families (Frost and Robinson, 2007). There is recognition that in order to fully understand the risk to children, there must be cooperation between children's and adults' services.

> Even the most effective integrated responses from children's services
> will only ameliorate the impacts of parent-based risk factors on a

Table 9.1: Bodies covered by key duties

Body (in addition to local authorities)	2004 Children Act (duty to cooperate)	2004 Children Act, Section 11 (duty to safeguard and promote welfare)	2002 Education Act, Section 175 and regulations under Section 157 (duty to safeguard and promote welfare)	2004 Children Act, Section 13 (statutory partnerships in LSBCs)	1989 Children Act (help with children in need)	1989 Children Act, Section 47 (help with enquiries about significant harm)
District councils	*	*				*
Police authority	*	*				
Chief officer of police	*	*		*		
Local Probation Board	*	*		*		
Youth Offending Team	*	*		*	*	*
Strategic health authority	*	*		*	*	*
Primary Care Trust	*	*		*		
Connexions Service	*					
Learning and Skills Council	*					
Special health authority		* (as designated by the Secretary of State)			*	*
NHS Trust	*	*		*	*	*
NHS Foundation Trust	*	*		*	*	*
British Transport Police	*	*				
Prison or secure training centre		*		* (which detains children)		
CAFCASS		*		*		
Maintained schools			*			
Further education colleges			*			
Independent schools			*			
Contracted services	*		*			

Source: HM Government (2006: 223)

child. To reduce the actual risk factor at source, joint working with adults' services is required to tackle the parents' problems. (Cabinet Office, 2007: 29)

The Common Assessment Framework (CAF) has been brought in as a means of assisting this 'joined-up working'. The CAF has been introduced as a means of helping agencies to identify unmet needs and encourage a proactive rather than reactive approach to the wellbeing of children (Children's Workforce and Development Council, 2007).

> The full range of measures brought in by the government in response to the Victoria Climbié inquiry can be found at www.everychildmatters.gov.uk

However, despite the introduction of new systems and protocols, inter-agency work to safeguard children remains a complex and demanding field and exemplifies many of the issues around partnership working that are raised in the other chapters of this book. The consequences of poor practice in this area, however, are incredibly damaging not only in terms of harm to children and families but also in terms of the professional credibility of agencies and individuals. The recent case of Peter Connolly (Baby P) again raised concerns that children are not being adequately protected and the high-profile media coverage of the case focused on poor practice by the agencies involved, particularly Haringey Social Services Department, the same department that was criticised following the death of Victoria Climbié. The joint area review into Haringey children's services following Baby P's death identified a number of inadequacies that contributed to children and young people being at risk of harm: 'Social care, health and police authorities do not communicate and collaborate routinely and consistently to ensure effective assessment, planning and review of cases of vulnerable children and young people' (Ofsted et al, 2008: 3).

Inquiries that have followed the deaths of children as a result of abuse and neglect, from Maria Colwell onwards, have consistently identified that problems in collaborative working have contributed to an environment in which opportunities to protect vulnerable children have been missed (Reder et al, 1993). Despite the recognition that partnership work is the best way to manage risk, the partnership approach does not always work as intended. It is necessary therefore to explore the professional issues that can undermine effective inter-agency working.

Communication

In their review of 35 major child abuse inquiries, Reder et al (1993) highlight that flawed inter-agency communication is the feature that stands out above all others. Their review alerts us to the fact that the issue is not just about lack of communication or poor information sharing but that it is also about the quality of information being shared, the meaning that is attributed to the information and the assumptions that may be made as a result. The inquiry into the death of Victoria Climbié was critical of the passive nature of some professionals in accumulating information, with one social worker described as 'a collecting bowl into which people pour observations' (Hall and Slembrouck, 2009: 289). The simple sharing of information is insufficient to manage risk effectively if meaning is not ascribed to this information and used to revise the assessment of the case.

Another barrier to effective communication can be uncertainty around policies and procedures that form the framework for inter-agency working (Reder and Duncan, 2003). If professionals are uncertain around issues such as confidentiality then this may hamper their willingness to engage with other agencies. Related to this can also be the contrasting policies of different agencies, which reflect the different priorities and values of these agencies. In terms of safeguarding children, for example, there can be discrepancies around beliefs regarding the nature of family life and how best to intervene to protect children. For example, there can be a persistent belief that a child should be kept in the family home where possible, with their natural parents. This belief contributed to Maria Colwell being returned to her mother without any clear assessment of the mother's new family circumstances (Reder et al, 1993: 92). In the case of Victoria Climbié, assumptions and beliefs linked to race and culture hindered accurate assessments. For, example, the disclosure that Victoria would 'stand to attention' in front of her great-aunt was interpreted as being part of African Caribbean family culture rather than an indication of fear (Laming, 2003: 345). Trying to work constructively with others who hold opposing views can be difficult and may lead to levels of mistrust that can damage communication and information sharing and ultimately damage the safeguarding process (Reder and Duncan, 2003).

Reder and Duncan (2003) argue that good communication is so fundamental to inter-agency working that it should be prioritised as a core skill and adopted as a key part of training. The suggestion is that changes to policies, technologies and the practicalities of communication will be irrelevant if professionals do not develop appropriate interpersonal skills. This is not just about how to convey information appropriately but also how to listen and interpret the information provided by others. A key point here is that it does not matter if a huge volume of information has been collected about a particular individual or family if the information has been given no meaning. In the Victoria Climbié case, there was communication between professionals and information was shared but the process was characterised by misunderstanding and misinterpretations and as a result vital connections were missed, which led to inappropriate assessments and ultimately the failure to protect a vulnerable child (Reder and Duncan, 2003). For example, there was a misinterpretation of the term 'fit for discharge' when Victoria was due to be released from hospital, with Victoria's social worker assuming this meant that North Middlesex Hospital had no further concerns about Victoria and hospital workers stating that this had simply meant that Victoria was physically ready to leave the hospital (Laming, 2003: 147).

Identify an incident in your personal or professional life where there has been misinterpretation of information. What caused this misinterpretation and how could it have been avoided?

Professional status and power

Effective inter-agency working requires trust, respect and a common sense of purpose. However, evaluations of the safeguarding children process have identified that partnership working is often undermined by clashes in values and ideologies, inconsistencies in categorisation of information and lack of participation or marginalisation of participants (Brandon et al, 2005; Hall and Slembrouck, 2009). These issues often link to the status ascribed to certain professions and the role that they play in specific inter-agency processes. Other linked issues may be reluctance by certain professionals to challenge the views of those who they perceive as being of a higher status. In the Victoria Climbié inquiry there was a very clear example provided when a social worker involved in the case defended her inaction by referring to the status of another professional. The social worker argued that she assumed that a senior consultant paediatrician would communicate any child protection concerns if there were any and that this was why she did not take a more investigative approach (Hall and Slembrouck, 2009: 289). The concern here is that individuals may defer to those they perceive to have a higher status and greater knowledge and in doing so may miss vital pieces of information or misinterpret the information because it has not been questioned. This can significantly undermine the risk management process.

What are your perceptions of the different agencies involved in the safeguarding process? How might this influence the way you work with these agencies?

Shared responsibility

Inter-agency working is premised on the assumption that shared knowledge and expertise will provide a more effective resolution to a problem (Nash, 2006: 154). It is not enough for agencies to have a common goal, for example the protection of a child; there must also be agreement on how this will be achieved. Effective working requires clarity with regard to the roles and responsibilities that each individual and agency will undertake (Nash, 2006). However, a key finding in the inquiry into the death of Victoria Climbié was that the notion of shared responsibility can lead to a lack of coordination and a reluctance to take lead responsibility (Laming, 2003). An efficient system is dependent on those who work within it and currently a consistent issue for those working to manage risk in child protection is the pressure to avoid mistakes. There is a high price to pay for professionals who make mistakes in risk management, as witnessed in the recent case of Baby P, where public outrage reached unprecedented levels.

Working within this blame culture can lead to defensive practice and, in some cases, inaction or professional paralysis (Nash, 2006: 149), which has huge implications for effective risk management.

Agencies also have competing priorities, which can have an impact on their ability to work collaboratively. Practitioners from health, social care and criminal justice are expected to work effectively together yet the priorities of their individual agencies may be very different. For example, a parent may be subject to probation supervision and the enforcement procedures that accompany this. Breach of a community order or post-release licence can lead to imprisonment, which would obviously have a huge impact on the safety and wellbeing of the child, but the probation practitioner may have little power to prevent this from occurring. The enforcement agenda within probation has also led to benefits sanctions for poor compliance in certain areas (BBC News, 2008). This measure reflected the emphasis on enforcing orders but failed to consider the wider impact on the children and families of offenders and seems in opposition to the current safeguarding remit, which includes the economic and social wellbeing of all children. Individual practitioners may feel that they are caught between the priorities of the multi-agency process and the demands exerted by their own agencies.

> Identify the particular demands of your own agency that might conflict with a multi-agency process. What strategies could you employ to achieve balance?

Professional relationships

Relationships are a key component of multi-agency working as they can enable or hinder communication and they contribute to the roles and responsibilities within the safeguarding process. Reder et al (1993) have reviewed professional relationships evidenced from child abuse inquiries and identified a number of patterns within professional networks that can hamper effective multi-agency working:

Closed professional system – A worker or workers develop(s) such fixed views about a case that they are unable to process information that contradicts that view. This may start as the passionate conviction of a conscientious worker but can become dogmatic and resistant to challenge. The worker may seek out other people who they believe hold the same views, which may be based on past working relationships. Information provided by individuals with an opposing view may be treated with distrust or overlooked.

Polarisation – This sees the development of divergent groups holding opposing views. This may link to fixed beliefs or mistrust of other agencies. This is problematic because it can result in poor information sharing and contradictory messages being provided to the families.

Exaggeration of hierarchy – Despite supposedly working towards a common goal, practitioners involved in multi-agency working can be influenced by the perceived professional hierarchy. Reder et al (1993) found that in some cases there was an exaggeration of professionals' perceived importance in the multi-agency process. At times this led to 'lower-status' individuals deferring to the opinions of those whom they perceived as holding 'higher-status' roles. In other cases the power of a particular role led to the marginalisation of other opinions.

Role confusion – The professionals who are involved in the process of safeguarding children may well have similar sets of skills and there may be some overlap in terms of responsibilities also. This does not necessarily have to be problematic, if there is open communication and a sense of collaborative working. However, a blurring of professional boundaries and ambiguity about specific responsibilities can cause tensions in the multi-agency process. Even though various professionals from different agencies may feel able to complete tasks, there needs to be clarity around statutory duties and powers so that there can be accountability for decisions. Individuals also need to be clear about what their responsibilities are so that there is no excuse for inaction. Clarity of purpose is also central to safeguarding children so that the focus is on the child rather than on the parents. This may be challenging for agencies whose primary function is to work with adults, for example the Probation Service.

> Consider how you might be able to avoid developing the type of networks identified above.

In the aftermath of serious incidents there is often a focus on the need to change systems and policies; to amend the protocols for inter-agency working. There may be strong arguments for such changes but they may also serve to undermine professional judgement and discretion, particularly if such changes are not supported by adequate resources and training. If such support is not in place, system changes result in increased levels of bureaucracy and a focus on accountability rather than improved practice that protects vulnerable children (Reder and Duncan, 2003; Nash, 2006). This is not likely to encourage increased responsibility and may lead to a situation whereby agencies seek to minimise their role and transfer blame onto others (Nash, 2006). Reder et al (1993: 69) emphasise the need for professionals to feel that they are working in a 'secure setting'; a practice context in which they feel 'valued, respected and supported'. The stress and anxiety provoked by continual change in the parameters of practice may contribute to further errors in judgement and increased risk to children (Reder et al, 1993: 69).

Table 9.2: Common core of skills and knowledge for multi-agency working

Skills	Knowledge
Communication and teamwork • Communicate effectively with other practitioners and professionals by listening and ensuring that you are being listened to • Appreciate that others may not have the same understanding of professional terms and may interpret abbreviations such as acronyms differently • Provide timely, appropriate, succinct information to enable other practitioners to deliver their support to the young person, the child or parent/carer • Record, summarise, share and feedback information, using IT skills where necessary to do so • Work in a team context, forging and sustaining relationships across agencies and respecting the contribution of others working with children, young people and families • Share experience through formal and informal exchanges and work with adults who are parents/carers **Assertiveness** • Be proactive, initiate necessary action and be able and prepared to put forward your own judgements • Have the confidence to challenge situations by looking beyond your immediate role and asking considered questions • Present facts and judgements objectively • Identify possible sources of support within your own working environment • Judge when you should provide the support yourself and when you should refer to another practitioner or professional **Your role and remit** • Know your main job and responsibilities within your working environment • Know the value and expertise you bring to a team and that brought by your colleagues	**Know how to make queries** • Know your role within different group situations and how you contribute to the overall group process, understanding the value of sharing how you approach your role with other professionals • Develop your skills and knowledge with training from experts, to minimise the need for referral to specialist services, enabling continuity for the family, child or young person while enhancing your own skills and knowledge • Have a greater knowledge and understanding of the range of organisations and individuals working with children, young people and those caring for them, and be aware of the roles and responsibilities of other professionals **Procedures and working methods** • Know what to do in given cases, eg for referrals or raising concerns • Know what the triggers are for reporting incidents or unexpected behaviour • Know how to work within your own and other organisational values, beliefs and cultures • Know what to do when there is an insufficient response from other organisations or agencies , while maintaining focus on what is in the child or young person's best interest • Understand the way that partner services operate – their procedures, objectives, role and relationships – in order to work effectively alongside them • Know about the Common Assessment Framework for Children and Young People (CAF) and, where appropriate, how to use it **Laws, policies and procedures** • Know about the existence of key laws relating to children and young people and where to obtain further information • Know about employers' safeguarding and health and safety policies and procedures, and how they apply in the wider working environment

Source: HM Government (2005: 18-20)

Effective multi-agency working

Multi-agency working can be fraught with tensions but is still considered to be the most effective way of safeguarding vulnerable children and young people. When agencies and practitioners communicate well and collaborate effectively, then it is likely that there will be better outcomes for children and families (Howarth, 2009: 114). Governmental guidance on the core skills and knowledge for effective multi-agency working with children and young people is outlined in Table 9.2.

Partnership with families

In order to safeguard children and young people from harm it is important for agencies not only to work in partnership with each other but also to work in partnership with families and communities. Gardner and Cleaver (2009: 41) identify that working with families is important not only because family members can provide key information but also because successful partnership can provide reassurance for the child and the parents may be more inclined to comply with a plan if they have played a part in its creation. Parents may understandably be defensive if questions have been raised about the welfare of their children and they may be reluctant to engage with services as a consequence. It can be a difficult process to address such anxieties but effective collaboration between agencies can help to alleviate this.

> I think if the parents see that professionals who are involved in the care of their child are all working together, and are making decisions you know are in the best interests of the child, and if they see that there's good communication between the professionals and that we are all saying the same things and we are heading towards the same goal, I think it can only help with gaining their cooperation. (Paediatrician, cited in Devaney, 2008: 250)

The extended family network can also be important in managing the risk to children. Family relationships are complex and varied and it is important to establish the key people in a child's life. There may be figures in the extended family who are emotionally significant to the child and who may be able not only to provide insight into the home environment but also be a source of respite and support (Gupta and McNeill-McKinnell, 2009).

Conclusion

Safeguarding children is a complex and difficult process where the risks of the wrong decision are severe. As a consequence, effective multi-agency working is essential in protecting vulnerable children and young people from harm. This chapter has outlined some of the tensions that can be involved in this process and some of the barriers to effective working.

> ## Summary of key points
>
> ■ Professionals need to be clear about their roles and responsibilities within the multi-agency process.
> ■ Assumptions should not be made about the importance of opinions based on professional status.
> ■ There needs to be a clear sense of purpose; the safety and welfare of the child is paramount.
> ■ Parents and family members should be viewed as key partners in the process of assessment and protection.

Case summaries

Maria Colwell (died 07/01/1973) Maria died aged seven as a result of neglect and abuse at the hands of her stepfather, William Kepple. Maria had been fostered by her aunt and uncle when she was 19 months old because her mother felt that she could not cope with her five children. Maria was returned to her mother five years later with the support of social services. The inquiry found that this decision had been based on insufficient evidence. All the agencies involved in the case were criticised in the inquiry report. William Kepple was sentenced to eight years for manslaughter.

Report: Department of Health and Social Security (1974) *Report of the Committee of Inquiry into the Care and Supervision Provided in Relation to Maria Colwell.* London: HMSO.

Victoria Climbié (died 25/02/2000) Victoria died aged eight of hypothermia following months of abuse and neglect at the hands of her great-aunt Marie Therese Kouao and her partner Carl Manning. Kouao and Manning were both given life sentences for Victoria's murder in January 2001. The inquiry that was held following Victoria's death found that there were 12 key occasions on which agencies could have intervened to save Victoria's life. Agencies and individuals involved were criticised for poor communication and there was found to be 'widespread organisational malaise' and poor leadership.

Report: Laming, H. (2003) *The Victoria Climbié Inquiry: Report of an Inquiry by Lord Laming*, Cm 5730. London: HMSO.

Peter Connolly (Baby P) (died 03/08/2007) Peter died aged 17 months following months of physical abuse resulting in over 50 injuries. His mother Tracey Connolly, her partner Steven Barker and his brother Jason Owen were convicted in 2008 of causing or allowing his death. The case sparked public outrage and led for calls for widespread reforms to the child protection system in England and Wales. A joint area review published in December 2008 identified inadequacies in assessment of risk and multi-agency working and also a lack of effective leadership.

Report: Local Safeguarding Children Board Haringey (2009) *Serious Case Review: Baby Peter*. Haringey: Local Safeguarding Children Board Haringey.

References

BBC News (2008) 'Community service plan "failing"'. Available from http://newsvote.bbc.co.uk/mpapps/pagetools/print/news.bbc.co.uk/1/hi/uk7658315.stm

Brandon, M., Dodsworth, J. and Rumball, D. (2005) 'Serious case reviews: learning to use expertise', *Child Abuse Review*, 14, 160-76.

Cabinet Office (2007) *Reaching Out: Think Family, Analysis of Themes from the Families at Risk Review*. London: Social Exclusion Task Force.

Cheminais, R. (2009) *Effective Multi-Agency Partnerships: Putting Every Child Matters into Practice*. London: Sage Publications.

Children's Workforce and Development Council (2007) *Common Assessment Framework for Children and Young People: Practitioners' Guide*. Leeds: CWDC.

Devaney, J. (2008) 'Inter-professional working in child protection families with long-term and complex needs', *Child Abuse Review*, 17, 242-61.

DfES (Department for Education and Skills) (2003) *Every Child Matters*. London: The Stationery Office.

DH (Department of Health), Home Office and Department of Education and Employment (1999) *Working Together to Safeguard Children: A Guide to Inter-Agency Working to Safeguard and Promote the Welfare of Children*. London: HMSO.

Frost, N. and Robinson, M. (2007) 'Joining up children's services: safeguarding children in multi-disciplinary teams', *Child Abuse Review*, 16, 184-99.

Gardner, R. and Clever, H. (2009) 'Working effectively with parents', in Cleaver, H., Cawson, P., Gorin, S. and Walker, S. (eds) *Safeguarding Children: A Shared Responsibility*. Chichester: Wiley-Blackwell.

Gupta, A. and McNeill-McKinnell, M. (2009) 'The wider family and community', in Cleaver, H., Cawson, P., Gorin, S. and Walker, S. (eds) *Safeguarding Children: A Shared Responsibility*. Chichester: Wiley-Blackwell.

Hall, C. and Slembrouck, S. (2009) 'Professional categorization, risk management and inter-agency communication in public inquiries into disastrous outcomes', *British Journal of Social Work*, 39, 280-98.

HM Government (2005) *Common Core of Skills and Knowledge for the Children's Workforce*. London: HMSO.

HM Government (2006) *Working Together to Safeguard Children*. London: The Stationery Office.

Home Office, Department of Health, Department of Education and Science and the Welsh Office (1991) *Working Together under the Children Act 1989: A Guide to Arrangements for Inter-Agency Co-Operation for the Protection of Children from Abuse*. London: HMSO.

Howarth, J. (2009) 'Working effectively in a multi-agency context', in Cleaver, H., Cawson, P., Gorin, S. and Walker, S. (eds) *Safeguarding Children: A Shared Responsibility*. Chichester: Wiley–Blackwell.

Laming, H. (2003) *The Victoria Climbié Inquiry: Report of an Inquiry by Lord Laming*, Cm 5730. London: The Stationery Office.

Nash, M. (2006) *Public Protection and the Criminal Justice Process*. Oxford: Oxford University Press.

Ofsted, Healthcare Commission and HM Inspectorate of Constabulary (2008) *Joint Area Review Haringey Children's Services Authority Area: Review of Services for Children and Young People, with Particular Reference to Safeguarding*.

Parton, N. (2006) *Safeguarding Childhood: Early Intervention and Surveillance in a Late Modern Society*. Basingstoke: Palgrave Macmillan.

Reder, P. and Duncan, S. (2003) 'Understanding communication in child protection networks', *Child Abuse Review*, 12, 82–100.

Reder, P., Duncan, S. and Gray, M. (1993) *Beyond Blame: Child Abuse Tragedies Revisited*. London: Routledge.

CHAPTER 10

Working together to tackle domestic violence

Jacki Tapley

Aims of the chapter
- To reflect on the shift in attitudes towards violence in the home, and the political importance of victims of crime.
- To examine multi-agency responses to victims of domestic violence.
- To review research into local projects in one English county.

> Today it is recognised that the divide between public and private violence is less distinct, and violence between intimates has become a more salient public policy issue than ever before. Increased public intervention has been legitimated by new legislation, new police powers, and changing attitudes towards state intervention. (Hoyle, 1998: 1)

Writing in 1998, Hoyle captures the gradual but extraordinary shift in political and public attitudes towards violence within the home. Once regarded solely as a private matter, it has increasingly become recognised as an essentially public concern, with serious consequences not only for the victims and their children, but also for wider society (Walby and Allen, 2004).

Indeed, there has been much activity in the way of new initiatives and policies with regard to victims of crime generally since 1990 (Tapley, 2005a), but of particular significance is how the issue of domestic violence has ascended the political agenda, from the frequently ridiculed margins of radical feminism to mainstream government policy making, which has steadily gathered momentum and resulted in frenetic government activity during the last decade. Most activity has centred on improving responses to victims of domestic abuse and sexual violence, through the creation of multi-agency partnerships, drawing on statutory and voluntary agencies from criminal justice, education, health, housing and social services. This activity can be evidenced by referring to the plethora of government consultations, campaigns, policies and legislation, listed as key achievements in one of the most recent government consultation documents, *Together We Can End Violence against Women and Girls* (Home Office, 2009: 35).

This chapter explores some of the factors that have contributed towards this political shift in attitude regarding state intervention in matters previously considered as 'private' and, based on research undertaken by the author during the last 12 years in a southern county of England, examines the development of multi-agency partnerships and their ability to respond to and improve the protection and support offered to those who suffer from what is now commonly referred to as domestic violence or domestic abuse.

Uncovering the nature and extent of domestic violence

Historically, violence within the home was not considered a criminal act. Patriarchal values supported the view that it was a man's responsibility and right to control his wife and family, and the use of violence 'within reason' was an accepted way of doing so. For too long society tolerated and ignored violence within the home, believing it to be a solely private matter. It was not until the 19th century, with the emergence of first-wave feminism, that women started the struggle to gain legal rights in marriage and reform in property laws, and to campaign for equal access to education and employment and for the vote. Harne and Radford (2008: 87) examined the work of the early feminists and their attempts to challenge the male monopoly of law, where 'women historically were totally excluded from law and law making' and where 'married women were denied the status of legal subjects', but instead whose legal existence, by marriage, was suspended and incorporated into that of the husband (Hoggett and Pearl, 1987, cited in Harne and Radford, 2008: 87). Deemed as such to be their legal property, it was thus acceptable for husbands to control their wives, to chastise them and 'to imprison and recapture them if they attempted to leave and, because they legally owned women's bodies, to rape them with impunity' (2008: 89).

While some limited changes in legislation were achieved, it was not until the emergence of second-wave feminism in the 20th century that the patriarchal values dominating gender relations in the UK started to be challenged. Violence against women was once again placed on the political agenda by activist feminist groups in the 1970s, supported by a range of feminist academic research, which 'laid the ground for the recognition of the widespread problem of domestic violence and the motivation to challenge it' (Hoyle, 2007: 147). In particular, both the activist and academic feminists were critical of the inadequate criminal justice response to domestic violence (Edwards, 1989; Dobash and Dobash, 1992). The state and, in particular, the police, were reluctant to intervene in domestic incidents, considering them not to be a matter for the police, but one of social welfare. But it was not only the police who failed to intervene; those agencies tasked with promoting social welfare, including social services, education and health professionals, also failed to acknowledge women's experiences of domestic violence (Stanko, 1985).

Although forms of victimisation within the home remained hidden, concerns with regard to victims of crime beyond the private sphere had started to emerge in the 1940s with the development of victimology, a subdiscipline of criminology. Early theorists of victimology argued that criminology focused solely on the offender and it was the work of Von Hentig (1948, cited in Walklate, 2007: 30) that began to focus attention on the relationship between the victim and the offender in contributing to an understanding of the perpetration of a crime. Eager to differentiate the victim from the non-victim, 'suggesting that there is a normal person such that, when the victim is measured against them, the victim falls short' (2007: 30), the early theorists developed typologies that introduced the concepts of victim proneness, culpability and precipitation (Mendelsohn, 1956, cited in Walklate, 2007: 30). These early positivist theories, which contributed to the development of conventional victimology, thus began to implicitly blame the victim for their own victimisation and 'to form the core of much victimological thinking' (Walklate, 2001: 30).

Consequently, it was the powerful combination of patriarchal beliefs and the predominant view in victimology that victims were culpable and precipitated their own victimisation that left victims of domestic abuse vulnerable, unprotected and abandoned, with no assistance to help them escape from the cycle of abuse. It was far easier to assume that wives who were abused by their husbands had done something to provoke their husband's anger and were therefore deserving of 'punishment', than to challenge the behaviour of the perpetrator and the very foundations of a patriarchal society.

Thus, the convenient truths surrounding domestic abuse were enshrined in myth. Those left suffering the abuse were frequently considered to have provoked the violence by their own actions and were therefore undeserving of any support. This could clearly be evidenced by the lack of response afforded to victims by the criminal justice system, as revealed in the attitudes of police officers (Hanmer and Saunders, 1984; Radford, 1987) and the Crown Prosecution Service (CPS) (Cretney and Davis, 1997). Nowhere is this demonstrated more clearly than in the lenient sentencing of men who have killed their partners, whereby nagging, infidelity or even suspected infidelity have all been considered as acceptable defences of provocation, thus reducing a charge of murder to manslaughter (Justice for Women, 2006, cited in Harne and Radford, 2008: 102). Such attitudes, reflected by the criminal justice response in even the most serious forms of violence, have assisted in the development of myths and stereotypes that squarely place the blame on the victim, without challenging the behaviour of the perpetrator, including questioning why they do not leave if they do not like it, that victims abuse alcohol and drugs thus contributing to the violence, that women move from one abusive relationship to another so it must be something about them, and that it only happens to women in lower socioeconomic classes (Richards et al, 2008).

However, the development of critical and feminist perspectives in victimology from the 1970s increasingly challenged these myths and stereotypes, in particular the patriarchal values and beliefs that underpinned them. The failures of criminal justice agencies and other statutory bodies to protect women from violence within the home led to the creation of women's groups and centres set up to provide practical support, assistance and protection (Malos, 2000, cited in Harne and Radford, 2008: 182), and in this informal way the Women's Aid Refuge movement was born (Hanmer, 2003, cited in Harne and Radford, 2008: 170). Academic research started to reveal the extent and truly insidious nature of intimate violence. Studies found that rather than domestic violence being a problem of anger management, it was far more selective than that (Kirkwood, 1993; Mullender, 1996; Hoyle, 2007). Instead, it is argued that domestic abuse is all about exercising and maintaining control over the victim using various methods and techniques, including jealous, mistrusting and intimidating behaviour, isolation from friends and family, financial control, verbal criticisms and gradually the use of escalating violence to maintain control, especially if there are any signs of control being lost.

Following changes in methodology and the use of self-completion questionnaires, the British Crime Survey started to raise awareness with regard to the nature and extent of violence suffered by women. It was revealed that women are more likely to be sexually attacked by men they know, often partners (32%) or acquaintances (22%), than by strangers (8%) (Myhill and Allen, 2002). Experiences of domestic violence since the age of 16 revealed that 45% of women and 26% of men recalled being subjected to abuse, threats and force in a domestic context (Walby and Allen, 2004). However, with regard to power differentials in intimate relationships, this research supported the findings of earlier feminist research, in that it found that women were overwhelmingly the most heavily abused group, suffered the most serious injuries and the greatest impact on health, housing and employment (Walby and Allen, 2004). More recently, the British Crime Survey found that domestic violence accounts for 16% of all violent crime and that an average of two women a week are killed by a partner or ex-partner (Home Office, 2007, cited in Blyth and Shaw, 2009: 179), a statistic that has not changed since the early 1980s.

The politicisation of domestic violence

The development of victimology as an academic discipline, consisting of a range of competing theoretical perspectives and the growth of activist campaigns in support of certain groups of victims, coincided with a period of penological pessimism in the 1980s. Despite political rhetoric promising to be tough on law and order, crime rates continued to rise together with an increasing fear of crime. Consequently, confidence in the police and confidence in the criminal justice system to work effectively with offenders began to be seriously questioned, and in response to the campaigning of disparate groups advocating on behalf of victims of crime, politicians began to realise the expedience of acknowledging those who suffered crime, resulting in the politicisation of victims' issues from 1990, with the publication of the first Victim's Charter (Tapley, 2005b).

The subsequent acknowledgement by the government of the need to improve the criminal justice response to victims of crime and the populist political rhetoric of putting victims at the heart of the criminal justice system made it increasingly difficult for the government to ignore the failure of the system to respond to victims of domestic violence, as supported by increasing evidence to be found in the findings of subsequent British Crime Surveys (Tapley, 2005b), thus resulting in the government finally accepting the arguments of the feminist campaigns, not so long ago considered as radical and anti-establishment. Evidence of this can be found in the most recent government consultation document, which acknowledges:

> the dedication of the women's voluntary sector [who] for almost four decades, have provided refuges, rape crisis centres, crisis lines, survivors' groups and other creative projects. It is due to their tireless work, both in terms of practical assistance and campaigning, that the issue of violence against women is now firmly on the public policy agenda, both nationally and internationally. More importantly, it is a movement to which thousands of women and children literally owe their lives. (Home Office, 2009: 3)

The politicisation of wider victims' issues helps to explain the more recent rapid ascendance of domestic violence on the political agenda, culminating in a range of reforms that now demand violence within the home be responded to as a 'real' crime, but what the government does not explain is why it took 40 years to start listening to the concerns and campaigns that voiced the experiences of thousands of women, whereby on average, two women a week were being killed by a partner or ex-partner. Blyth and Shaw (2009: 178) argue that it was a number of high-profile female Members of Parliament (MPs) and the effectiveness of their advocacy for women's issues, following the election of a Labour government in 1997, which resulted in domestic violence achieving greater recognition.

This can be evidenced by observing the rise of female MPs in government from 9% in 1992 to 18% in 1997, with 28% of female Labour MPs in government in 2005, compared with 9% and 16% of female MPs in the Conservative and Liberal Democratic Parties respectively (Cracknell, 2005). Perhaps the most notable and effective female MP at raising awareness regarding domestic violence is Harriet Harman, who was appointed as Secretary of State for Social Security and Minister for Women and Equality from 1997. In 2001, Harriet Harman was appointed Solicitor General and led a drive within government to make tackling domestic violence a priority, and continued this in her role as Minister for Justice from 2005. Other female MPs who have contributed to achieving a higher political profile for domestic violence victims, and victims of crime more generally, have been Baroness Scotland, Vera Baird, and Jacqui Smith in her role as Home Secretary in 2009. A number of national campaigns were launched by female ministers to raise awareness of the extent and impact of domestic violence, including *Living Without*

Fear (Home Office,1999), *Break the Chain* (Home Office, 2001) and the *Safety and Justice* (Home Office, 2003) consultation paper that, together with the White Paper *Justice for All* (Home Office, 2002), informed the 2004 Domestic Violence, Crime and Victims Act, which introduced policies and legislation focusing on improving the protection and support of victims of domestic violence.

Improving the criminal justice response to domestic violence

As the increasing literature now shows, domestic violence is an extremely complex issue, involving a diverse range of controlling and coercive behaviours that have not always been recognised or accepted as forms of abusive behaviour. For this reason, defining what 'domestic violence' is has itself been problematic (Richards et al, 2008). Research by the author has found that while the physical injuries sustained through physical violence have an undoubtedly serious impact on the victim, it is the emotional and psychological abuse that has the most pervasive long-term impact on the victim and their ability to recover. Therefore, it is essential that the different forms of abusive behaviour are recognised by all the agencies now involved in working with victims of domestic violence at the different stages, and that it is acknowledged that abuse can still be occurring even when there is no evidence of physical harm. This is particularly important when undertaking risk assessments (Richards et al, 2008: 109). The term 'victim' has also been contested, with feminist groups preferring to use the term 'survivor', but in this chapter the term 'victim' is used.

Following the introduction of Home Office guidelines and policies since 1990, it became clear that some agencies were having difficulties identifying what situations involved domestic violence and that many of the agencies were using different definitions. As there is no offence of 'domestic violence', cases involving domestic violence could result in charges with a wide range of different offences – from criminal damage, common assault, actual or grievous bodily harm, or harassment to attempted murder – and it would not always be obvious, particularly to the CPS, that a case involved a domestic context. With the introduction of specialist courts and statutory charging, this has now changed and all domestic cases must be flagged as such. Some areas have introduced the use of different colour files to distinguish them. For clarity, the shared Association of Chief Police Officers (ACPO), CPS and government definition of domestic violence is:

> Any incident of threatening behaviour, violence or abuse (psychological, physical, sexual, financial or emotional) between adults, aged 18 or over, who are or have been intimate partners or family members, regardless of gender or sexuality. (ACPO, 2008: 7)

As outlined in its published *Guidance on Investigating Domestic Abuse* (ACPO, 2008: 7), the stated priorities of the Police Service in responding to domestic violence are as follows:

- to protect the lives of both adults and children who are at risk as a result of domestic abuse;
- to investigate all reports of domestic abuse;
- to facilitate effective action against offenders so that they can be held accountable through the criminal justice system;
- to adopt a proactive multi-agency approach in preventing and reducing domestic abuse.

The above priorities are underpinned by legal obligations, including the 1998 Human Rights Act and the European Convention on Human Rights, to protect life and to protect individuals from inhuman and degrading treatment (ACPO, 2008: 7).

The definition of domestic violence has also broadened to include other human rights abuses, including female genital mutilation (2003 Female Genital Mutilation Act), forced marriages and so-called honour crimes (2007 Forced Marriages and Civil Protection Act).

As indicated above, since the late 1990s there have been a plethora of initiatives and policies aimed at creating a criminal justice response to domestic violence. This has included the Police Service, the CPS and the Probation Service developing their own policies in accordance with government guidelines. Government activity culminated in the introduction of the 2004 Domestic Violence, Crime and Victims Act, which introduced a Code of Practice for Victims of Crime and also promised to introduce a range of measures that would offer victims of domestic violence greater protection and support. Central to this strategy was the continuation of earlier legislation, including the 1998 Crime and Disorder Act, which placed a responsibility on local authorities and a range of statutory and voluntary agencies to adopt a multi-agency approach when working with victims of domestic violence. This is essential as it has become widely recognised that individuals suffering from domestic abuse have a range of needs that go beyond what the police and criminal justice system can provide, including housing, health, finance and support for their children (Harne and Radford, 2008; Richards et al, 2008; Blyth and Shaw, 2009).

The last decade has seen a range of initiatives introduced that have required both statutory and voluntary agencies to work in partnership to improve the protection and support of individuals suffering from domestic abuse. This has included the development of domestic violence forums, perpetrator programmes and the formulation of women's groups for the partners of perpetrators. In the area where the author has undertaken her research, the co-location of police and CPS staff in criminal justice departments to prepare prosecution files took place in 2003, the Witness Care Unit was introduced in 2004 and two Specialist Domestic Violence Courts were introduced in April 2006. The remainder of this chapter draws on the findings of four separate studies undertaken by the author in a southern county of England, the latest of which is still ongoing. These studies offer a helpful but critical analysis of the development of partnership working in this county over a 10-year period.

Evaluating the development of multi-agency working in a domestic context

The first of the studies formed part of a PhD thesis and involved a qualitative, longitudinal study, focusing on the experiences of victims of violent crime in a southern county in England (Tapley, 2003). The research essentially revisited an earlier study undertaken by Shapland et al (1985) and the original aim was to evaluate the impact of reforms on the actual experiences of victims as their cases progressed through the criminal justice system. The research was undertaken and the cases followed during the period 1998 to 2002. Despite the plethora of initiatives introduced during this period, the findings of the research were strikingly similar to those of the earlier study. While the majority of victims were satisfied with their initial contact with the police, levels of satisfaction steadily declined as their cases progressed, the major cause of this being the lack of information provided regarding criminal justice procedures and the progress of their case. While this was a small-scale piece of qualitative research, it followed in-depth the cases of 13 participants from the initial reporting through to the final outcome, 12 of which resulted in a conviction. The research involved repeat in-depth interviews with participants, court observations and interviews with criminal justice professionals.

One of the 12 cases involved the physical assault of a female by her estranged husband. The assault took place one evening in early December 1998. On hearing the disturbance, neighbours called the police and they attended shortly afterwards. However, despite the appearance of physical injuries to the face and hands of the woman, and the presence of three small children in the home, the police did not arrest the perpetrator and allowed him to leave the home still in possession of the keys to the house. This case raised serious concerns, particularly regarding levels of risk, as the perpetrator was already known to the criminal justice system, was in breach of a current Probation Order, had alcohol and drug addiction problems and there were concerns regarding his mental health. Despite a range of the relevant agencies becoming involved, including the police, probation, courts and social services, it took over six weeks for the perpetrator to be arrested, no action was taken when the perpetrator breached bail conditions, and in the meantime the children were put on the 'at risk' register and the victim was put under scrutiny for her apparent failure to protect her children. This can be evidenced by the frustration voiced to the researcher at different stages during the process. The following quote is taken from the first interview:

> It makes me feel so tense, I'm terrified they're going to take my children away. They've offered him to go to the alcohol counselling clinic and he just turns it all down. I said it's so unfair, nobody's making him sort

himself out, they're all coming to me. I mean, it's like I've said, if the police can't stop him, they [social services] can't stop him, how in God's name do they expect me to? I feel like I'm getting doubly punished for something he's doing. I'm doing everything I can to keep him away, then they're [social services] saying he's a danger, but writing up a contract saying if he's sober he can come round and see the kids....
It's just like ... turning into a living nightmare really. (Tapley, 2003: 163)

In this case, it was only because of a case conference held to decide on whether to put the children on the 'at risk' register, that the failure to arrest the actual perpetrator arose:

If it hadn't been for the fact that the domestic violence officer pushed the police, I don't think he'd be arrested now. Um ... one of the police officers at the conference did turn round, um, in a more roundabout way than I'm gonna say, but he basically said 'it's just domestic violence', his whole attitude was 'it doesn't count'. (Tapley, 2003: 164)

At the final interview held in July 1999, the participant summarised her views of the whole multi-agency approach to her case:

I just seemed to be fighting a losing battle with these people, y'know. I mean, I just feel like one person's always contradicting another. I mean, they contacted Social Services because they said he was a threat to the children and then it took them over six weeks to arrest him. I mean, quite honestly, I'd think twice about phoning the police, I really would. I feel ... not badly treated, but it's like they're acting in ignorance, they're not thinking about how I felt, how my children felt ... fair enough, they may have a job to do and they might have a certain way they've got to go about doing it, but I think it would put most women off doing it again. (Tapley, 2003: 164)

The evidence arising from this case appeared to support the conclusions of earlier studies, including Cretney et al (1994) and Crawford and Enterkin (1999). The delays in arrest and prosecution, with the lack of clarity, confused and conflicting aims and overlapping priorities, resulted in the agencies focusing only on their own specific core tasks with no one taking overall responsibility for the victim (Tapley, 2003). As a consequence, there is little wonder that victims find it difficult to fulfil their obligations of pursuing a complaint and then sustaining a commitment to the prosecution process, when the agencies involved fail to fulfil their own. In this case, the perpetrator pleaded guilty on the day of the trial, but the letter sent to the victim advising her of the outcome of the case arrived so late, that the perpetrator had in fact already been released following his sentence of 25 weeks' imprisonment.

The dissatisfaction specifically of victims of domestic violence was also revealed in a later study undertaken in the first quarter of 2004. The author undertook a Witness Satisfaction Survey using postal questionnaires, followed up by semi-structured interviews with a purposive sample of victims who had been required to attend court as a witness (Tapley, 2005c). The respondents had suffered a range of offences, with 17% of the sample having suffered domestic violence. The study found that while there had been improvements in the way victims had been provided with information from the police and CPS, there were still gaps in provision, leaving victims feeling vulnerable and dissatisfied with how they were treated and the outcome of their case. However, the most striking finding was that, despite the introduction of policies to protect victims of domestic violence, including police and CPS domestic violence policies, special measures and Victim Personal Statements, it was found that only 44% of the victims of domestic violence would be prepared to go to court again, compared with 66% of the total sample (Tapley, 2005c). What this research found was that there was a reluctance to acknowledge victims of domestic violence as vulnerable and intimidated, as applications for special measures in these cases were turned down. This demonstrated a lack of understanding of the nature of domestic violence and the fear of victims giving evidence in court against the perpetrator. In one case the police failed to tell the victim that the application had been refused, because they knew she would not want to give evidence without special measures: 'The police could have been more helpful and not lied to get me to court. It was very stressful and it would have helped if I had been told that the request for a screen had been denied before arriving at court' (Tapley, 2005c: 50).

The research also identified that one of the smaller courts being used for domestic violence cases was not appropriate as it could not offer adequate protection for those victims attending. This provided an example of good professional practice by the prosecution lawyer in the case, who requested an adjournment and that the hearing be held at a court that could provide adequate protection for the victim (Tapley, 2005b). As a result of the research, only very few domestic violence cases are now being heard at this court, and this is on the request of victims who do not require special measures and for whom it is more convenient for them to attend this court.

In 2007, the researcher was asked by the Police Service to undertake research with victims of domestic violence and their satisfaction with the police response. As part of this research a focus group was undertaken with women whose abusers were taking part in a perpetrators programme. This research found that the victims still felt that on occasions the police were not taking domestic violence seriously and that the police tended to try to negotiate with the perpetrator, rather than make an arrest, which on occasions would only fuel the problem: 'It was obvious he was not in the mood for negotiating, their attempts were just fuelling the situation. The problem is, the worst the arrest situation, the worse you think it is going to be when they are released' (Tapley, 2007).

This research also found that officers did not appear to be aware of their own Police Force's policies, with victims advising that they had been told by the police that they could not tell victims when the perpetrator had been released following arrest, that perpetrators were not being arrested or charged for breaching bail conditions and that proactive arrest policies were not being enforced when offences had taken place.

In one case, involving a woman who had also suffered violence from a previous partner, the victim appeared to have received a poor response from a range of the agencies involved. On first attending, despite children being present, the police were reluctant to arrest the perpetrator and kept moving him on, rather than arresting him for harassment, which they could have done. During one of the initial hearings at court, there was no application for bail conditions, which the prosecutor and police later agreed should have been applied for. In addition, the victim also received judgemental advice from her social worker: 'she made me feel awful, she really upset me. She said my kids had too many toys and told me that I was awful at picking men. I just took it all in then exploded when she went' (Tapley, 2007).

This reflects an attitude that blames the victim for the violence rather than holding the perpetrator accountable. This view was only perpetuated when the case finally went to court for trial. First, the victim turned up at the court late, as she had been advised to go to a different court by the witness care officer. In the meantime, the agent acting for the CPS had been negotiating with the perpetrator's defence lawyer, a conversation that the author overheard while waiting in court, and this was heavily laden with a view that did not consider the case to be serious. Although the victim did arrive at court prepared to give her evidence, the agent for the CPS persuaded her that it was in her best interests to accept a guilty plea to a lesser charge, especially as she had experienced domestic violence in the past and there was no guarantee that the perpetrator would be found guilty in this case. Following the court hearing, the victim expressed disappointment at the final outcome, which was a bind over for 12 months to the sum of £500, which did not reflect the seriousness of the offence, and which the Chair of the Magistrates actually commented on in his final summing up. Sounding resigned, the victim commented on the body language of the prosecutor, which had made her feel that 'he didn't really want to be there and just wanted to get it out of the way, but I suppose at least this will keep him off me....' (Tapley, 2007). This case demonstrates that attitudes towards people suffering from domestic violence still reflect a lack of understanding of the nature of domestic violence and still place blame on the victim. It also demonstrates that the interests and procedures of the organisations involved often still take priority over the interests of the victim, similar to the findings of the earlier research (Tapley, 2003).

Evidence of an improved response to victims

In 2009, the author was asked to undertake some further research regarding the satisfaction of victims of domestic violence and their contact with the police. It can be argued that the commission of research itself demonstrates a commitment by the police to be accountable for how they respond to victims of domestic violence and a willingness to listen to victims' experiences. This study started in May 2009 and focuses on those victims who have been assessed as being at a high risk of further abuse. Participants have been randomly selected from police records regarding cases that have been referred to a MARAC (Multi-Agency Risk Assessment Conference). Participants have been contacted by letter, followed up by a telephone call. Semi-structured interviews have taken place with some participants, the majority in their own homes. While the study is still ongoing, the preliminary findings indicate that, following the introduction of Witness Care Units in 2004, the implementation of specialist domestic violence courts in 2006, and the subsequent introduction of independent domestic violence advisors (IDVAs) and the setting up of MARACS, there is now evidence of a more coherent, cohesive response being provided to individuals suffering from domestic abuse (Cook et al, 2004). This appears due to the setting up of more formalised partnerships between statutory and voluntary agencies, as a requirement of the core components needed for the implementation of specialist domestic violence courts (Home Office, 2008). This has led to an increase in awareness training for many professionals and the creation of working groups with representatives from a range of the relevant agencies, including local authorities, health, social services, police, probation, courts, the CPS and voluntary agencies, including Victim Support, Refuges and Relate.

Participants interviewed so far have commented on the levels of support being offered by police officers from the Domestic Violence Units, the provision of alarms and home safety strategies, being kept up to date with the progress of their case, the use of special measures if required to give evidence in court and the ongoing support provide by the IDVAs and their outreach services. However, participants have commented on the lack of availability of counselling services for themselves, as these are limited to a certain number of sessions and there is sometimes a waiting list:

> "... and when there is help, it always seems several months away, past when you need it."

> "I waited for about three months for counselling but it has helped ... been fantastic. I've had to start spreading them out though, as you only get 12 one-to-one sessions, and I'm going to probably need some more counselling after the trial."

Another issue emerging is the need for more supportive services for children. Some of the children involved are receiving help from professionals provided through social services, and some schools are attempting to help, but are limited by the resources they can provide. The impact of domestic abuse on children is becoming more widely acknowledged and, as a result, services for children and parental support are starting to emerge, but this is only available in some areas and is an area that requires further investment (Harne and Radford, 2008; Blythe and Shaw, 2009).

Another theme emerging from all the studies is the response provided to male victims of domestic abuse. The sample of male victims in the studies is very small, therefore it is difficult to generalise the findings, but the studies reveal that the police response is often unsympathetic and lacks sufficient understanding. One male victim in the current study who has been suffering ongoing harassment felt that the police were not taking it that seriously:

> "I felt the call-handler had taken it seriously, but they did not contact me to advise that it was unlikely someone would come out that day, I had to call them twice again before I was told. By the time she was arrested I'd had quite a lot of contact with the police, but I was only aware she had been arrested when I received a message from her saying she wouldn't be able to collect the children. Even though I was advised to contact the police if another incident happened, the sergeant I spoke to was very off with me. He had not read any of the history and assumed I was the perpetrator. Even when he realised I was the victim, there was no apology. It just made me feel like I was bothering them, so you don't end up reporting every incident."

As there are relatively few studies relating to male victims and in some cases it has been difficult to distinguish who is the perpetrator and who is the victim, this is an important area that requires far greater research. Unfortunately, in some cases the male perpetrator makes counterclaims and presents himself as the victim, as in a case recently reviewed at a Hate Crime Scrutiny Panel, on which the author sits as the independent facilitator, but this only came to light following further investigation, thus indicating the levels of complexity sometimes found in cases of domestic abuse.

While it is too early in the current study to draw conclusions, the preliminary findings do indicate that for victims of domestic violence considered at 'high risk', the protection and services being provided have improved, but the final conclusions will be discussed fully in a future publication. However, the research to date has also found that the nature of multi-agency partnerships is still fraught with difficulties and tensions. The availability of funding and who controls the funding is an ongoing concern and this often reflects the power differentials between some statutory and voluntary agencies, as also found by Harne and Radford (2008). As acknowledged by Blythe and Shaw (2009: 191):

The fundamental point that government guidance and local strategies often gloss over is that partnership work is difficult. There are differences in organisational culture, terminology, practice, operational priorities and training.... Each partner regards the other with a degree of professional scepticism and sometimes with downright distrust. Different interests, priorities and practice in multi-agency groups make collaborative work difficult.

It is essential that these tensions be acknowledged and the difficult reality of multi-agency partnerships addressed. Many effective partnerships depend on the personalities of champions within each agency and their ability to work together, but can equally be adversely affected by uncooperative partners and those motivated by their own organisational agendas, often losing sight of the very individuals their organisation is there to assist.

A current initiative being proposed in the area where the author has undertaken her research is to introduce a panel to review domestic abuse cases, similar to the Hate Crime Scrutiny Panel, but rather than scrutinise cases, it would undertake a review of the cases and how they were responded to. Cases of domestic abuse make up the majority of cases put before the Scrutiny Panel, but these panels, following their introduction nationally by the CPS in 2008, mainly focus on the role of the police and the CPS, and the reviews often require input from the other agencies that may be involved with cases focusing on domestic abuse. As well as the Panel reviewing cases that have failed to result in a successful prosecution (given that the focus is on the CPS), successful cases are also put before the Panel to illustrate examples of good practice. It is felt that reviewing domestic abuse cases by a multi-agency panel would result in the sharing of good practices and the identification of gaps in the provision of services that may still remain.

Conclusion

This chapter has examined the change in political and professional attitudes towards domestic abuse, mainly as a result of the efforts by the voluntary sector. The demand by government that a multi-agency approach be adopted to assist in the prevention of domestic abuse and the protection and support of those suffering it has given rise to some tensions, in particular with regard to power differentials and resources, but more recent research is starting to reveal the benefits of such an approach, and the goodwill that does exist to ensure that victims of abuse are treated with respect and afforded the rights that have relatively recently been introduced to protect them.

The government's ongoing commitment to improving their response to domestic violence is reflected in the aims and objectives stated in the *National Domestic Violence Delivery Plan* (HM Government, 2009). While it has not been possible in this chapter to examine comprehensively the range of policies and legislation that have been introduced, it has demonstrated that domestic abuse is at last being responded to as a 'real' crime and that people should no longer have to suffer in silence and should feel confident in reporting the abuse to the police.

In fact, recent evidence from the British Crime Survey indicates that following years of little change, the prevalence of both men and women experiencing (non-sexual) partner and family abuse in the previous year decreased between the 2006/07 and 2007/08 British Crime Survey interviews (from 2% to 1% for men and from 3% to 2% for women (Povey et al, 2009).

While these results appear encouraging and could reflect the changing attitudes towards violence within the home, and the more proactive criminal justice response, it could be argued that it is too early to be optimistic that incidents of domestic violence are indeed falling (and it is definitely too early for agencies and their partnerships to become complacent) but it is certainly something that we should all be hoping to aspire to.

Consider the importance of shared values and ethics regarding multi-agency approaches to tackling domestic abuse effectively and how these should be included in the core value statements of criminal justice organisations and voluntary sector agencies working in this area.

Further reading

Blyth, L. and Shaw, S. (2009) 'Not behind closed doors: working in partnership against domestic violence', in Carnwell, R. and Buchanan, J. (eds) *Effective Practice in Health, Social Care and Criminal Justice: A Partnership Approach.* Maidenhead: McGraw-Hill/ Open University Press.

References

ACPO (2008) *Guidance on Investigating Domestic Abuse*, London: National Police Improvement Agency.

Blyth, L. and Shaw, S. (2009) 'Not behind closed doors: working in partnership against domestic violence', in Carnwell, R. and Buchanan, J. (eds) *Effective Practice in Health, Social Care and Criminal Justice: A Partnership Approach.* Maidenhead: McGraw-Hill/Open University Press.

Cook, D., Burton, M., Robinson, A. and Vallely, C. (2004) *Evaluation of Specialist Domestic Violence Courts/Fast Track Systems.* Cardiff and Leicester: University of Cardiff and University of Leicester.

Cracknell, R. (2005) *Social Background of MPs.* London: Social and General Statistics Section, House of Commons Library. Available from www.parliament. uk/commons/lib/research/notes/snSG-01528.pdf

Crawford, A. and Enterkin, J. (1999) *Victim Contact Work and the Probation Service: A Study of Service Delivery and Impact.* Leeds: Centre for Criminal Justice Studies, University of Leeds.

Cretney, A. and Davis, G. (1997) 'Prosecuting domestic assault: victims failing courts, or courts failing victims?', *The Howard Journal*, 36(2), 146-57.

Cretney, A., Davis, G., Clarkson, C. and Shepherd, J. (1994) 'Criminalising assault: the failure of the "Offence Against Society" model', *British Journal of Criminology*, 34(1), 15-29.

Dobash, R.E. and Dobash, R.P. (1992) *Women, Violence and Social Change*. London: Routledge.

Edwards, S. (1989) *Policing Domestic Violence, Women, the Law and the State*. London: Sage Publications.

Hanmer, J. and Saunders, S. (1984) *Well-founded Fear: A Community Study of Violence to Women*. London: Hutchinson.

Harne, L. and Radford, J. (2008) *Tackling Domestic Violence: Theories, Policies and Practice*. Maidenhead: McGraw-Hill/Open University Press.

HM Government (2009) *National Domestic Violence Delivery Plan: Annual Progress Report 2008–09*. London: HM Government.

Home Office (1999) *Living Without Fear*. London: Home Office.

Home Office (2001) *Breaking the Chain*. London: Home Office.

Home Office (2002) *Justice for All*. White Paper. London: Home Office.

Home Office (2003) *Safety and Justice: A Consultation Document*. London: Home Office.

Home Office (2008) *Justice with Safety: Specialist Domestic Violence Courts Review 2007–2008*. London: Home Office.

Home Office (2009) *Together We Can End Violence against Women and Girls*. London: Home Office.

Hoyle, C. (1998) *Negotiating Domestic Violence: Police, Criminal Justice and Victims*. Oxford: Clarendon Press.

Hoyle, C. (2007) 'Feminism, victimology and domestic violence', in Walklate, S. (ed) *Handbook of Victims and Victimology*, Cullompton: Willan Publishing.

Kirkwood, C. (1993) *Leaving Abusive Partners*. London: Sage Publications.

Mullender, A. (1996) *Rethinking Domestic Violence*. London: Routledge.

Myhill, A. and Allen, J. (2002) *Rape and Sexual Assault on Women: The Extent and Nature of the Problem*. Home Office Research Study 237. London: HMSO.

Povey. D., Coleman, K., Kaiza, P. and Roe, S. (2009) *Homicides, Firearm Offences and Intimate Violence 2007/08*. Statistical Bulletin 02/09. London: Home Office.

Radford, J. (1987) 'Policing male violence: policing women', in Hanmer, J. and Maynard, M. (eds) *Violence and Social Control*. London: Macmillan.

Richards, L., Letchford, S. and Stratton, S. (2008) *Policing Domestic Violence*. Oxford: Oxford University Press.

Shapland, J., Willmore, J. and Duff, P. (1985) *Victims in the Criminal Justice System*, Aldershot: Gower.

Stanko, E.A. (1985) *Intimate Intrusions: Women's Experiences of Male Violence*. London: Routledge.

Tapley, J. (2003) 'From "good citizen" to "deserving client": the relationship between victims of violent crime and the state using citizenship as the conceptualising tool'. PhD thesis, University of Southampton.

Tapley, J. (2005a) 'Public confidence costs – criminal justice from a victim's perspective', *British Journal of Community Justice*, 3(2), 25-37.

Tapley, J. (2005b) 'Confidence in criminal justice: achieving community justice for victims and witnesses', in Pakes, F. and Winstone, J. (eds) *Community Justice: Issues for Probation and Criminal Justice*. Cullompton: Willan Publishing.

Tapley, J. (2005c) 'Political rhetoric and the reality of victims' experiences', *Prison Service Journal*, 158, 45-52.

Tapley, J. (2007) 'Domestic abuse and the police response'. Unpublished research.

Walby, S. and Allen, J. (2004) *Domestic Violence, Sexual Assault and Stalking: Findings from the British Crime Survey*. Home Office Research Study 276. London: HMSO.

Walklate, S. (2001) *Gender, Crime and Criminal Justice*, Cullompton: Willan Publishing.

Walklate, S. (2007) *Imagining the Victim of Crime*. Maidenhead: McGraw-Hill/ Open University Press.

CHAPTER 11

Unlocking prisoners: does multi-agency working hold the key to the successful resettlement of released prisoners?

Gerry Parkinson

Aims of the chapter

■ To explore the development of the resettlement of prisoners from a position of neglect to one of priority due to the high rate of reoffending.

■ To critically examine the government's response based on the *Reducing Re-offending National Action Plan* (Home Office, 2004) and regional reducing reoffending strategies emphasising a multi-agency response addressing the seven pathways to crime.

■ To consider the support offered to released prisoners in accessing services and the contribution of theoretical ideas around desistance, particularly agency, in establishing a stable, crime-free lifestyle.

■ To highlight the tensions, between control and care, within the government's response to meeting the needs of released prisoners.

■ To examine the success of the above multi-agency approach.

Resettlement: what's in a name?

The current priority given to the resettlement of prisoners is an inevitable result of a punitive agenda, adopted by successive governments, in the response to criminal offending. It is easy to remember the Labour mantra of 'being tough on crime, tough on the causes of crime' (Labour Party, 1997), but it would seem that the government has found it easier to be tough on crime, as indicated by the dramatic and continuing increase in rates of imprisonment, from approximately 48,000 in 1990 to just fewer than 83,000 in 2009 (Ministry of Justice, 2009). The second part of the slogan has remained difficult to achieve, particularly for that group of the population who present the greatest risk of offending, namely those recently released from prison. This chapter examines the neglect and rediscovery of what has become known as the 'resettlement agenda' and the cornerstone of that agenda, the provision of high-quality, local services from a range of private, not-for-profit and voluntary providers.

It is not disputed that a range of resources is required to assist and develop a crime-free lifestyle, but a context of nurture and support is also vital if released prisoners are to develop the confidence and self-belief to establish and maintain contact with these service providers. Over the years, resettlement policy has been beset with the same dilemmas evident in virtually every aspect of society's response to criminal behaviour, namely the equally convincing but opposing arguments around punishment, public protection and rehabilitation. These arguments are most clearly evident in Section 142(1) of the 2003 Criminal Justice Act, which provides the five statutory aims of sentencing, including punishment of offenders, protecting the public and reform and rehabilitation. The punishment and public protection aims are easier to implement through the length of prison sentence; however, achieving the aim of reform and rehabilitation presents greater challenges, particularly any attempt to improve the social position of offenders, as opposed to improving their behaviour. As Maguire (2007: 398) states, 'imprisonment may actually compound the difficulties and add new problems to those they [the offender] face when they leave ... even if they fully intend to "go straight", many will face distrust or rejection from ordinary members of the community....'

Take a few minutes to consider what images the word 'resettlement' evokes.

The vocabulary used to describe the supervision of those released from prison reflects the dilemma discussed in the previous paragraph, with words such as 'throughcare', 'aftercare', 'reintegration' and 'resettlement' having been used at various times to describe the support offered to released prisoners. The word 'resettlement' was used more often in official publications possibly because, as Raynor (2004), cited by Maguire (2007: 405), suggests, it avoided the word 'care'. 'Resettlement' is preferred by those organisations developing policy and practice in this area, but as Hedderman (2007: 9) indicates, the contexts within which it is used are so varied as to suggest little agreement of what is meant by the term. Nor does 'resettlement' reflect the experiences of ex-prisoners who often face severe obstacles in establishing a settled and crime-free lifestyle as a result of the social isolation and rejection of the community into which they hope to be resettled. As Raynor (2007: 27) points out, the former community and the ex-prisoner's position within it may be the cause of their offending, suggesting that settlement elsewhere would be more appropriate, and not resettlement. The definition of resettlement provided by the Association of Chief Officers of Probation (Her Majesty's Inspectorate of Prisons, 2001: 12) avoids the above arguments by defining it as:

> a systematic and evidence-based process by which actions are taken to work with the offender in custody and on release, so that communities are better protected from harm and reoffending is significantly reduced. It encompasses the totality of work with prisoners, their families and significant others in partnership with statutory and voluntary organisations.

The re-emergence of resettlement

Whatever word is used to describe the support provided to ex-prisoners, official acknowledgement of the neglect of ex-prisoners, particularly short-term, was recognised in the Social Exclusion Unit report, *Reducing Re-offending by Ex-prisoners* (SEU, 2002). This report detailed the significance of the social exclusion faced by prisoners over a range of indicators, including unemployment (67%), no qualifications (60%), drug misuse (over 50%) and homelessness (32%). Further, those receiving shorter periods of custody had higher rates of reconviction within two years of release: 61% for males and 56% for females, compared to the figure of 56% for male and 35% for female longer-term prisoners (SEU, 2002: 14). The voluntary support to ex-prisoners once provided by the Probation Service had been reduced as a consequence of the 1991 Criminal Justice Act, which restricted statutory supervision to those prisoners serving 12 months or more. Those receiving less than 12 months, who represented a significant proportion of sentenced prisoners, were directed to conventional support agencies available to all or to particular voluntary agencies addressing the needs of ex-offenders, such as NACRO. Probation statistics noted a dramatic in drop in the voluntary contact provided by the Probation Service from over 26,500 individuals in 1991 to only 4,500 in 1996 (Home Office, 2001). Few short-term prisoners took up the support offered by voluntary agencies (Maguire, 2007). The Social Exclusion Unit report concluded that those who required the most support received the least. Attempts to tackle these issues by utilising mainstream statutory agencies were unsuccessful as released prisoners were either a low priority in the relevant agency or failed to take up post-release offers of support. These difficulties were compounded by the fact that short-term prisoners received little or no individual counselling, either in prison or following release, to enable them to access the limited available services.

The government's response to the above again highlighted the tension between the competing claims of punishment and reform, in relation to separate provision or priority for ex-prisoners. Raynor (2007: 27) summarised the argument that if ex-prisoners have welfare needs they should be met by the appropriate community agency available to all, not just within the criminal justice system, otherwise resettlement practice is susceptible to the charge of preferential treatment for offenders. If ex-prisoners have increased needs due to imprisonment, then the taxpayer is paying both to create the need and to alleviate it. This highlights a further tension between the government's approach to social exclusion and its policies for criminal justice. New Labour has developed a range of strategies aimed at promoting social inclusion, at the same time as expanding the range of the criminal law and the sanctions imposed by it, heightening the exclusion of those who fall foul of the law (Faulkner, 2007). As Gardener et al (1998: 27) noted, 'it strikes us as strange that a government which purports to be interested in tackling social exclusion at the same time promotes legislative measures destined to create a whole new breed of outcasts'.

What policies within the criminal justice system promote the exclusion of offenders?

The conclusion of the Social Exclusion Unit report was clear, the involvement of a range of service providers, drawn from the statutory, voluntary, business and faith communities, was essential to the resettlement of offenders, avoiding the revolving door of further exclusion, reoffending and imprisonment (SEU, 2002). The government's response to the report was the *Reducing Re-offending National Action Plan* (Home Office, 2004), highlighting, among other things, the resettlement needs of prisoners, particularly short-term, and reinforcing the message that ex-prisoners should be regarded as a priority group, the meeting of whose needs would benefit the community in general in terms of reduced reoffending. The National Action Plan aimed to bring together, at both a national and regional level, relevant statutory, voluntary and private agencies that could contribute to alleviating deficiencies in seven key areas or pathways linked to reoffending: accommodation; education, training and employment; mental and physical health; drugs and alcohol; finance; children and families of offenders; attitudes, thinking and behaviour (Home Office, 2004). The National Action Plan was to be implemented at a regional level through regional partnerships of relevant agencies, coordinated by the regional offender managers and charged with delivering those services crucial to each strategic pathway. Each Regional Reducing Reoffending Plan would require a coordinated multi-agency response to each of the identified pathways, drawing on a wide range of local public, private and voluntary providers, increasing the services available to all offender groups, both in prison and those serving community sentences, but the core focus was support for the resettlement of ex-prisoners.

What obstacles could arise in establishing a coordinated multi-agency response, such as the ones mentioned above?

Creating a multi-agency response

There is no intention here to consider the regional response to each pathway, but a brief overview will be offered of how three of the pathways were addressed: accommodation, employment, and drugs and alcohol. The Social Exclusion Report (SEU, 2002), National Action Plan (Home Office, 2004) and the various Regional Plans all highlighted accommodation as a significant problem for prisoner resettlement. Approximately one third of prisoners lost their accommodation as a result of the sentence, with a further third entering prison from temporary accommodation (SEU, 2002). These problems were particularly acute for female offenders, black and minority ethnic offenders, and those with substance misuse and/or mental health problems (NACRO, 2000, 2001, 2002). Those leaving prison without secure accommodation faced considerable difficulties in establishing a stable lifestyle from which to gain employment or address any of the other problems underpinning their offending (Maguire and Nolan, 2007).

The accommodation pathway acknowledged that access to secure accommodation was the key to successful rehabilitation. The Regional Strategies detailed the action to be taken at each stage of the sentence, in the case of prisoners before, during and post custody. An assessment of a prisoner's accommodation would be made at the reception point, which then informed the support offered during the custodial sentence to secure appropriate accommodation on release. However, crucial to success was the supply of suitable accommodation and partnership arrangements were essential to making the most of available housing stock. Two projects have been highlighted as examples of a partnership response to accommodation: the South West Accommodation Gateway and the Housing and Returning Prisoners (HARP) protocol in the North East. The Gateway project provides a series of multi-agency one-stop shops, both in the community and in prison, offering easy access to advice and other support. HARP brings together statutory and voluntary providers of accommodation with the Prison and Probation Services to create a common approach to planning for the housing of returning prisoners, from the point of prison reception to the offender's eventual release. Both projects aim to maximise the contribution of the statutory and voluntary housing sector in meeting the accommodation needs of released prisoners.

Lack of employment is acknowledged as being associated with reoffending, which also correlates with low school achievement, limited or no qualifications and no experience of stable employment (Nescott, 2007). The link between unemployment and crime was noted by the Cambridge Study in Delinquent Development, a longitudinal survey of 411 males (Farrington et al, 1986, cited in Farrall, 2004: 58). The employment pathway aimed to provide a coordinated response involving training to improve employment opportunities coupled with strategies for engaging with employers in providing jobs for ex-offenders. Offenders will have individual learning plans highlighting learning need and ensuring that such needs are met as the offender progresses through the criminal justice system. Underpinning the above is the provision of high-quality learning and skills training through the Offenders' Learning and Skills Unit supported by both the National Offender Management Service (NOMS) and the Department for Education and Skills. The key to success will be the partnerships with employers in providing jobs for ex-offenders. To illustrate, in the North East, partnership arrangements between the statutory sector and industry have enabled successful completers of unpaid work to be guaranteed job interviews for advertised vacancies. Laing O'Rourke Construction has pledged to reserve a small number of apprenticeship opportunities for offenders (NOMS, 2007).

Numerous studies have indicated the extent of alcohol and drug misuse within the prison population. The Office for National Statistics claimed that 63% of men and 39% of women were classed as hazardous drinkers in the year before coming to prison (Singleton et al, 1999, cited in Farrant, 2008: 9). Wheatley (2007: 400) refers to research suggesting that between 60% and 70% of prisoners had abused drugs in the 12 months prior to custody. In addition, 53% regarded their drug use as problematic, with some 32% of sentenced and 40% of remand prisoners having severe dependency. The drugs and alcohol pathway identifies a range of multi-agency responses including Drug Action Teams, Criminal Justice Integrated Teams and CARAT teams undertaking the assessment and support of offenders' substance-related needs, within the prison. The Regional Strategies clearly identify the importance of aftercare following release from prison and either the provision or brokering of services available in the community. Once again, effective partnerships with a range of voluntary and community organisations are key components of success in this area (see Heath, this volume).

In November 2005, Baroness Scotland launched the Reducing Reoffending Alliances, which together with the Regional Re offending Action Plan, aimed to promote a multi-agency response by increasing the number of partnerships within the community and across government with the clear priority of reducing reoffending. A range of alliances under three different heading was created:

- the NOMS Corporate Alliance, addressing the training and employment needs of offenders by public, private and voluntary agencies;
- the NOMS Civic Alliance, focusing on accommodation, health, arts, leisure and sport;
- the NOMS Faith and Voluntary and Community Sector Alliance, providing practical and spiritual support to a range of offender groups.

The Alliances provide a structure for the comprehensive development of partnerships to meet the needs of offenders generally and ex-prisoners in particular. Each region has reviewed its partnership arrangements and summaries of these are available from the NOMS website (http://noms.justice.gov.uk/noms-regions/) under the heading 'Working in partnership'. While examples of good practice are evident, at the present time a number of the actions appear more an aspiration than a reality, such as strengthening links with employers, increasing housing provision, and developing effective partnerships with voluntary and community sector organisations, with limited reference to agreements with specific organisations. Assessing the success of the partnership or Alliances agenda is not easy given the complex framework of NOMS and the various other agendas and initiatives within it. The Alliances agenda will take time to come to fruition and will be hampered by the conflicting priorities of other agencies, particularly in a time of recession when cutbacks in funding may lead to a reordering of priorities to the disadvantage of offenders (Hudson et al, 2007).

Beyond the provision of services

The partnership arrangements, discussed above, are clearly important in promoting social inclusion among ex-prisoners, but they are only part of the answer. What is equally important is the level of support offered to released prisoners to enable them to take advantage of the opportunities provided by partnerships. The lack of support for short-term prisoners has already been discussed and the impact on reconviction rates noted. However, Maguire (2007) summarises a number of official reports as concluding that even when released on licence, ex-prisoners often received an impersonal service from probation officers, geared to ensuring that basic requirements were in place upon release. Financial and time constraints limited contact with both the individual prisoner and the institution, which meant that any rehabilitative work that was commenced in prison was not communicated to the supervising probation officer and not continued. Probation Service targets around enforcement led to a priority being given to enforcement. The Halliday Report (2001) began the process of addressing the above criticism by extending statutory supervision to all released prisoners, proposing the 'seamless sentence' for those serving less than 12 months, served partly in the community and partly in prison. In addition, Halliday emphasised the importance of rehabilitation and proposed making supervision a more coherent and meaningful experience. These proposals formed the basis of Custody Plus within the 2003 Criminal Justice Act, which was due to be introduced in autumn of 2006, but has been postponed indefinitely.

Carter (2003) undertook a comprehensive review of the correctional services of prison and probation and acknowledged, among numerous other things, the lack of integration between what he described as 'the current silos of prison and probation' (2003: 5). He proposed a new approach that would merge the Prison and Probation Service under the NOMS, focusing on the management of offenders throughout the whole of the sentence providing for the 'end-to-end management of offenders regardless of whether they are given a custodial or community sentence' (2003: 34). As well as creating a single organisation, Carter proposed that a single offender manager would be assigned to each offender with the overall responsibility of assessing, planning and directing the case. The acronym ASPIRE was used to define the role of the offender manager: Assess, Sentence, Plan, Implement (Intervention), Review, Evaluate (NOMS, 2005: 7). The National Offender Management Model talked of an Offender Management Team of key personnel, headed by the offender manager, but also including others who could provide day-to-day support or deliver a range of interventions (NOMS, 2006). The availability of a range of interventions drawn from the voluntary, private and public sector is a key to the success of the above structure and links the partnership or Alliances agenda to the Offender Management Model (see Gough and also Skinner, this volume).

The Offender Management Model also highlighted the tension between an emphasis on punishment or reform, by expressly stating the aims of offender management as being punishment, control, change and help, with little advice on how to resolve these competing aims. In addition, NOMS (2005: 39) makes explicit the requirement on offender managers to use Core Correctional Practices in their supervision of offenders 'characterised by open, warm and enthusiastic relationships' (Dowden and Andrews, 2004: 205). These practices are described as just as important as the technical content of the programme (NOMS, 2005: 39). The above tension has implications for those supervising released prisoners on licence between the short-term objectives of managing the risks posed by offenders through ensuring that the requirements of the licence are rigorously enforced, against the long-term creation of a stable, crime-free lifestyle based on such things as employment prospects and addressing substance misuse (Hedderman, 2007: 19).

In addition to the above, Maruna and LeBel (2002), cited in Hucklesby and Wincup (2007: 55), identified the limitations of a needs-based resettlement strategy focusing on the immediate practical requirements of ex-prisoners in creating a stable lifestyle. While being valuable, such strategies ignore the longer-term requirement of promoting personal responsibility through developing the offender's belief in their ability to take control of their life. Such a belief, known as 'agency' within the growing body of desistance literature, is crucial for the long-term desistance from crime (Maruna et al, 2004). Desistance theory considers the processes involved in the long-term desistance from crime and has focused on a number of issues, particularly the development of social bonds and narrative approaches. Social bonds in terms of family support, important relationships, educational achievement and employment are important in avoiding crime, not only in terms of satisfying needs in this area, but also in developing a narrative script against offending. Research by Maruna into the characteristics of those who avoided reoffending (desisters) and those who reoffended (persisters) highlighted the importance of thinking and self-belief in their ability to avoid reoffending. Offenders constructed a narrative in order to make sense of their lives that impacted on individual optimism, the view of themselves and others and the future. Desisters saw themselves as relatively successful, in control and having options, whereas persisters expressed a much more pessimistic narrative (Maruna et al, 2004).

It is the interplay between the above perspectives of social bonds, narrative script as well as maturation that results in desistance from crime. As McCulloch and McNeill (2008: 158) conclude, 'desistence resides somewhere in the interfaces between developing personal maturity, changing social bonds associated with certain life transitions and the individual subjective narrative constructions which offenders build around these key events and changes'.

The desistance paradigm moves away from what intervention is provided by the various partnership arrangements and addresses the issue of how it is provided and the involvement of the offender in the process of decision making, as well as the outcome. Such an approach, it is argued, would increase not only the short-term take-up of services but also the long-term desistance from crime.

How can a sense of personal responsibility and self-belief be developed in offenders?

The merging of the multi-agency response with the Offender Management Model

In an effort to base probation practice on evidence of what was effective in reducing reoffending, the government funded four Probation Pathfinders into specific areas of probation practice: offending behaviour programmes; basic skills; enhanced community service; and the resettlement of short-term prisoners. Those pathfinders focusing on resettlement were originally designed to examine responses to the resettlement of adult prisoners sentenced to less than 12 months. Within resettlement, seven pathfinder projects were established in seven different prisons; three of the projects were run by the voluntary sector, with the remaining four being probation led (Clancy et al, 2006). The intention of these pathfinders was to address the needs of ex-prisoners by improving the availability and take-up of the key services addressing accommodation, low educational attainment, unemployment and substance misuse. In addition to the above, an additional element was added to three of the four probation-led projects, namely the 'FOR-A Change' programme. This programme drew on motivational interviewing principles, in terms of prisoners setting their own goals and plans, reinforcing the offender's motivation to access relevant services on release. In addition, a cognitive-behavioural component developed improved thinking skills that underpinned their decision making, specifically in relation to offending behaviour, and generally in promoting resettlement (Clancy et al, 2006). The programme comprised 12 group sessions and one individual session, one of which was a 'market place' involving representatives from a variety of local organisations offering support to released prisoners, covering among other things employment, accommodation, financial advice, drugs and alcohol.

The research report into the above was short on firm, conclusive evidence given the relatively low numbers involved and the follow-up period of only one year. However, the importance of post-release contact to reinforce the work begun in custody was clearly identified, in that those who had post-release contact with any project staff had significantly lower rates of reconviction than those who had no contact. A comparison between actual reconviction rates and predicted scores generated through OGRS2 (the Revised Offender Group Reconviction Scale) indicated that those in contact with project staff after release were convicted at a lower rate, 1% below that predicted, whereas those who had no contact were reconvicted at 6% above that predicted. Contact after release was greater among those who attended probation-led projects, although the volunteer mentors provided by voluntary sector-led programmes were also associated with significantly lower reconviction rates (Clancy et al, 2006). This latter conclusion reinforces the importance of the individual relationship between the probation officer and the prisoner offering challenge, support and commitment. Hudson et al (2007) summarise the conclusions of the pathfinder in identifying the broad themes underpinning effective practice with this group of offenders: support with practical problems; work on motivation and thinking skills; and continuity of support from prison to the community following release. These conclusions have parallels with the developing theory of desistance in highlighting the factors and processes of personal change supporting the avoidance of further offending (Maguire, 2007; Raynor, 2007).

Evaluating the success of the above policies in terms of reoffending rates is difficult, as they are relatively new and require time to bed down. The government is claiming some success with reoffending rates, published in March 2007, indicating that proven reoffending rates reduced by 6.9% between 1997 and 2004 (Cunliffe and Shepherd, 2007). These figures suggest that NOMS is over halfway towards its long-term ambition of a 10% reduction in reoffending by 2011. The report also examines reoffending rates by disposal and notes that proven reoffending rates are higher among those sentenced to imprisonment compared with most community disposals, apart from Drug Treatment and Testing Orders. Within custodial disposals, prisoners sentenced to less than 12 months have the highest proven reoffending rate, at over 70%, a figure that has only marginally altered over the four years under examination. The researchers warn that 'these results should not be compared to statistics published before 2002 as there has been a move from reconviction to proven reoffending and a more comprehensive data source is now in use' (Cunliffe and Shepherd, 2007: 11).

Despite the above caveat, the figures suggest that the experiences of short-term prisoners have not materially altered since the publication of the Social Exclusion Unit report (SEU, 2002). Ex-prisoners continue to experience some of the greatest social need, exacerbated by the most extreme form of social exclusion – imprisonment. They have often led chaotic and personally destructive lifestyles, compromising their ability to engage with the people and processes that would lead to a more structured, stable and crime-free life. Multi-agency initiatives aimed at meeting the identified needs of all prisoners are vitally important, but the context within which support or supervision is provided is equally important.

Conclusion

Throughout this chapter, the tension between a punitive response to offenders and their rehabilitation has been highlighted, particularly in terms of where the emphasis lies. The influence of more punitive responses supporting the political image of being 'tough on crime' – demanding supervision, close monitoring and rigorous enforcement – has the potential to push offenders away from mainstream services, compounding the social exclusion experienced by them. A more inclusive strategy needs to focus on the offender as a fellow human being, a member of the community, as opposed to being stigmatised and marginalised. Engaging with ex-prisoners in promoting their resettlement requires exploration of the implications of 'open, warm and enthusiastic relationships' (Dowden and Andrews, 2004: 205) on the everyday practice and support offered to ex-prisoners. Without an emphasis on care in the contemporary correctional practice with ex-prisoners, a multi-agency response will not be accessed by released prisoners, who will remain socially excluded and at high risk of reoffending.

Summary of key points

■ A multi-agency approach to meeting the needs of released prisoners is essential to successful resettlement.

■ Equally important is a context of nurture and support that involves released prisoners in their decision making, promoting individual confidence and self-belief.

■ The development of the above context has been hampered by the care/control dilemma, which prioritises public protection, exacerbating the exclusion faced by released prisoners.

Further reading

Carlen, P. and Worrall, A. (2004) *Analysing Women's Imprisonment*. Cullompton: Willan Publishing.

Hucklesby, A. and Hagley-Dickinson, L. (eds) (2007) *Prisoner Resettlement Policy and Practice*. Cullompton: Willan Publishing.

Jewkes, Y. (ed) (2007) *Handbook on Prisons*. Cullompton: Willan Publishing.

Liebling, A. and Maruna, S. (eds) (2005) *The Effects of Imprisonment*. Cullompton: Willan Publishing.

Maruna, S. and Immarigeon, R. (eds) (2004) *After Crime and Punishment: Pathways to Offender Reintegration*. Cullompton: Willan Publishing.

References

Carter, P. (2003) *Managing Offenders, Reducing Crime: A New Approach*, Correctional Services Review. London: Home Office.

Clancy, A., Hudson, K., Maguire, M., Peake, R., Raynor, P., Vanstone, M. and Kynch, J. (2006) *Getting Out and Staying Out: Results of the Prisoner Resettlement Pathfinders*. Bristol: The Policy Press.

Cunliffe, J. and Shepherd, A. (2007) *Re-offending of Adults: Results from the 2004 Cohort*. London: Home Office.

Dowden, C. and Andrews, D. (2004) 'The importance of staff practice in delivering effective correctional treatment: a meta-analytical review of core correctional practices', *International Journal of Offender Therapy and Comparative Criminology*, 48(2), 203-14.

Farrall, S. (2004) 'Social capital and offender reintegration: making probation desistance focused', in Maruna, S. and Immarigeon, R. (eds) *After Crime and Punishment: Pathways to Offender Reintegration* (pp 57-84). Cullompton: Willan Publishing.

Farrant, F. (2008) 'Alcohol', in Jewkes, Y. and Bennett, J. (eds) *Dictionary of Prisons and Punishment* (pp 9-10). Cullompton: Willan Publishing.

Faulkner, D. (2007) 'Social exclusion', in Canton, R. and Hancock, D. (eds) *Dictionary of Probation and Offender Management* (pp 297-99). Cullompton: Willan Publishing.

Gardener, J., von Hirsch, A., Smith, A., Morgan, R., Ashworth, A. and Wasik, M. (1998) 'Clause 1 – the hybrid law from hell?', *Criminal Justice Matters*, 31, 25-7.

Halliday, J. (2001) *Making Punishments Work*. London: Home Office.

Hedderman, C. (2007) 'Rediscovering resettlement: narrowing the gap between policy rhetoric and practice reality', in Hucklesby, A. and Hagley-Dickinson, L. (eds) *Prisoner Resettlement Policy and Practice* (pp 9-25). Cullompton: Willan Publishing.

Her Majesty's Inspectorate of Prisons (2001) *Through the Prison Gate: A Joint Thematic Review by HM Inspectorates of Prison and Probation*. London: Home Office.

Home Office (2001) *Probation Statistics England and Wales, 1999*. London: Home Office

Home Office (2004) *Reducing Re-Offending National Action Plan*. London: Home Office.

Hucklesby, A. and Wincup, E. (2007) 'Models of resettlement work with prisoners', in Hucklesby, A. and Hagley-Dickinson, L. (eds) *Prisoner Resettlement Policy and Practice* (pp 43-66). Cullompton: Willan Publishing.

Hudson, K., Maguire, M. and Raynor, P. (2007) 'Through the prison gate: resettlement, offender management and the "seamless sentence"', in Jewkes, Y. (ed) *Handbook on Prisons* (pp 629-49). Cullompton: Willan Publishing.

Labour Party (1997) *The Labour Party Manifesto*. London: Labour Party.

McCulloch, P. and McNeill, F. (2008) 'Desistance-focused approaches', in Green, S., Lancaster, E. and Feasey, S. (eds) *Addressing Offending Behaviour: Context, Practice and Values* (pp 154-89). Cullompton: Willan Publishing.

Maguire, M. (2007) 'The resettlement of ex-prisoners', in Gelsthorpe, L. and Morgan, R. (eds) *Handbook of Probation* (pp 398-424). Cullompton: Willan Publishing.

Maguire, M. and Nolan, J. (2007) 'Accommodation and related services for ex-prisoners', in Hucklesby, A. and Hagley-Dickinson, L. (eds) *Prisoner Resettlement Policy and Practice* (pp 144-73). Cullompton: Willan Publishing.

Maruna, S., Immarigeon, R. and LeBel, T. (2004) 'Ex-offender reintegration: theory and practice', in Maruna, S. and Immarigeon, R. (eds) *After Crime and Punishment: Pathways to Offender Reintegration* (pp 3-26). Cullompton: Willan Publishing.

Maruna, S., Porter, L. and Carvalho, I. (2004) 'The Liverpool Desistance Study and probation practice: opening the dialogue', *The Probation Journal*, 51(3), 221-32.

Ministry of Justice (2009) *Prison Population and Accommodation Briefing for 15th May 2009*. London: Ministry of Justice.

NACRO (National Association for the Care and Resettlement of Offenders) (2000) *The Forgotten Majority: The Resettlement of Short-term Prisoners*. London: NACRO.

NACRO (2001) *Women Behind Bars: A Positive Agenda for Women Prisoners' Resettlement*. London: NACRO.

NACRO (2002) *Resettling Prisoners from Black and Minority Ethnic Groups.* London: NACRO.

Nescot (2007) *Opening Doors: Research Reports 2007, Surrey and Sussex.* Surrey: Nescot College.

NOMS (National Offender Management Service) (2005) *The NOMS Offender Management Model.* London: NOMS.

NOMS (2006) *End-to-End Offender Management.* London: NOMS. Available at http://noms.justice.gov.uk/managing-offenders/end-to-end/

NOMS (2007) *Reducing Reoffending Alliances in the North East Region.* London: NOMS.

NOMS (2008) *Agency Framework Document,* London: NOMS.

Padfield, N. and Maruna, S. (2006) 'The revolving door at the prison gate: exploring the dramatic increase in recalls to prison', *Criminology and Criminal Justice*, 6(3), 329-52.

Raynor, P. (2007) 'Theoretical perspectives on resettlement: what it is and how it might work', in Hucklesby, A. and Hagley-Dickinson, L. (eds) *Prisoner Resettlement Policy and Practice* (pp 26-42). Cullompton: Willan Publishing.

SEU (Social Exclusion Unit) (2002) *Reducing Re-Offending by Ex-Prisoners.* London: Office of the Deputy Prime Minister.

Wheatley, M. (2007) 'Drugs in prison', in Jewkes, Y. (ed) *Handbook on Prisons* (pp 399-422). Cullompton: Willan Publishing.

CHAPTER 12

Offenders with mental health problems in the criminal justice system: the multi-agency challenge

Francis Pakes and Jane Winstone

Aims of the chapter

- To argue that providing services to offenders with mental health problems is a matter that requires multi-agency collaboration throughout.
- To highlight the importance of definitions of what constitutes a mentally disordered offender.
- To demonstrate the prevalence of mental health problems in offender populations.
- To highlight the challenges in identifying and meeting mental health needs in these populations.
- To introduce the key recommendations of the Bradley Report on people with mental health problems or learning disabilities in the criminal justice system.

Introduction

The provision of services to individuals with mental health needs who pass through the criminal justice system is a quintessential multi-agency matter. The term 'offender' (or 'suspect' or 'defendant') demonstrates that these individuals are at least partly defined by their involvement in the criminal justice system but at the same time, it is health providers that are best placed to meet their needs (NACRO, 2004). That makes multi-agency work a necessity: the individuals find themselves in one system but need services from another.

However, the differences between criminal justice and health and social care agencies are such that multi-agency work is far from straightforward. Stone (2003) stated that where multi-agency collaboration works well it is the most effective way of providing for the multiple and complex needs of offenders with mental health difficulties. However, he went on to add that such arrangements often collapse under the weight of festering personal differences rooted in the poor articulation of roles and responsibilities, restricted resources and professional and philosophical differences.

First of all there is a fundamental difference in perception of the same individual. They are labelled as 'service users' in many healthcare settings, but 'offenders' (or 'defendants') in criminal justice. The former places emphasis on identification of treatment and motivation to comply with medication, the latter on coercion, punishment and motivation of compliance with sentence provisions and behaviour change. In addition, both health and criminal justice agencies form a myriad of organisations themselves with differing priorities, cultures and discourses. Inter-agency work within both realms is already difficult, let alone cross-boundary efforts. Finally, there are differing principles and organisational pressures that underlie how offenders with mental health problems are dealt with in either health or criminal justice. Within health and criminal justice agencies there are different ways in which caseloads and delays are managed. Health agencies tend to emphasise the importance of voluntary participation and may have a restrictive admissions criteria and restricted availability of bed space. In contrast, the police and prisons can hardly pick and choose their clientele and an individual sentenced to prison must be found a place immediately. Because of such differences, health and criminal justice agencies relate very differently to the same individual, including differing views on their entitlements, what constitutes quality service and the importance of certain outcomes.

It is well known that offender mental health is no marginal concern. Many individuals who are kept either in police cells or in holding cells at Magistrates' Courts or who are on remand, in prison, in approved premises or serving a Community Order have needs in the area of mental health and emotional wellbeing. For example, a 2004 study looked at residents of approved premises in Greater Manchester and found that just over a quarter had a known psychiatric diagnosis (HMIP et al, 2008). Whether that qualifies them as a 'mentally disordered offender' is subject to an issue of definition. The Reed Report (1992) looked at provision for mentally disordered offenders and defined a mentally disordered offender simply as 'A mentally disordered person who has broken the law' (1992: 4). That definition avoids the issue of what constitutes a mentally disordered person. A rather narrow definition would be the one utilised by National Statistics where the term 'mentally disordered offender' refers to people who have been compulsorily admitted to hospital under the following Acts:

- Part V of the 1959 Mental Health Act;
- Part III of the 1983 Mental Health Act;[1]
- the 1964 Criminal Procedure (Insanity) Act, as amended by the 1991 Criminal Procedure (Insanity and Unfitness to Plead) Act;
- the 2004 Domestic Violence, Crime and Victims Act.

Less than 2,000 entered hospital compulsorily from court or from prison in 2007/08 (NHS Information Centre, 2008). This group comprises a small subset of all individuals passing through the criminal justice system with identified or identifiable mental health needs and predominantly represents those with severe and enduring mental illness. These are individuals whose behaviour did not legally fulfil the requirements for the imposition of statutory punishment, this being to demonstrate a guilty intent/act (*actus reus*) or being in possession of a reasoning mind (*mens rea*).

We can juxtapose this definition with that of the National Association for the Care and Resettlement of Offenders (NACRO), which reads:

> Those who come into contact with the criminal justice system because they have committed, or are suspected of committing, a criminal offence and:- who may be acutely or chronically mentally ill; those with neuroses, behavioural and/or personality disorders; those with learning difficulties; some who, as a function of alcohol and/ or substance misuse, have a mental health problem; and any who are suspected of falling into one or other of these groups. It also includes those in whom a degree of mental disturbance is recognised, even though that may not be severe enough to bring it within the criteria laid down by the Mental Health Act 1983, and those offenders who, even though they do not fall easily within this definition – for example, some sex offenders and some abnormally aggressive offenders – may benefit from psychological treatments. (NACRO, 2006: 2)

This arguably is a description rather than a definition, but looking at mental illness from this definitional perspective allows the inclusion of a majority of all individuals with identified mental health concerns who pass through the criminal justice system in any given year. As there are over one million sentences (including fines) imposed annually (Pakes and Pakes, 2009), the number of people in the criminal justice system who might need mental health provision could be in the order of tens of thousands or even more (78,700 people were dealt with by Crown Court for indictable offences in 2007, and 123,000 were arrested and held in custody until their first court appearance (Ministry of Justice, 2007). It highlights that definitions are important. Two options present themselves: either mentally disordered offenders can be defined through a narrow legal definition and these individuals are often locked away in hospital settings or a definition can be adopted to include many if not most offenders and defendants. It is the latter that we have chosen for the purposes of this chapter.

The tenet of this chapter is as follows. Mental health problems are rife in offender and defendant populations, in particular in prison. However, mental health needs are frequently overlooked when individuals enter the criminal justice system. Police officers are usually not trained to recognise mental health problems and when individuals are transferred to court to face magistrates their mental health needs are frequently not taken fully into account. That is likely to lead to delays if at some point during prosecution mental health difficulties are flagged up. That in turn can lengthen time spent on remand (James et al, 2002). In addition, there is a risk of inappropriate disposals. For example, prisons have frequently been argued to be unsuitable places for those with mental health problems to regain mental wellbeing (see, for example, Bradley, 2009; Sainsbury Centre for Mental

Health, 2009) in order to maximise the opportunity to lead a self-supporting prosocial lifestyle upon release. Equally, Community Orders may be unworkable where resources and specialist mental health support are difficult to access post sentence. As Blackburn (2004) states, interventions for offenders with mental health problems frequently lie outside of the provisions usually found within the criminal justice system.

In short, multi-agency mental health support for offenders and defendants requires an overhaul and it is hoped that the Bradley Report (Bradley, 2009)[2] will provide impetus for this. The chapter concludes by discussing the key findings and recommendations of that report and how the implementation of the recommendations might change provision for this vulnerable group of individuals.

> Do offenders with mental health problems need help or deserve punishment? How might you decide whether treatment or punishment should get priority?

Rates of mental health problems within the criminal justice system

For multi-agency intervention to take place, a mental health need has first to be identified and for those entering the criminal justice pathway through arrest it is the police who will be the first agency of contact. It is well known that mental health problems at police stations are frequently overlooked. Nemitz and Bean (2001) argue that no one actually knows the numbers of mentally disordered suspects passing through the police stations in England and Wales each year although estimates vary from 2% to 20%. Data are also available to suggest that between 1.6% (Revolving Doors, 1994) and 2.7% (Robertson et al, 1995) of those held in police stations suffer from a serious mental illness. The available research has focused on severe and 'obvious' mental health problems (Revolving Doors, 1994; James, 2000). That might have led to an underestimation of the overall prevalence of mental health problems experienced in police cells. After all, many detainees will suffer from anxiety brought about by either the arrest or the events leading up to it. A reason for non-detection might be that mental disorder is often co-morbid with alcohol or substance abuse problems, so that the former might be overlooked due to the prominence of the latter (see Heath and also Rees, this volume). Based on an analysis of 1,575 custody records, a third of all arrests involved an arrestee who had been drinking (Man et al, 2002).

James (2000) looked at police station diversion schemes in operation in three areas (Charing Cross, Marylebone and West End Central) in London. He found that 1.1% (in total 712 cases) of those in police custody were suspected of suffering from a mental disorder. Of these, and using James's terminology, 42.1% were diagnosed with schizophrenia or allied states, 9.0% with substance dependence, 8.5% with personality disorder, 7% with depression, 6.6% were manic, while 1.3% had a mental handicap or learning disability.

There is no doubt that sentencing that does not take into account mental health problems is rife within the criminal justice system. Starting with the secure estate, the now seminal study of Singleton et al (1998) identified a high prevalence of mental health problems in prison (see Table 12.1). Data from Fazel and Danesh (2002) demonstrate that the UK is not unique in this respect and that prisons all over the world are populated with detainees who suffer from one or more diagnosable mental health problem. The cost of this may well be reflected in rates of suicide and self-harm. In the UK the suicide rate in prisons in 2007 was 114 per 100,000 inmates. The figure for the general population is 8.3. Thus, the suicide rate for those imprisoned is 13 times higher, which is staggering when it is considered that these are people looked after and contained in cells where every effort is made to minimise the opportunities for self-harm and suicide. Around 30% of all offenders engage in some form of self-harm while in custody (Brooker et al, 2002) amounting to over 6,000 incidents per year (*Hansard*, 2009). It highlights what is well known but still easily forgotten, namely that prisons are places of suffering. The neglect of mental health problems in both identification and management can be argued to significantly contribute to that.

Table 12.1: Mental health problems in UK prisons

	Remand males (%) n=1,250	Prison males (%) n=1,121	Remand females (%) n=187	Prison females (% n=584
Psychosis	10	7	14 (combined)	
Personality disorders	78	64	50 (combined)	
Neurotic disorders	59	40	76	63

Source: Singleton et al (1998)

It is important to note that prevalence figures for remand are higher than for prison inmates post conviction. This could be due to the fact that remand can be a particularly stressful time. It also highlights the impression that the system is insufficiently proactive in identifying mental health problems, meaning that many of these go unnoticed, despite the existence of well-established screening tools (Grubin et al, 2002; Noel et al, 2003).

Forty per cent of offenders on a Community Order are thought to have at least one identifiable mental illness. This suggests that mental illness is rarely given prime importance in the sentencing process judging by the fact that Community Orders with a Mental Health Treatment Requirement (MHTR) are relatively rare (Khanom et al, 2009), one of the problems cited being the difficulty in obtaining appropriately qualified medical professionals to implement a MHTR. Only 725 have been imposed nationally out of nearly 200,000 offenders (Seymour and Rutherford: 2008: 13), while in one Probation Area alone 109 of the 6,835 offenders on a Community Order had an identified mental health need, of whom only 37 had a MHTR. In addition, as mentioned above, the incidence of one in four offenders in approved premises in Greater Manchester with a known psychiatric diagnosis suggests that this situation is likely mirrored across other approved premises. Of those in Greater Manchester, 5.4% had a diagnosis of psychosis, 41% had a secondary diagnosis as well, and about one in three had an alcohol or drugs misuse problem (HMI Probation et al, 2008).

Together these figures show that in some criminal justice settings, mental health problems are the norm, not the exception. In others, they are a frequent occurrence. It is striking that training, let alone multi-agency training, on mental health awareness or any education beyond that, is rare throughout the criminal justice system. Winstone and Pakes (2008) argue that this is contributory to why so many offenders pass through the sentencing process without specific provision made for their mental health needs and adds to the problems posed for those responsible for supervising and supporting offenders with a mental health problem post sentence.

> It is clear that offenders very frequently suffer from mental health problems. In what ways should prison officers, judges and juries be better informed about mental health?

The identification of mental health need

In most custody suites, no standard dedicated mental health support is available despite the fact that there are just over 100 Assessment, Diversion and Liaison Schemes that serve police stations and/or Magistrates' Courts (NACRO, 2005; Winstone and Pakes, 2008) although they are far from a universal provision. These schemes tend to involve a psychiatric nurse and sometimes a psychiatrist who are adept at identifying mental health needs within populations. The question is the extent to which they have access to individuals and information about individuals that allows them to do that effectively once a person has entered the criminal justice system.

The identification of need can be thought of as a three-tier process. It is simply impractical to subject every person who finds themselves in police custody or who is due to appear in court to a thorough mental health assessment. Instead, what is required is something quick and easy to identify individuals who are likely to benefit from a fuller assessment. This process is called screening. Screening can take various forms. It can be based on information from the individual in question and will involve simple questions such as 'Are you on medication?' or 'Have you ever been diagnosed with a mental illness?'. It can also involve, where possible, an examination of information about the individual, such as information from the Police National Computer or NHS records. This already raises issues that health information is sought without the individual's consent. Practically, many an individual is not screened but is in fact 'referred' to these schemes through custody staff identifying an individual as 'odd' or having had previous dealings with them or being aware of existing mental health problems.

Screening only marks the beginning of identification of need. Further to a positive screening outcome, a further and more comprehensive assessment can take place. It tends to involve an interview with the individual of up to an hour and usage of a formal assessment tool. Where necessary, an assessment of fitness to plead, fitness to be detained and interviewed, and an assessment of mental health needs and ways in which those needs can be met or managed will be made. These assessments are reported to court in written or oral form and might serve as a lever to unlock services for these individuals. Such assessments are still short of formal diagnosis. At the same time it must be recognised that many offenders and defendants will have a multitude of other needs in areas such as substance misuse, housing, debt management, physical health and personal relationships.

Should the mental health needs be more serious and further reporting be required, the 2007 Mental Health Act might come into play and a psychiatric report can be requested. This is the third tier of assessment. In practice, however, most individuals are screened, assessed and dealt with without resort to the Mental Health Act. The level of need is often relatively minor and can be managed without bringing the legal machinery of the Mental Health Act to bear.

It is often mentioned that offenders need mental health help but courts frequently require mental health input from mental health professionals in order to secure certain disposals, such as a disposal under the 2007 Mental Health Act or the imposition of a Community Order with a MHTR. The relationship between criminal justice agencies and health agencies or mental health professionals is therefore multifaceted. A simple example will demonstrate the intrinsic difficulty of these relationships. Consider an offender sentenced to a Community Order with a MHTR that requires him/her to attend regular sessions with a local Community Mental Health Team. The offender must have agreed to that sentence, and must realise that failing to attend can constitute a breach of that Order. A breach can lead to imprisonment. When a client indeed fails to turn up for a health appointment, should the community psychiatric nurse tell the relevant probation officer, knowing that that information could be used to place the client behind bars? Would health professionals become jailers by default, knowing full well that prison is more likely to exacerbate than ameliorate mental health issues? It is such blurring of roles and professional objectives that highlights the difficulty between mental health and criminal justice bodies.

Addressing need

Where mental health needs are identified early there is an opportunity to address them. Many individuals with mental health problems are picked up for low-level nuisance transgressions such as public order offences and discharged without follow-up. This represents a lost opportunity to connect or reconnect those individuals with services. The process of linking up is not necessarily multi-agency work as much as multi-agency awareness: those who refer on need awareness of both the individual's mental health needs and knowledge of existing services if the person is to be effectively 'signposted'. If, however, a mentally disordered individual is pointed in the right direction of services, only one in three actually makes an appointment and many will disappear from view prior to any sustained engagement with these services (Shaw et al, 2001).

It is here where multi-agency work can be highly beneficial. This work can take the role of advocacy: rather than leaving a vulnerable individual to fend for themselves within a myriad of social and community mental health services, scheme workers can make appointments on behalf of that individual and, where appropriate, accompany them. This enhances the chance of successful engagement (Winstone and Pakes, 2008). Many defendants will not require care beyond community mental health services but will need to register with a general practitioner before such services can be accessed. A link worker can help unlock these doors that many defendants find difficult to open themselves. Individuals might already have a care coordinator if they are on a Care Programme Approach (CPA). A CPA can be utilised for individuals who need specialist community mental health interventions. It will involve the formulation of a care plan and the individual is assigned a key worker. Should it be necessary, a CPA can involve a multidisciplinary team, but even at this point the issues of which agency is to undertake and pay for which part of the resources, input and support and how liaison and management functions are to be allocated can lead to multi-agency tensions, which are difficult to resolve (Stone, 2003).

There are also issues that even the most dedicated link worker cannot solve, for example the patchy provision of psychological, counselling and housing services. Services for women (Hunter et al, 2007), black and minority ethnic groups and those with personality disorder or learning disability are also, at best, in short supply and at worst, non-existent. Although multi-agency work cannot solve the lack of resources, it does provide the individual with the best chance of linking up with services where they do exist. That said, long waiting lists are likely to exacerbate levels of need with defendants feeling, as a senior probation officer once put it to us, "as a ball between bats".

Where the offending is not so serious and where there is a lower risk of harm to self or others, arrangements tend to rely on goodwill and informal relationships, with provision being notoriously patchy and piecemeal. That provision has probably become more rather than less piecemeal over the years since the Reed Report (1992), judging by the decrease in the number of Assessment, Liaison and Diversion Schemes that we have documented (Winstone and Pakes, 2008, Pakes and Winstone, 2009). It is not our intention to replicate the debate on the fragility of such schemes here but suffice it to say that where statutory arrangements are found wanting, arrangements seem precariously lacking in protocol, with insecure funding arrangements, little oversight and not much more than the most basic data collection and analysis (Winstone and Pakes, 2008). This can only add to the problems faced by multi-agency provision and it is little wonder that so many schemes fail to survive over the long term, falling as they do between the health and justice sectors and often not fully supported by either.

For the seriously ill and serious and dangerous offenders, statutory arrangements are in place. The 2007 Mental Health Act covers severe and enduring mental illness, fitness to plead and can provide for Hospital Orders as a disposal. Similarly, Multi-Agency Public Protection Arrangements (MAPPA) will cover the mentally disordered individual judged to pose a sufficiently serious risk to be covered by the MAPPA framework. The multi-agency work of MAPPA (see Clift and also Nash, this volume) has undoubtedly been a success story, but it is interesting to note that until a statutory responsibility was placed on collaborating agencies, the multi-agency arrangements for this group of offenders had been as prone to founder as any other. Finally, Community Orders with supervision allow for mental health problems to be addressed as part of a sentence plan. That can occur via probation supervision, through the formulation of Specified Activities or as part of a MHTR. The effectiveness of these Community Order provisions, as mentioned above, tends to suffer from a lack of comprehensive local resources for the management of mental health but also includes such day-to-day frustrations as difficulties in securing regular contact with psychiatrists and other medical professionals, such as general practitioners, in order to get the mental health aspect of the identified need fully supported.

A more comprehensive multi-agency strategy for dealing with offenders with mental health difficulties throughout the criminal justice system is essential. The reasons for this include the following core considerations:

- effectiveness: sentencing options that ignore mental health difficulties are more likely to be ineffective;
- expedience: unrecognised mental health difficulties may prove to be an obstacle at the sentencing stage, causing delays;
- quality of justice: mental health problems should be addressed to secure a just disposal;
- reducing reoffending and risk of self harm: it is likely that mental health problems properly addressed and effectively managed are likely to reduce reoffending and risk of self-harm directly or indirectly as mental wellbeing will be conducive to engagement with intervention designed to promote behaviour change.

> What factors need to be taken into consideration regarding a defendant's mental health condition at the point of sentencing?

A driver for change: the Bradley Report

The Secretary of State for Justice Jack Straw asked Lord Bradley to undertake this independent review in December 2007 under the following terms of reference:

- to examine the extent to which offenders with mental health problems or learning disabilities could, in appropriate cases, be diverted from prison to other services, and the barriers to such diversion;
- to make recommendations to government, in particular on the organisation of effective court liaison and diversion arrangements and the services needed to support them.

The Bradley Report came out on 30 April 2009. It contains no less than 82 recommendations and the good news is that the immediate government response stated that none of these 82 recommendations had been rejected and that in fact there is a good degree of cross-party support for the implementation of Lord Bradley's recommendations.

Central to Bradley's vision is the development and strengthening of Criminal Justice Mental Health Teams (CJMHTs). All police stations and courts should have access to diversion and liaison services. These multi-agency teams should provide continuity of care for individuals throughout the criminal justice system. They should have responsibility for information sharing between all the agencies. In addition, they should have direct involvement with MAPPA. A minimum dataset should be developed for collection by CJMHTs to provide improved information to assess need, plan and performance-manage services and inform commissioning decisions. Clearly, the vision is for such teams to be hub of all multi-agency efforts (Pakes and Winstone, 2008; see also, Spurgeon, 2005).

It is important that the commissioning of services becomes more multi-agency. It is recommended that Primary Care Trusts and partners should jointly plan services for offenders. This will hopefully ensure that the services that are needed will also be available. In addition, the suggestion has been made that inspections could be carried out jointly by criminal justice and health inspectorates.

A further pillar for reform concerns training. Training needs have been identified across the criminal justice spectrum as well as outside it. This has led to a substantial number of recommendations, including mental health training for all staff in schools. Those in primary healthcare, including general practitioners, should have mental health and learning disability awareness training in order to identify individuals (children and young people in particular) needing help and refer them to specialist services. In addition, community support officers and police officers should link with local mental health services to develop joint training packages for mental health awareness and learning disability issues. Training should also be available to Appropriate Adults. Their role is recognised as important in supporting vulnerable people at the police station. Mental health awareness and learning disabilities should be a key component in the police training programme and should also be available for prison staff and all probation staff, as well as the judiciary. Such training should be developed with the input of service users. Joint training has indeed been identified as a way of smoothening inter-agency relations at the level of practitioners (Winstone and Pakes, 2008; Pakes and Winstone, 2009). The lack of specific training on mental health issues for professionals is a longstanding complaint. The focus on training to identify mental health needs will not only allow for mental health needs to be more quickly identified and hence addressed, it will also empower criminal justice professionals, who often feel ill-equipped at best and overwhelmed at worst, in dealing with acute mental health difficulties of which they feel they have insufficient knowledge and skills to deal with effectively.

Finally, Lord Bradley is looking to secure a clear national framework to focus on this agenda that transcends traditional organisational boundaries. He therefore recommends the establishment of a National Programme Board. This Board should bring together all the relevant government departments covering health, social care and criminal justice. The Programme Board should be directly responsible to ministers. In addition, the Programme Board should be supported by a National Advisory Board. It should provide independent, evidence-based advice, act as an independent challenge to the development and progress programme and highlight examples of good practice and commission studies in areas of particular interest.

Although it is clear that a national structure of accountability is essential, change will occur through effective local partnerships. Services need to be commissioned locally taking account of local needs through needs assessments. Local Criminal Justice Mental Health Teams will be the vehicle for that change. In order for these teams to be effective they need to be bolstered. The Programme Board should oversee the development of national standards including:

- core minimum standards;
- a national network;
- a reporting structure;
- a national minimum dataset;
- performance monitoring;
- local development plans;
- key personnel.

The last of these is of obvious importance. NACRO has documented that about half of all such schemes in operation at present do not have access to a forensic psychiatrist. Winstone and Pakes found in their national survey (Winstone and Pakes, 2008) that very few teams have representatives from black and minority ethnic organisations, housing, psychology, and drugs and alcohol services including the voluntary sector. There is no doubt that the multi-agency and inter-disciplinary nature of these teams will need to be strengthened. That said, the intention is clearly that what already exists should be built on, and good practice in CJMHTs certainly exists. Lord Bradley (2009: 167) mentions the Manchester Mental Health Criminal Justice Liaison Service as an example of good practice.

Thus, the recommendations of the Bradley Report look at strengthening local provision, provide for increased mental health awareness both within and beyond the criminal justice system, provide for multi-agency informed commissioning of services informed by needs assessment and a national overseeing structure to ensure that the provision of mental health services to individuals passing through the criminal justice system will not fall off the governmental agenda as it has done in the past. It is an ambitious, possibly even an inspired report. If it does bring about the envisaged change, the report will be the best thing that has happened to this field in the last 20 years. It indeed received a very positive reception from many statutory and non-statutory stakeholders including the Sainsbury Centre for Mental Health and NACRO (www.nacro.org.uk/templates/news/newsItem. cfm/2009043000.htm).

Conclusion

There is considerable world-weariness among professionals and policy makers alike with regard to failed efforts in the past to address the mental health problems of those passing through the criminal justice system. It has been argued that the social and political trend has been one of criminalising mental health and of prioritising security and punitive responses over care. The Bradley Report emphasises that public protection should remain the overriding priority and it is clear that the legitimacy of the report throughout health and criminal justice is enhanced by stating that commitment clearly. However, the wider social and political context in which these recommendations need to be implemented may not be conducive to wholesale change for the better.

The other obvious issue is inevitably one of money. A spokesperson for the Mental Health Foundation was quoted as saying: 'The risk is that these essential reforms will never get out of the starting blocks without serious investment' (Mental Health Foundation, 2009). Many of the recommendations, not least the extensive training programme to increase mental health awareness both inside criminal justice and in other agencies, will be expensive. It may well be the case that the new monies to implement the recommendations will be highly limited. Two responses to that are worth making. The first is that it requires creativity in the configuration and reconfiguration of services. The second is that a successful programme of provision for mentally disordered offenders should save money in many places. It should reduce unnecessary prison sentences, and time spent on remand. Indeed, a report by Tribal (2009) to support the Bradley Report found that millions of pounds can be saved by effective liaison and assessment services to reduce the amount of time and numbers on remand. More effective commissioning of psychiatric reports could save almost three million pounds annually. The biggest cost reduction is, however, the avoidance of short prison sentences for people with mental health problems who may eligible for a Community Order. That could save £40 million annually (Tribal, 2009). It highlights that money can be found by effective implementation, which in turn can be used to fund the more expensive parts of the reform programme – provided there is continued political will to effect the changes.

The projected savings will enhance the perceived feasibility of the programme of reform. However, much continues to rely on political will. As the Mental Health Foundation is quoted as saying:

It would be a disgrace for this report to be filed under good intentions, especially given the high financial and human cost of doing nothing. To have all the evidence of what needs to be done so clearly demonstrated and not to act would be inexcusable. (Mental Health Foundation, 2009)

Notes

[1] The 1983 Mental Health Act was revised in 2007. The term 'mental illness' was replaced by the term 'mental disorder'.

[2] Lord Keith Bradley was commissioned by the Secretary of State for Justice to review the provisions for offenders passing through the criminal justice system with mental health needs.

Summary of key points

- Providing services for individuals with mental health problems in the criminal justice system is quintessentially a multi-agency matter.
- Unfortunately, provision for these individuals is patchy and often reliant on goodwill or haphazard arrangements.
- The need among these offenders is both complex and high. It is therefore encouraging that Lord Bradley has reported so comprehensively on this.
- The government is at present setting out a plan of action after initially having accepted all 82 recommendations of the Bradley Report.

Further reading

Bradley, Lord (2009) *Lord Bradley's Review of People with Mental Health Problems or Learning Disabilities in the Criminal Justice System*. London: Department of Health.

Pakes, F. and Winstone, J. (2009) 'Effective practice in mental health liaison and diversion', *Howard Journal of Criminal Justice*, 48, 158-71.

Sainsbury Centre for Mental Health (2009) *Diversion: A Better Way Forward for Criminal Justice and Mental Health*. London: Sainsbury Centre for Mental Health.

References

Blackburn, R. (2004) '"What works" with mentally disordered offenders', *Psychology, Crime and Law*, 3, 297–308.

Bradley, Lord (2009) *Lord Bradley's Review of People with Mental Health Problems or Learning Disabilities in the Criminal Justice System*. London: Department of Health.

Brooker, C., Repper, J., Beverley, C., Ferriter, M. and Brewer, N. (2002) *Mental Health Services and Prisoners: A review for the Department of Health*. Sheffield: SCHARR: University of Sheffield.

Fazel, S. and Danesh, J. (2002) 'Serious mental disorder in 23 000 prisoners: a systematic review of 62 surveys', *The Lancet*, 359, 545-50.

Grubin, D., Carson, D. and Parsons, S. (2002) *Report on New Reception Health Screening Arrangements: The Result of a Pilot Study in 10 Prisons*. London: Department of Health.

Hansard (2009) 'Prisoners and self harm'. HC Deb, 3 June 2009, col 529W. Available at www.theyworkforyou.com/wrans/?id=2009-06-03a.274144.h

HMI Probation, HMI Prisons and HMI Constabulary (2008) *Joint Inspection of Approved Premises*. London: HMI Probation, HMI Prisons and HMI Constabulary

Hunter, G., Boyce, I. and Penfold, C. (2007) *Evaluation of Criminal Justice Liaison and Diversion Schemes: A Focus on Women Offenders*. London: King's College London.

James, D. (2000). 'Police station diversion schemes: role and efficacy in central London', *Journal of Forensic Psychiatry*, 11, 532-55.

James, E.D., Farnham, F., Moorey, H., Lloyd, H., Hill, K., Blizard, R. and Barnes, T.R.E. (2002) *Outcome of Psychiatric Admission through the Courts*. London: Home Office.

Khanom, H., Samele, C. and Rutherford, M. (2009) *Missed Opportunity: Community Sentences and the Mental Health Treatment Requirement*. London: Sainsbury Centre for Mental Health.

Man, L.-H., Best, D., Marshall, J., Godfrey, C. and Budd, T. (2002) *Dealing with Alcohol-related Detainees in the Custody Suite*. Home Office RDS Findings 178. London: HMSO.

Mental Health Foundation (2009) 'Lord Bradley's report on prisons and mental health must not be left on the shelf', Press Release 30-04-2009. London: Mental Health Foundation.

Ministry of Justice (2007) *Sentencing Statistics 2006*. London: Home Office/ Ministry of Justice.

NACRO (National Association for the Care and Resettlement of Offenders) (2004) *Information Sharing – Challenges and Opportunities: A Guide to Sharing Confidential Information Regarding Mentally Disordered Offenders*. London: NACRO.

NACRO (2005) *Findings of the 2004 Survey of Court Diversion/Criminal Justice Mental Health Liaison Schemes for Mentally Disordered Offenders in England and Wales*. London: NACRO.

NACRO (2006) *Liaison and Diversion for Mentally Disordered Offenders*. London: NACRO.

Nemitz, T. and Bean, P. (2001) 'Protecting the rights of the mentally disordered in police stations: the use of the appropriate adult in England and Wales', *International Journal of Law and Psychiatry*, 24, 595-605.

NHS Information Centre (2008) 'In-patients formally detained in hospitals under the Mental Health Act 1983 and other legislation, England: 1997-98 to 2007-08'. Available at www.ic.nhs.uk/

Noel, G., Parson, S. and Grubin, D. (2003) 'Reception screening and mental health needs assessment in a male remand prison', *Psychiatric Bulletin*, 27, 251-3.

Pakes, F. and Pakes, S. (2009) *Criminal Psychology*. Cullompton: Willan Publishing.

Pakes, F. and Winstone, J. (2009) 'Effective practice in mental health liaison and diversion', Howard Journal of Criminal Justice, 48, 158–71.

Reed, J. (chair) (1992) *Review of Health and Social Services for Mentally Disordered Offenders and Others Requiring Similar Services*, Cm 2088. London: HMSO.

Revolving Doors (1994) *The Management of People with Mental Health Problems by Paddington Police*. London: Revolving Doors.

Robertson, G. (1994) 'A follow up of remanded mentally ill offenders given hospital orders', *Medicine, Science and Law*, 34, 61–6.

Sainsbury Centre for Mental Health (2009) *Diversion: A Better Way Forward for Criminal Justice and Mental Health*. London: Sainsbury Centre for Mental Health.

Seymour, L. and Rutherford, M. (2008) *The Community Order and the Mental Health Treatment Requirement*. London: Sainsbury Centre for Mental Health.

Shaw, J., Tomenson, B., Creed, F. and Perry, A. (2001) 'Loss of contact with psychiatric services in people diverted from the criminal justice system', *Journal of Forensic Psychiatry*, 12, 203–10.

Singleton, N., Meltzer, H. and Gatward, R. (1998) *Psychiatric Morbidity among Prisoners in England and Wales*. London: Office for National Statistics.

Spurgeon, D. (2005) 'Diversionary tactics', *Safer Society* (summer), 24–6.

Stone (2003) *A Compendium Guide to Mentally Disordered Offenders* (2nd edn). Crayford: Shaw and Sons.

Tribal (2008) *Financial Report to the Bradley Review*. London: Department of Health.

Winstone, J. and Pakes, F. (2008) *Report on National Criminal Justice Mental Health Team Audit (England)*. London: Department of Health.

CHAPTER 13

The partnership approach to drug misuse

Bernie Heath

Aims of the chapter

- To describe the historical development of drug policy and strategy that has resulted in the current partnership approach to drug misuse.
- To discuss the meaning of partnership in relation to drug treatment.
- To explore the nature of partnerships in relation to the delivery of coerced treatment, giving consideration to ethical and value dilemmas.
- To explore provision to those who have complex and diverse needs.
- To outline what is effective in the treatment of drug misuse and consider whether the current partnership approach reflects this.

Collaboration and partnership is central to this government's philosophy of modernisation (see Pycroft, this volume) and it is arguable that nowhere is it more apparent than in the strategic response to drug misuse. The need to build service capacity to meet the target of increasing the number of drug users in 'treatment' by 100% over the 10-year period 1998 to 2008 (Home Office, 1998) has resulted in a plethora of partnership arrangements between the public, private and voluntary sectors. Indeed the government views the third sector agencies as key players in relation to criminal justice responsibilities, 'playing a full role in supporting the effective management of offenders' (Ministry of Justice, 2008: 7). Historically, agencies within the National Health Service (NHS) and the voluntary sector have voiced their unease in relation to allying themselves to the coercive treatment of drug misusing offenders, believing that it is an ethically inappropriate approach (Gibbs, 1999: 285; Unell, 2002: 229). Yet despite moral misgivings, the coalition between health services and criminal justice agencies is now a strategic imperative. Given such an unlikely marriage it is worth exploring how such 'collaborative' arrangements have come into existence.

Strategic responses informed by perceptions of drug users

The shift in the approach to drug misusers from treatment and rehabilitation to the current focus on punishment and social control can be traced through policy and legislative initiatives that today aim to direct drug users into treatment at every stage of the criminal justice process (NTA, 2006: 8). However, such a shift can only have taken place if the *perception* of the drug user in today's society has been transformed. Historically, drug users were viewed sympathetically and seen as in need of help and treatment – a notion reinforced by the fact that up until the 1960s, drug users were largely middle class, did not generally commit crime to fund their habit and were treated by their own doctors via prescribed morphine and heroin. Addiction was viewed as 'a personal vice, practiced by those with a mental disorder', which posed no threat to society as a whole (Unell, 2002: 225).

Drug use did not remain within the realms of the middle classes and alarm bells began to ring in the 1960s when recreational drug use expanded and was perceived as a threat to young people of any class. A shift towards social control is observed in recommendations from the 2nd Brain Committee 1965 (Bennett and Holloway, 2005: 20), which required the notification of addicts to the Home Office and restricted the prescribing of controlled drugs to doctors licensed by the Home Office practising from agreed premises – thus treatment centres were established. The 1980s in particular saw a further change in emphasis towards social control with the rapid expansion in the availability of drugs in the UK, especially heroin, which gained popularity with new users as a result of its 'marketing' as a smokeable drug. Increasingly, drug misuse began to be linked to poverty, deprivation and, in particular, crime. The growing incidence of HIV among intravenous drug users also focused policy towards public health concerns and harm reduction. Thus, drug-related harm was no longer seen as the sole remit of the person under treatment but society itself was viewed as a source of risk, with drug users viewed not only as transmitters of disease but also as a risk to the public in terms of drug-driven crime. These concerns are reflected in the then Conservative government's first genuinely strategic response to the drug problem, *Tackling Drugs Together: A Strategy for England 1995–1998* (Home Office, 1995), which emphasised the need for stronger action to reduce the supply and demand of illegal drugs (Bennett and Holloway, 2005: 26). The means of achieving this was to be a strong partnership approach via the introduction of 149 Drug Action Teams, which would implement the strategy and adapt it to local circumstances. New Labour continued to build on this partnership approach, launching its strategy, *Tackling Drugs to Build a Better Britain* (Home Office, 1998), the focus of which included major objectives in three areas: crime, young people and public health. Significantly, the role of an anti-drug coordinator was created whose office was to 'combine all the resources of the state in the fight against drugs' (Unell, 2002: 233), thus setting the tone in relation to a 'war on drugs' and clarifying that the Home Office rather than the Department of Health was to have authority in relation to the social control of drugs.

Despite the association between drugs and crime being extremely complex, government policy, as evidenced in the *Updated Drug Strategy* (Home Office, 2002), *Confident Communities in a Secure Britain* (Home Office, 2004) and *Drugs: Protecting Families and Communities* (HM Government, 2008), has increasingly reflected the 'drug use causes crime' viewpoint. This is summed up by David Blunkett, Home Secretary from 2001 to 2004, who asserts that 'drugs damage health ... and turn law abiding citizens into thieves' (Home Office, 2002: 3). The cause of the problem is therefore perceived as a synthesis of illegal drugs and individual drug users rather than in wider social problems. The solution then is the elimination of drug misuse via treatment, which if not accessed via voluntary means, will be coerced.

Hammersley (2008: 72-97) offers a useful chapter on the drugs–crime connection, which extends beyond the above approach, while Bennett and Holloway (2005: 115) also offer further insight into this complex association, which suggests that, contrary to government perceptions, 'criminal behaviour precedes the onset of harder drug use (such as heroin, crack and cocaine)'. Alternatively, Buchanan (2009: 119) sees problematic drug use as symptomatic of serious difficulties and problems associated with social exclusion.

> Consider the drugs–crime connection in relation to those offenders whom you are currently supervising. To what extent is this a clear and straightforward connection?

The development of the partnership approach to drug misuse

The Probation Service has a strong record of working collaboratively with other agencies on an ad hoc basis (Gibbs, 1999: 283). As a result of substance misuse being highlighted as a priority by the incoming New Labour government (Rumgay, 2000: 3), this approach (albeit more formalised in nature) has continued to be the way forward. The National Drug Strategy (Home Office, 1998) stated that, 'because of the complexity of the problem, partnership really is essential at every level'. The emphasis on partnerships has been furthered by the government instructing Drug Action Teams to amalgamate and pool resources with their Crime and Disorder Reduction Partnerships to 'provide the right framework to enable the more effective delivery of the crime reduction and drugs agendas' (Home Office, 2003: 1).

Given the complex arrangements required for the delivery of drug services, it is perhaps unsurprising that collaborative working can be a challenge. The meaning of partnership may also be interpreted differently by those involved in the delivery and can confuse issues in relation to responsibility and accountability. The descriptions used to describe partnership working within the drugs field is also wide and is summarised in Box 13.1.

> **Box 13.1: Definition of partnership working (adapted from NTA, 2005: 1)**
>
> **Partnership work**: organisations with 'differing goals and traditions, linking to work together' (Home Office, 1992).
>
> **Joint working**: involves drug services developing working relationships with other drug-related organisations or services to 'help establish the broadest range of seamless service delivery' (NTA, 2002).
>
> **Shared care**: the joint participation of specialists and primary care, especially general practitioners and pharmacists, in the planned delivery of care for patients with a drug misuse problem 'informed by an enhanced information exchange beyond routine discharge and referral letters' (DH, 1995).
>
> **Integrated care pathways**: used to *define* and *describe* parts of the care process, which involve a number of activities, tasks, procedures or choices. They apply equally to care delivered by one person, one agency or a number of agencies working simultaneously with an individual (Effective Interventions Unit, 2003: 2).
>
> **Multi-agency working:** Involves different agencies cooperating on panels, formal secondments to a different agency to work to common goals or a range of separate services that share a location and work in collaboration (Alcohol Concern, 2006: 1).

The above definitions suggest that a variety of agencies should participate in a planned, coordinated process to deliver a broad range of services tailored to meet the needs of the individual. Partnerships should presumably be advantageous to the person at the receiving end of the process; they should enhance and complement existing provision and seek to supplement rather than supplant the agencies with which they are working. In relation to services for drug misusers, however, the emphasis on what should be prioritised by agencies involved in the delivery of services can be in stark contrast. Health-related policy makes reference to the 'care' process, which involves personal choice reflecting 'client needs and experience' (Effective Interventions Unit, 2003: 2), while criminal justice policy unsurprisingly reflects agencies joining forces and 'exploiting diverse skills and knowledge' to resolve crime for the benefit of the wider community (Crawford, 1997, cited in Minkes et al, 2005: 255). Rumgay (2007: 551) reinforces this, stating that the *enforcement* of a partnership approach by policy makers 'threatens to undermine the value of a good idea through indiscriminate application' and little consideration of what partnership is good *for*. Indeed, much of the literature commending the partnership approach concentrates on benefits to agencies and the improved outcomes that can be expected (economic efficiency, skills enhancement, breaking down barriers, improving communication between services) and there is less emphasis on whether such improved outcomes (if they can be measured) reflect a better and more effective service for service users.

Partnerships involving coerced treatment

Coerced treatment concerns an individual being faced with a choice of consenting to 'comply with what is required of them or facing criminal sanctions' (NTA, 2006: 9). Coerced treatment will therefore involve encouragement and information giving regarding the benefits of engaging with drug services and treatment but it will also involve detailing the likely, less pleasant consequences should the individual decide not to accept the *option* on offer. Seddon (2007: 271) suggests that this reference to *options* 'marks the distinction between coerced and compulsory treatment', as coerced treatment implies an element of choice whereas compulsory treatment does not. This choice has, however, been described as a sham by those opposed to coerced treatment (Seddon, 2007: 272). Consequently, agencies that have not previously been aligned with the criminal justice service but have now been commissioned to deliver interventions with drug misusers will need to embrace this approach (see Gough, this volume).

Table 13.1 outlines the potential differences in perceptions of drug-misusing offenders and the resultant emphasis between criminal justice sector services and drug treatment services.

Table 13.1: Differing perceptions of drug misusing offenders

Criminal justice sector	Drug treatment services
Perceived as an offender who makes rational choices	Perceived as a patient with an illness
Emphasis on punishment/public protection/crime reduction	Emphasis on treatment/harm reduction
Coerced change via strict enforcement	Change promoted via motivation
Time-limited programme of interventions	No time constraints on treatment
Victim's needs prioritised	Patient's needs prioritised although choices may be limited
Focus on risk management	Focus on relapse management
Little emphasis on social factors	Little emphasis on social factors

The facility to *impose* (albeit with consent) treatment in respect of drug misuse was introduced via Section 1A(6) of the 1991 Criminal Justice Act but little use was made of this disposal, with a 1997 thematic inspection suggesting that the reasons for this included a lack of guidance to practitioners, poor communication to sentencers, a lack of funding for treatment and a reluctance by treatment providers and probation staff to engage with legally coerced treatment (Turnbull et al, 2000: 1). Nevertheless, the coerced treatment of drug misusers gained favour based on research evidencing a link between problematic drug use and acquisitive crime, which was said to exceed £1.5 billion per year (Turnbull et al, 2000: 1), with the social and economic costs increasing this figure to 'between £10 billion and £18 billion' (Home Office, 2002: 6). Such figures seemed to require a more drastic response and the 'treatment works' message was reinforced by the National Treatment Outcome Research Study (NTORS), whose findings not only pointed to improved health but also a 25% drop in crimes committed by those who had entered treatment. This reduction was especially marked in relation to the 10% of drug misusers who demonstrated the highest level of criminal activity. This client group who were frequent users of cocaine and heroin were said to be responsible for 76% of crime (Gossop et al, 2001: 19) and clearly were worthy of special measures.

As a response to drug-driven offending, Drug Treatment and Testing Orders (DTTOs) were launched as a new community sentence in 2000, being replaced in April 2005 by the Drug Rehabilitation Requirement (DRR). Like its predecessor, the DRR is delivered by the Probation Service in partnership with drug treatment services and other selected agencies and therefore comprises of a package of interventions addressing offending behaviour alongside treatment, drug testing and court reviews.

Alongside the introduction of the DRR, the government also launched the Drug Interventions Programme (DIP), which was initiated in 2003 and set up Criminal Justice Integrated Teams (CJITs). Their aim is to identify and work with non-statutory cases that might benefit from support, advice, assessment and treatment both before and after they come into contact with the criminal justice system. Typically, teams comprise of arrest referral workers based in custody suites, specialist housing advice workers, and outreach and family support workers. Potential offenders suitable for DRRs are referred and the CJIT works with them to sustain motivation before sentence. According to the Drug Interventions Programme (nd: para 3), over £500 million has now been invested in CJITs.

There are, however, penalties for those who choose not to accept the opportunity of being referred for assessment. Tough Choices, an extension of the Drug Interventions Project and reinforced by the 2005 Drugs Act, introduced sanctions such as the refusal of bail for those who refused tests or failed to attend assessments. The Welfare Reform Bill, which, at the time of writing, is progressing through Parliament, requires drug users to participate in measures (such as drug treatment) aimed at improving their ability to find work and allows for benefit sanctions to be applied to people who fail to comply with the programme without 'good cause' (Coles, 2009: 4).

> Consider proposals in the Welfare Reform Bill. To what extent might benefit sanctions lead to greater compliance with treatment and the ability to access work and training?

Lessons learned in relation to partnerships that involved coerced treatment

The final evaluation report on DTTOs (Turnbull et al, 2000) offers a valuable insight into the difficulties that arise when enforcement agencies and treatment agencies combine to deliver an integrated service. Despite the lessons learned from this it would appear that many of the issues that were apparent then remain unresolved in current arrangements. Turnbull et al (2000: 1) point to effective inter-agency working as being the 'single most important factor to address'. The author's experience as a senior probation officer with responsibility for one of the comparator sites included in the final evaluation report and the subsequent roll-out of DTTOs across a geographically large area would reinforce this. In contrast to the pilot areas the evaluation report highlighted that the comparator sites had established 'more robust partnership approaches which reflected the origins of the projects which were "bottom up" initiatives and had enjoyed longer developmental periods' (Turnbull et al, 2000: 55). Looking back it is evident that the time and effort taken on clarifying roles, responsibilities, confidentiality protocols, assessment and recording procedures and of particular importance ethical issues and differences was well spent. Issues of concern were not restricted to enforced treatment but also included the *amount* of urine tests that should be carried out and the requirement that these tests should be observed. Additionally, major (clinical) decisions concerning the withdrawal of substitute prescribing were no longer to be determined solely by the treatment provider without recourse to the other members of the partnership (namely the Probation Service and the court).

Turnbull et al (2000: 53) refer to problems within the pilot sites that include:

* nurses feeling 'downgraded, undervalued and sometimes feel[ing] their main role is simply to carry out urine tests';
* a high turnover of staff resulting from 'an inability to adapt to inter-agency work' and a degree of personal conflict between individuals from different agencies;
* different working cultures and differing expectations in relation to workloads;
* staff undertaking each other's tasks for which they were not qualified;
* the threat to clinical independence;
* different agency expectations regarding client motivation, treatment and punishment.

Disputes in relation to enforcement and breach can generally be overcome by appropriate discussion and realistic expectations in relation to anticipated progress. Nevertheless, it could be argued that the imposition of targets has tended to focus the attention of the agencies on processes and accountability rather than service provision. McSweeney et al (2007: 482) suggest that research points to coerced treatment methods such as DRRs being hampered by 'an emphasis on bureaucracy, accountability and performance management', with staff morale suffering as a result of the loss of professional discretion. Such difficulties are, however, unlikely to be overcome as the emphasis on enforcement has been strengthened and, as a result of the 2003 Criminal Justice Act, the consequences of breach will result in more onerous conditions being imposed. Additionally, the adverse publicity associated with poor enforcement practice, as in the case of Elliott White, who, while subject to a DRR, was involved in the murder of John Monkton (HMIP, 2006: 21), will naturally result in practitioners tending towards defensive practice and being less flexible (see Clift and also Nash, this volume).

It would be surprising if no resistance were met from treatment agencies, when discussing human rights issues and the erosion of clinical independence. However, issues related to agency priorities and the management of risk and public protection could be equally if not more significant and this is highlighted in the following example.

> Mr A. is on licence after serving four years for theft and a serious assault involving a firearm. He has previous convictions for violence, has a long history of opiate misuse, has no desire to stop using drugs and has continued to misuse drugs while in prison. His relationship with his probation officer is good and he has acknowledged the difficulty in adhering to his licence conditions, which include drug treatment and testing. He has cooperated with drug treatment in the past, during which time he was prescribed injectable diamorphine. His risk of harm during this period was significantly reduced. The dilemma for the partnership was:
>
> - The responsible clinician was not prepared to prescribe injectable diamorphine without having first attempted methadone maintenance. His view was that he was ethically bound to minimise harm and act in the best interest of the patient. His opinion was that he would be no better than a 'dealer' if he prescribed injectable diamorphine. Additionally, he did not want his clinical authority undermined.
> - Mr A. was not prepared to accept methadone and gave good reasons based on past experience. He was clear that he was likely to become involved in drug networks if not treated. He was willing to accept treatment, had cooperated with assessment but wanted choice.
> - Probation Service staff were predominantly concerned with Mr A's risk of harm to the public. It was of lesser concern whether Mr A. was prescribed methadone or heroin as long as he cooperated with treatment and as a consequence the level of risk he posed was reduced.
> - The police's priority was similar to that of the Probation Service in that the social control of Mr A. was their primary concern.

The above highlights problems in relation to ethical practice and the difficulty of resolving disputes which threaten the integrity of other agencies. The resolution of this dilemma was in hindsight resolved by the Probation Service and the police utilising their combined weight under the auspices of Multi-Agency Public Protection Arrangements (MAPPA), which place a duty on other agencies to cooperate in order to protect the public. Thus, the clinician was persuaded to prescribe injectable diamorphine (with added provisions). As Nash (2006: 160) suggests, the combined authority available to MAPPA can result in coercive practice in relation to offenders, other agencies and professionals as well (see Nash, this volume). Turnbull et al (2000: 56) highlight that difficulties in such partnership arrangements are not generally a function of clashes of personality or skills deficits but 'a consequence of joint working on a difficult enterprise by organisations with big differences in working styles, traditions and values'.

Roles and responsibilities

There is a danger that, in establishing close working relationships with other agencies, professional roles and responsibilities become blurred, with drug workers/ nurses undertaking Probation Service responsibilities and vice versa. This is more likely to happen when agencies combine into a team under one roof or long-term secondments occur. The strengths of the partnership approach would suggest that collaboration should bring additional qualities, skills and resources together for the benefit of the service user while also enhancing practitioners' knowledge and understanding of the focus and approach of other agencies. Probation officers can therefore expect to gain insight into health-related issues and in turn health workers will gain understanding of public protection and offender management. However, Rumgay (2000: 138) refers to the potential of workers to lose their professional identity and suggests that specialist posts should be time limited and rotated and seconded staff should retain a presence in their own agency. It is, however, the reality that those commissioning the services of other agencies can use their contractual power to organise service delivery to their own benefit and thus diminish the professional autonomy of partners.

> Requiring criminal justice competence from CPNs [community psychiatric nurses] and medical skills from Probation Officers is an inefficient use of the skills of both groups. (Turnbull et al, 2000: 57)
>
> Reflect on this statement, giving consideration to the model of delivery in your area.

Responding to complex needs

Problematic drug users have complex needs, which may, in addition to drug and alcohol addiction, include:

- mental health problems;
- poor physical health and emotional wellbeing;
- accommodation issues;
- literacy problems;

- debt;
- unemployment.

Additionally, problematic drug use among women is linked to violence, sexual abuse, exploitation, intimidation and poverty (Drugscope, 2005:21). The associated lifestyle may also bring many individuals into situations that are potentially dangerous. This is especially the case for those (predominantly women) involved in prostitution (see Goldhill, this volume). The result is that the anticipated profile of a problematic drug user is an individual with few social bonds who is socially excluded and potentially vulnerable. Such individuals will also have 'criminogenic' needs, which are those needs assessed as being directly linked to offending behaviour and may include drug use, poor problem solving, poor decision making, pro-criminal attitudes and networks and a lack of victim empathy.

Given the above it would seem that a partnership approach that is purposefully structured to meet individual needs is the way forward. The voluntary sector, which has historically been less constrained by cash-linked performance targets, has a good record of responding to local need and supporting individuals in flexible and innovative ways. However, Vennard and Hedderman (2009:237) suggest that the current government arrangements that require adherence by partners to a national framework fail to respond to diversity at a local level and '[runs] the risk of demoralising front line staff' who rather than prioritising service provision that reflects the core values and unique strengths of their own agency find themselves having to fit into and respond to criminal justice priorities. Consequently, if such agencies become solely dependent on government funding, they run the risk of becoming just another business venture that offers an undifferentiated service.

Although there has been considerable investment in tackling problematic drug use, little attention has been given to the sequencing of integrated social support (Audit Commission, 2004:3). In particular, it is suggested that failure to attend to needs in relation to accommodation, employment, training and education and aftercare is likely to undermine progress in other areas. Unfortunately, this is in direct conflict with the Offender Management Model, which instructs offender managers to give priority to punitive sanctions when sequencing interventions: 'If the punitive elements in the sentence are not put into effect briskly and delivered effectively, the credibility of NOMS – and all of its other objectives – is put at risk' (NOMS, 2006:32).

In responding to complex needs, there is a danger of multi-agency overload in that individuals who have previously had few commitments become overwhelmed with agency support. McSweeney and Hough's (2006) five-year research aimed to coordinate statutory and voluntary provision across 12 Inner London boroughs and employed 120 practitioners. The agencies received over 5,000 referrals from individuals with multiple needs and assessed over 3,000 but found that half of service users only engaged with one service (2006:112). It is suggested that it is unrealistic for those with multiple needs to be sufficiently organised and motivated to access a number of services simultaneously and there is a danger in overloading services in response to high needs and thus in the context of coerced treatment and enforcement, setting offenders up to fail. Implementation failure was deemed to be a further reason for poor uptake and this included poor sequencing of services, problematic assessment processes that involved the individual being subjected to separate assessment procedures by each agency and 'funding regimes that eroded mutual trust and did too little to foster joint working' (2006: 112).

What is effective?

Current literature points to drug misuse treatment (accessed voluntarily or via court-mandated sanctions) as being effective in terms of a reduction in the use of illegal drugs and associated crime, with improvements in health, social and personal functioning (McLellan, 1997, cited in Gossop, 2006: 4). However, regardless of the route of access, attention should be given to realistic expectations (McSweeney et al, 2007: 485) and the appropriate coordination and sequencing of services that gives consideration to social and personal needs, without which, Buchanan (2009: 12) suggests, relapse is inevitable. However, in relation to care planning, only 26% of local partnerships are reported as being 'good or excellent' with this measure, reflecting the *existence* of a plan rather than the quality of it (NTA, 2008, cited in Clinks et al, 2008: 10) or the experience of those using the service.

For further information on care planning and the treatment journey, see NTA (2006).

Treatment retention is indicative of effectiveness, and individualised treatment choice and the *quality* of the professional relationship are the strongest predictors of patient drop-out or treatment retention (Najavits et al, 2000: 2163). This is supported by Burnett and McNeill (2005: 232), who suggest that a 'person-centred' approach is necessary for effective work and arguably this approach should be elicited from all the agencies that are involved in the process of treatment, reintegration and change. Nevertheless, Rassool (1998), cited in Eley et al (2005: 404), suggests that many care professionals hold negative attitudes and stereotypical perceptions of drug misusers.

The notion of a more holistic, one-stop shop is supported by service users (Eley et al, 2005: 407). However, current provision within drug treatment clinics does not fit into this model and cannot generally offer practical help such as debt counselling, assistance with accommodation and benefits, parenting classes and crèches – arguably provisions that could be supported by partnership arrangements. Although measures are being taken to improve accessibility, current provision has been criticised for:

- emphasising substitute prescribing rather than abstinence, detoxification or residential rehabilitation;
- responding primarily to the needs of white male opiate users;

- not being sufficiently welcoming to women;
- not responding to the needs of minority ethnic groups.

It could also be argued that the current arrangements perceive drug misusers as troublesome, time consuming and different from normal citizens and as such they are corralled into discrete services (drug clinics, structured day care, accredited programmes) with others like them, which takes little account of the different stages of change, levels of motivation or the wish to follow other routes to address their drug misuse. Reintegration that may of necessity require individuals to disassociate themselves from other drug users can therefore be compromised.

Conclusion

Healthy partnerships should allow agencies to maintain their uniqueness and should further the aims of all the agencies rather than the most powerful. However, arrangements in relation to coerced treatment do not always reflect an approach based on equality and negotiation. Services that may previously have been defined as 'help', such as drug treatment, counselling, education, training and employment, are now wrapped up in notions of punishment, a situation that very few agencies would have formerly tolerated but have had to accommodate for financial survival. McSweeney and Hough (2006: 121) suggest that the government's vision to deliver a 'mixed economy' of providers is beset with difficulties, which are largely due to competitive tendering. The emphasis on value for money results in contracting out, which is characterised by 'caution, greed and meanness' (McSweeney and Hough, 2006: 121), with agencies having to look after their own interests to prove their worth rather than working in genuine partnership.

Summary of key points

- The effectiveness of partnerships should be measured in terms of advantages to service users rather than the benefits to the agencies involved.
- The true spirit of partnership, which concerns an equal relationship between agencies, is unlikely to be possible within the context of coerced treatment or where partners compete for resources.
- Rewarding good partnership work in addition to meeting single agency targets is likely to encourage collaboration and discourage competitiveness (McSweeney and Hough, 2006: 120).
- There is a need for a 'generic assessment' or assessments that are able to cross-reference so that the same information is not gathered many times over.
- Careful attention should be given to the sequencing and amount of interventions that the offender is expected to attend – prioritising punishment is not deemed to be effective.
- Effective drug treatment initiatives are likely to be undermined by bureaucratic processes and target-driven outcomes.

Further reading

The following document offers a good insight into the delivery of drug treatment services: National Treatment Agency for Substance Misuse (2009) *The Story of Drug Treatment: Effective Treatment Changing Lives*. London: National Treatment Agency. Available at www. nta.nhs.uk/publications/documents/story_of_drug_treatment.pdf

The New Bridge Foundation (founded in 1956) offers a good example of long-term, voluntary support, mentoring and practical help for prisoners both during their sentence and after release. See full details on their website at: www.newbridgefoundation.org.uk

A strong example of a coordinated response to a specific issue – drug-related deaths – is offered in the following article: Bennett, J., Stevens, G., Walker, A., Williams, H., Winter, A. and Hamilton-Deeley, V. (2006) 'A co-ordinated response to the high drug death rate in Brighton and Hove', *Probation Journal*, 53(3), 265-77.

The bureaucracy that threatens to undermine the provision of drug services is fully explained by Nick Davies in a *Guardian* special investigation: 'How Britain is losing the drugs war'. *The Guardian*, 22 May 2003. Available at www.guardian.co.uk/uk/2003/may/22/drugsandalcohol.ukcrime

References

Alcohol Concern (2006) *Multi-Agency Working: Guidance for Professionals Working with Problem Drinking Parents*. London: Alcohol Concern. Available at www.alcoholandfamilies.org.uk/briefings/13.14.pdf

Audit Commission (2004) *Drug Misuse 2004: Reducing the Local Impact*. Wetherby: Audit Commission Publications.

Bennett, T. and Holloway, K. (2005) *Understanding Drugs, Alcohol and Crime*. Maidenhead: Open University Press.

Buchanan, J. (2009) 'Understanding and misunderstanding problem drug use: working together', in Carnwell, R. and Buchanan, J. (eds) *Effective Practice in Health, Social Care and Criminal Justice: A Partnership Approach*. Maidenhead: Open University Press.

Burnett, R. and McNeill, F. (2005) 'The place of the officer–offender relationship in assisting offenders to desist from crime', *Probation Journal*, 52(3), 221-43.

Clinks, DrugScope, Homeless Link and Mind (2008) *In from the Margins: Making Every Adult Matter*. Available at www.drugmisuse.isdscotland.org/publications/abstracts/meam_report.htm

Coles, A. (2009) *Liberty's Second Reading Briefing on the Welfare Reform Bill in the House of Lords*. London: Liberty. Available at www.liberty-human-rights.org.uk/pdfs/policy-09/welfarereform-2nd-reading-lords.pdf

Drug Interventions Programme (nd) *Strategy*. London: Home Office. Available at http://drugs.homeoffice.gov.uk/drug-interventions-programme/strategy/

Drugscope (2005) *Using Women.* London: Drugscope. Available at www.drugscope. org.uk/Resources/Drugscope/Documents/PDF/Other/UWreport.pdf

Effective Interventions Unit (2003) *Integrated Care Pathways Guide 1: Definitions and Concepts.* Edinburgh: Scottish Executive Health Department. Available at http://learnx.iriss.ac.uk/IntraLibrary?command=open-previewandlearning_object_key=i9262n30641t

Eley, S., Beaton K. and McIvor, G. (2005) 'Co-operation in drug treatment services: views of offenders on court orders in Scotland', *The Howard Journal*, 44(4), 400-10.

Gibbs, A. (1999) 'The forgotten voice: Probation Service users and partnerships', *The Howard Journal*, 38(3), 283-99.

Gossop, M. (2006) *Treating Drug Misuse Problems: Evidence of Effectiveness.* London: National Treatment Agency.

Gossop, M., Marsden, J. and Stewart, D. (2001) *The National Treatment Outcome Research Study: Changes in Substance Use, Health and Criminal Behaviour during the Five Years after Intake.* London: National Addiction Centre.

Hammersley, R. (2008) *Drugs and Crime.* Cambridge: Polity Press.

HM Government (2008) *Drugs: Protecting Families and Communities: The 2008 Drug Strategy.* London: Home Office.

HMIP (Her Majesty's Inspectorate of Probation) (2006) *An Independent Review of a Serious Further Offence Case: Damien Hanson and Elliott White.* London: HMIP.

Home Office (1992) *Partnership Working in Dealing with Offenders in the Community.* London: Home Office.

Home Office (1998) *Tackling Drugs to Build a Better Britain: The Government's Ten-Year Strategy for Tackling Drugs Misuse.* London: Cabinet Office. Available at www.archive.official-documents.co.uk/document/cm39/3945/strategy.htm

Home Office (2002) *Updated Drug Strategy 2002.* London: Home Office Drug Strategy Directorate.

Home Office (2003) *Drug Action Team and Crime and Disorder Reduction Partnership Integration/Closer Working: Further Guidance.* London: Crime Reduction Delivery Team/Partnership and Regions (Drugs Unit). Available at www.crimereduction. homeoffice.gov.uk/integration_a.pdf

Home Office (2004) *Confident Communities in a Secure Britain: The Home Office Strategic Plan 2004–2008.* Norwich: The Stationery Office.

McSweeney, T. and Hough, M. (2006) 'Supporting offenders with multiple needs: lessons for the "mixed economy" model of service provision', *Criminology and Criminal Justice*, 6(1), 107-25.

McSweeney, T., Stevens, A., Hunt, N. and Turnbull, P.J. (2007) 'Twisting arms or a helping hand? Assessing the impact of "coerced" and comparable "voluntary" drug treatment options', *British Journal of Criminology*, 47, 470-90.

Ministry of Justice (2008) *Working with the Third Sector to Reduce Re-offending: Securing Effective Partnerships 2008–2011.* London: Ministry of Justice.

Minkes, J., Hammersley, R. and Raynor, P. (2005) 'Partnership in working with young offenders with substance misuse problems', *The Howard Journal*, 44(3), 254-68.

Najavits, L.M., Crits-Christoph, P. and Dierberger, A. (2000) 'Clinician's impact on the quality of substance use disorder treatment', *Substance Use and Misuse*, 35(12-14), 2161-90.

Nash, M. (2006) *Public Protection and the Criminal Justice Process*. Oxford: Oxford University Press.

NOMS (National Offender Management Service) (2006) *The NOMS Offender Management Model*. London: Home Office.

NTA (National Treatment Agency for Substance Misuse) (2002) *Models of Care for the Treatment of Drug Users: Promoting Quality, Efficiency and Effectiveness In Drug Misuse Treatment Services in England: Part 2: Full Reference Report*. London: NTA.

NTA (2005) *Working in Partnership*. Developing Drug Service Policies: 8. London: NTA.

NTA (2006) *Models of Care for Treatment of Adult Drug Misusers: Update 2006*. London: NTA. Available at www.nta.nhs.uk/publications/documents/nta_modelsofcare_update_2006_moc3.pdf

NTA (2009) *The Story of Drug Treatment: Effective Treatment Changing Lives*. London: NTA. Available at www.nta.nhs.uk/publications/documents/story_of_drug_treatment.pdf

Rumgay, J. (2000) *The Addicted Offender*. Basingstoke: Palgrave Macmillan.

Rumgay, J. (2007) 'Partnerships in probation', in Gelsthorpe, L. and Morgan, R. (eds) *Handbook of Probation* (pp 542-64). Cullompton: Willan Publishing.

Seddon, T. (2007) 'Coerced drug treatment in the criminal justice system: conceptual, ethical and criminological issues', *Criminology and Criminal Justice*, 7(3), 269-86.

Turnbull, P.J., McSweeney, T., Webster, R., Edmunds, M. and Hough, M. (2000) *Drug Treatment and Testing Orders: Final Evaluation Report*, Home Office Research Study 212. London: Home Office Research, Development and Statistics Directorate.

Unell, I. (2002) 'Controlling drug use: where is the justice?', in Ward, D., Scott, J. and Lacey, M. (eds) *Probation Working for Justice* (pp 220-37). Oxford: Oxford University Press.

Vennard, J. and Hedderman, C. (2009) 'Helping offenders into employment: how far is the voluntary sector expertise valued in a contracting-out environment', *Criminology and Criminal Justice*, 9(2), 225-45.

CHAPTER 14

Dual diagnosis: issues and implications for criminal justice partnerships

Anne Rees

Aims of the chapter

- To consider language and labels.
- To discuss theoretical perspectives on dual diagnosis and their implications for practice.
- To analyse policy in relation to mental health legislation, and guidance from the Department of Health and the National Treatment Agency for Substance Misuse on working with dual diagnosis issues.
- To review the development of separate services provision, and the lack of integrated approaches, and the implications for service users and practitioner alike within the criminal justice system.
- To present what the research evidence suggests is effective practice in working with dual diagnosis.

Dual diagnosis is not a new phenomenon, but has become more visible since the 1980s with the 'care in the community' programme leading to hospitalised psychiatric patients being housed in the community. Along with this development, psychiatric services have developed accordingly and there has been a move from a traditionally medical bias to more of a focus on the social aspects of mental health problems (Boardman, 2005). As an increasing number of people with mental health problems have tended to be housed in the more deprived areas of cities, where accommodation is cheapest, they have as a consequence come into contact with illicit drugs and alcohol. This combination of mental health problems, drug and alcohol use and social deprivation has given rise to apparently complex and intractable needs, with more professional groupings involved in the planning and delivery of services. The issue of dual diagnosis continues to be a major challenge to the commissioning and delivery of services.

The partnership focus on the care and management of people with a dual diagnosis is a recent policy-led initiative developed primarily with those working within the National Health Service (NHS), social services and the voluntary sector. However, these partnership initiatives are beginning to filter through to the criminal justice system, with schemes involving both the Prison and the National Probation Service. As dictated by policy, these initiatives continue to be primarily led by the NHS. Despite these innovations there continue to be concerns about the fragmentation of service provision (DH, 2002a, 2007; Hawkings and Gilburt, 2004). This chapter seeks to consider the implications of the different developments of service provision for those with dual diagnosis within the criminal justice systems and the implications for multi-agency working.

One of the biggest factors influencing work with people with dual diagnosis is the 'mission' of a particular agency and their own perceptions of what support they can actually offer, with for example mental health services often holding the view that substance misuse is either the contributing factor or the causal factor of the person's mental disorder. As a consequence, many operate under the premise that once the misuse is dealt with, a more comprehensive assessment can be made. Those working within the substance misuse field often comment that they lack the expertise in coping with such disordered individuals and thus 'bat them back' to mental health services. Hawkings and Gilburt (2004: 23) argue that the first hurdle that practitioners need to overcome is the assessment process because individuals become 'preoccupied' with identifying whether the mental health issue or the substance misuse is the primary problem. This may then inform who takes the lead in developing interventions (see Pakes and Winstone, and also Heath, this volume).

Language and labels

Terminology has an impact on practitioners' common understanding when discussing those who experience both mental health and substance misuse problems. The terms 'co-morbidity', 'dual diagnosis' and 'complex needs' are used interchangeably both in the literature and between and within different agencies. The term 'co-morbidity' is used to describe two or more disorders that occur in the same person either simultaneously or sequentially (Volkow, 2008: 1). This is also referred to as 'concurrent co-morbidity' and 'successive co-morbidity' (Hodges et al, 2006: 8). The term 'co-morbidity' is more commonly used in (American) literature from both the health and the psychiatric field.

The term 'dual diagnosis' implies two existing problems; these could be two mental health conditions such as schizophrenia and depression, or a mental health condition and a learning disability. However, the term is more commonly used to refer to the combination of a mental disorder and substance misuse such as drugs and alcohol. The confusion around the term has been discussed extensively in the literature and the majority of writers set out by defining both the complexities of the terms used and also the definitions underpinning the term they intend to use. For example, Afuwape (2003: 5) states that the term 'dual diagnosis' is often 'restricted to specify a more serious mental illness and a substance misuse disorder', while El Guebaly (1990, cited in Afuwape, 2003: 5) 'proposes that the term dual diagnosis should include two over-lapping but clearly separate groups of individuals. One subgroup with major substance and psychiatric illnesses, whilst the other subgroup uses substances in ways that effect the course and treatment of mental illness'.

The World Health Organization (WHO, 1994) and the United Nations Office on Drugs and Crime (UNODC) define dual diagnosis as 'a person diagnosed as having an alcohol or drug abuse problem in addition to some other diagnosis, usually psychiatric such as a mood disorder or schizophrenia' (Hodges et al, 2006: 8). For the diagnosis of mental health and substance-related disorders such as substance abuse and dependency, the *Diagnostic and Statistical Manual of Mental Disorders* (4th revised edition) (DSM-IV-TR) (American Psychiatric Association, 2000) is used. The *International Statistical Classification of Diseases* (ICD-10) (WHO, 2007) identifies mental and behavioural disorders due to psychoactive substance use (F10–F19). It identifies a wide range of disorders attributable to psychoactive substances that are not clinically prescribed and very clearly states that it *excludes* the abuse of non-dependence-producing substances (WHO, 2007, chapter 5).

Although labels can be stigmatising and often unhelpful for the individual concerned, it is important to have a clearly agreed definition as this will influence decisions of intervention, resource allocation and service provision. The *Dual Diagnosis Good Practice Guidance* issued by the Department of Health (DH, 2002a), dictated that local areas develop their own focused definition to enable local areas to achieve an agreed definition that reflects local levels of need. However, it has simultaneously created a lot of the confusion around terminology, definitions, roles and responsibilities both within and between agencies.

Theoretical perspectives on dual diagnosis and their implications for practice

There is a range of theoretical perspectives that individually focus on mental disorders and substance misuse. Mental disorders include psychotic disorders, anxiety disorders, neurosis and personality disorders and there is a range of differing theoretical perspectives on their aetiology, for example that they are hereditary, due to stress vulnerability, due to biological factors, are drug induced or are socially constructed. Similarly, substance misuse varies from experimental, recreational, dependent (physical and psychological) and poly use, and there is a range of theoretical models on aetiology from the disease model, to the alcohol or drug syndrome model, to social learning models of addiction.

Although not as widely researched, many of the theoretical models for dual diagnosis are a variance of some of the models identified above. Mueser et al (1998) suggest four general models.

Common factor models

Common factor models consider genetic vulnerabilities, which may predispose individuals to developing both addictions and other mental illnesses. It is estimated that '40-60% of an individual's vulnerability to addiction is attributable to genetics'

(Volkow, 2008: 4) by either genetically increasing the likelihood of developing addictions and mental health disorders or acting indirectly by altering how an individual responds to stressful factors. However, Mueser et al (1998) have found inconclusive evidence to support this theory, arguing that factors such as poverty, socioeconomic status and cognitive functioning may be the contributing factors rather than genetic predisposition.

Secondary substance use disorder models

These models comprise two broad categories: the supersensitivity model and the psychosocial risk factor model. The latter contains three components: self-medication, alleviation of dysphoria and multiple risk factors. It is a commonly held assumption that self-medication with illicit substances is used to alleviate psychotic symptoms or to counteract the side effects of prescribed medication. However, Banerjee et al (2002: 5) found little evidence to support this as investigations into patterns of substance abuse found little relationship between specific symptoms and the use of particular substances.

The supersensitivity model claims that a combination of genetic and early environmental events, when coupled with environmental stress, can cause the onset or trigger a relapse of a mental disorder. This is not be confused with the 'supersensitive' model identified by Banerjee et al. This model suggests that some individuals are 'supersensitive' to the effects of substances; hence a small quantity of a substance could have powerful effects and may result in the early onset of mental health disorders (Banerjee et al, 2002: 6).

Secondary psychiatric disorder models

This approach begins from the premise that substance misuse can lead to mental disorders. This is an ongoing debate, which has focused on the links between stimulants, hallucinogenics and cannabis misuse and the development of mental disorder. Rethink (2009) reports that people who use cannabis are 40% more likely to experience psychosis than people who do not use cannabis. Banerjee et al (2002: 6) report similar findings – that heavy and long-term use of drugs can result in physical and mental health problems. McMurran (2002: 17) acknowledges that hallucinogenics can induce a variety of psychotic symptoms, and that cannabis use is linked to panic and paranoia. However, she maintains that this area needs much more careful investigation as there may be a multitude of causal factors involved. This theory is an influential factor underpinning the development of policies and legislation, for example the reclassification of cannabis from a class C to a class B drug in January 2009 (Home Office, 2009).

Bi-directional models

This model contains elements of some of the above models and suggests an interactional effect – substance misuse causes mental disorder and the mental disorder influences the continued misuse of substances.

These differing theories can influence a range of factors inherent in both individual or agency cultures and philosophies, which can hinder the effectiveness of working together. For example, Buchanan (2009: 121) states that there are four key aspects to working with drug misusers: health, social, legal and psychological. Although generally agreed that all four aspects need to be addressed, what is disputed is the importance given to each aspect. So, for example, if the problem is viewed primarily as a health issue, there will be a belief that an individual will not be able to address their mental health needs until they have begun work on becoming drug free.

The development of policy provision for dual diagnosis within the criminal justice system

The early 1990s saw a plethora of government directives driving the criminal justice partnership agenda, such as *Partnerships in Dealing with Offenders in the Community* (Home Office, 1990a) and *Partnerships in Crime Prevention* (Home Office, 1990b) (Rumgay, 2007: 545). However, there is little in terms of strategic documents related to the criminal justice system and multi-agency partnerships with a specific focus on dual diagnosis. Much of the policy and good practice guidelines have been developed by the Department of Health and have a specific remit of focusing on mental disorder and substance misuse as two parallel developments. Where dual diagnosis and criminal justice are considered, they are often embedded in mental health documents and only mentioned briefly. However, it is also due to the notion that 'The statutory mental health sector has the responsibility for co-ordinating and providing a multi-agency approach to people with co-morbidity' (Substance Misuse and Mental Health Co-Morbidity [dual diagnosis] Health Advisory Service, 2001, cited in Ministry of Justice and and DH, 2009: 19).

Although dual diagnosis was recognised as an important and challenging issue for the mental health services, the *National Service Framework for Mental Health* (DH, 1999) gave no guidance on the standards or service models with which to work with those dually diagnosed. The first and most prominent policy, introduced to plug this gap in service provision, is the *Mental Health Policy Implementation Guide: Dual Diagnosis Good Practice Guide* (DH, 2002a). This acknowledged that 'substance misuse is already part of mainstream mental health services and there was a need to work closely with specialist substance misuse services' (2002a: 3). It acknowledged the complex relationship between mental health and substance misuse and clarified that the misuse of substances by mental health clients should be taken as the norm rather than the exception. This document clarified that the prime responsibility for those with mental disorders and substance misuse problems lay with the mental health teams and that clients would benefit from an integrated model of care by one team rather than parallel or sequential models of care (Abou–Saleh, 2004: 352).

Acknowledging that this would not meet the needs of all, the guide stipulated the requirement that Local Implementation Teams work in partnership with Drug Action Teams. It also outlined the need for both services to provide 'specialist' support and training to the other when and where needed. There was little reference to co-working with criminal justice agencies; however, this later became one of the four programme areas of focus for the National Institute for Mental Health (England) (NIMHE). NIMHE is part of the Care Services Improvement Partnership, which was developed from the Department of Health's commitment to joint working (DH, 2002a). NIMHE's main aim is to break down barriers and develop flexible ways of working in order to improve the quality of life of people who experience mental distress and there are eight regional development centres with a remit to establish dual diagnosis networks (Gorry and Todd, 2008).

More recently we have seen the development of good working practices in terms of good practice guidelines developed by the Ministry of Justice and Department of Health *Guide for the Management of Dual Diagnosis for Prisons* (2009), which provides a comprehensive guide to working with dual diagnosis both within the prison and on release. The guide is focused on multi-agency work between prison mental health workers and prison staff or external agencies such as mental health or substance misuse services; however, there is little discussion of the role of the offender manager and the responsibility of the National Probation Service.

The Bradley Report (2009) acknowledged that dual diagnosis is common in the prison system, and Lord Bradley found that 'mental health services and substance misuse services in prison do not currently work well together' (2009: p 16: section 50) and recommended the urgent development of services for those dually diagnosed. Throughout the report Lord Bradley makes clear recommendations for closer agency working and coordinated responses. However, these were not necessarily inclusive of the National Probation Service, and reference to the role of offender managers was in terms of ensuring they were aware of their role in the Care Programme Approach.

The development of separate service provision, and the lack of an integrated approach; implications for service users and practitioners alike within the criminal justice system

It has been acknowledged that partnership working is an essential component to working with those who are dual diagnosed (McMurran, 2002: 18). However, the developments of separate policies have influenced differing models and philosophies of working practices. The mental health services have developed the Care Programme Approach, while the substance misuse services have implemented

Models of Care. Both models encourage the active participation of the client in the development of their care plan and in fact encourage service user participation at all levels in terms of service user representatives, planning groups and forums, right up to board level and active participation in decision making (DH, 2002b, 2008).

Although these policies have similar aims and objectives, the joint working between the drug services, alcohol services and mental health services is not without problems. Hawkings and Gilburt (2004: 30) found that, in practice, these services continue to experience a range of problems in coordinating care across professional disciplines. Staff may hold different views of priorities and needs and there is difficulty in planning joint arrangements, resulting in delayed assessments and reviews. Furthermore, when services are under pressure, those service users not deemed a priority are not receiving the appropriate levels of care and contact. Some service users may be under the care of a psychiatrist but not actually engaging with them. Added to this, those not deemed to be in sufficient need may not have an identified Care Programme Approach in place. An overriding conflict in joined-up practices is in the ethos of the services; mental health services are required to treat all patients, whether consensual or not, and substance misuse services work with those who want to be helped, are motivated to change or have been coerced by the courts into agreeing to access treatment as a condition of a Court Order.

The difficulties experienced above are reflected further when agencies from the criminal justice system are involved. Two models are about care and rehabilitation while the National Probation Service has moved to a law enforcement agency, with a dominant focus on criminogenic risk assessment in order to identify reoffending and harm (Nash, 2005). The Care Programme Approach and the models of care have a strong ethos of service user participation, whereas the main role of the National Probation Service is one of public protection and risk management, with no specific focus of offender participation in the development of policies. From the outset, one obvious barrier to joint working is language and labels: two agencies identify their client group as 'clients' or 'service users', while probation uses the term 'offender', reflecting the different viewpoints of the organisations.

Some examples of good partnership practices have been developed within different criminal justice agencies such as the Youth Justice Teams, the Prison Service and the Multi-Agency Public Protection Arrangements (MAPPA) within the National Probation Service, the Prison Service and the police. Youth justice already has very close multi-agency collaboration with alcohol, drugs and mental health workers working within the teams or based on the same premises where contact with the medical staff and visiting psychiatrist makes the whole process of referral and joint working much easier but these too have their problems.

The Prison Service has made inroads to developing multi-agency working in terms of dual diagnosis (Ministry of Justice and DH, 2009); in HMP Liverpool, dual diagnosis nurses worked closely with a range of prisons initially developing working protocols and more recently this has evolved to see the creation of two specialist dual diagnosis posts. The in-reach teams pick up the majority of those with mild to moderate mental health problems and the dual diagnosis teams sieve through approximately 25 referrals a week, picking up about six of those cases. (As a rough estimate, of possibly 1,400 inmates, 800 may have a mental disorder, of whom 600 could be identified as having a dual diagnosis.) In terms of partnership working the dual diagnosis team have built up relationships with those primarily working in the mental health field; they attend MAPPA panels, work closely with the prison's probation team and are developing good working relationships with prison officers, which has then paved the way to provide training.

A probation practitioner case study

To give an overview of some of the practical issues involved in working with dual diagnosis the author has had discussions with probation practitioners in a large metropolitan area in the north of England. These discussions can be placed within an Action Research framework, to identify the links between practice and policy in this difficult and complex area of work. Action Research is defined by Reason and Bradbury (2008: 4) as 'a participatory process concerned with developing practical knowing in the pursuit of worthwhile human purposes. It seeks to bring together action and reflection, theory and practice, in participation with others, in the pursuit of practical solutions to issues of pressing concern….'.

Of the probation officers spoken to, the average caseload was 75 cases. Of these, an average of 25/26 cases were being supervised in the community and subject to licence conditions. Six offender managers were able to identify between two and four cases with a diagnosis of mental health problems, in comparison with those officers who had an expressed interest in mental health who identified approximately 10 cases. These were cases with either a diagnosed or suspected mental health problem.

However, these figures do not correlate with published figures, which suggest that almost 90% of adult prisoners are likely to have a mental illness (DH and HMPS, 2001, cited in Minogue, 2009: 213), suggesting that more of the 25/26 cases would have a mental disorder. This highlights a major issue of assessment, either within the prison setting or upon release. It could be the case that these issues may not be recognised due to the substance misuse masking the mental health problem, or vice versa. Furthermore, practitioners may not feel qualified to diagnose such issues or they may not have sufficient knowledge or confidence to ask for an assessment.

Of the cases where there was a clear dual diagnosis, they were managed in accordance with their risk classification. Those offenders assessed as posing a high risk of serious harm were being managed in accordance with the MAPPA guidelines, whereas those who were assessed as posing a low/medium risk of harm, were in contact with psychiatric services, and managed in accordance with the Care Programme Approach, which was integrated with their sentence plan (see Clift and also Nash, this volume).

Those with identified substance misuse problems and with 'possible' mental health problems were managed in partnership with the relevant substance misuse service. Possible reasons for this closer alliance with drugs partnership agencies (rather than mental health services) could be that probation officers feel more confident and better informed in dealing with substance misuse, and also because mild anxiety and depression are not viewed as a mental health problem. Furthermore, the substance misuse may be seen as the primary/influencing factor for intervention; "… it's hard to work out what's really going on because they [offenders] have used drugs and alcohol as a mask for so long" (conversation with probation officer).

The cases managed under the MAPPA framework tended to have a prior historical diagnosis of mental disorder and substance misuse problems, and they possibly had a history of involvement with mental health services. These were usually identified prior to or during serving a custodial sentence, and therefore had gone through the referral process with the management of the licence being guided by multi-agency agreements. Feedback from offender managers showed a good level of inter-agency partnership as a direct result of statutory agreements and legislative frameworks. An observation of a MAPPA meeting demonstrated the strengths of partnership working when there were clear role definitions, a format and process for information sharing and joint planning of interventions, including who would do what.

Other than the cases dealt with under MAPPA, very few cases being jointly worked with mental health services could be identified. From the probation officers spoken to there was a mixed response in regard to the level of communication, and the effectiveness of those arrangements. Comments ranged from "we work well together coz I've got to know him [community psychiatric nurse; CPN]" through to that of lone working practices: "They [CPNs] just get on with it [mental health visits and contact] but I find I have to chase them [CPN] up for information and stuff". The probation officers tended to work more closely with the drug services as they reportedly had good links with them.

Those cases with a range of agencies involved such as CPNs, drugs workers, probation officers and accommodation providers "require everyone to know what the other is doing and this is not often the case". The lack of coordination of services resulted in the offender becoming 'partnershipped out' by too many appointments. This would appear to support Rumgay's (2007: 555) view that while there appears to be a universal agreement that partnerships are a good thing … what is it good for?

Those probation officers working in the drug rehabilitation teams reported little in the way of partnership working with mental health workers and felt they focused on drug issues with the drugs partnerships making the relevant assessments and referrals: "we continue to focus on drug use and can then liaise with mental health if needed". This reflects the findings of Khanom et al (2009: 6) in their research into the low-level use of Mental Health Treatment Orders; they found that courts were more likely to make a Drug Rehabilitation Requirement (DRR) rather than a mental health treatment requirement. Some explanations offered were that they were more familiar with the DRR, knew it was a dedicated team and processes were in place for making and managing a DRR. Yet probation staff working in DRRs have had little or no training in managing those with mental health problems.

What is effective in working with dual diagnosis?

Throughout this chapter the need for a close inter-agency approach to working with those dually diagnosed has been emphasised. It is clear that the co-existence of a range of problems needs to be addressed in order to achieve a reduction in both harms to the individual and harms to the community.

There are three identified models of working with those dually diagnosed: the sequential/serial model, the parallel model and the integrated model. The sequential treatment model is the least favoured; it implies treatment in stages, dealing with one problem at a time, that is, dealing with the substance misuse then referring on to the relevant mental health team for further treatment. Fraught with difficulties, it assumes that the problem dealt with first is the primary problem and once addressed the other will be alleviated. However, as we know, the two are often mutually interactive. Those that have proved the more popular with policy makers and researchers are the parallel and integrated models.

The parallel model focuses on both treatments at the same time by different agencies, which while it sounds more effective is not without its problems. It requires the individual to attend appointments on different days with different agencies, different staff and more commonly at different venues. Individuals often find it difficult to comply with the range of appointments and as motivation reduces they are more likely to disengage with services. The Department of Health (2002a: 22) believes that this model would be more effective in delivering a joined-up service if delivered on one site. This suggestion has been taken forward in the *Improving Health, Supporting Justice* consultation document (DH, 2007) and the Department has advocated for a 'one-stop shop' model of service delivery. This model enables closer working between agencies for a more focused, joined-up delivery of service; increases access to a range of services for those excluded from mainstream services and reduces disengagement. However, this needs to be taken forward cautiously and it may not alter the differing ethos of those agencies. There is the danger that this approach may exclude people from services when they have failed to attend one of the other services and if behaviour is unacceptable within the building then they may be excluded from all services.

> What are the ethical implications of this approach?

If services were to be integrated under one roof, Drake and Mueser (2000) suggest that multidisciplinary specialists, based not just in the same building but in the same team, could use their skills and knowledge to develop combined common procedures. They argue that the research repeatedly demonstrates this approach as being successful in engaging and retaining dual diagnosed patients. This moves us towards the integrated model, which builds on the latter concurrent provision of services but is delivered by one member of staff in the same team within the same setting. This model has been introduced in the Prison Service with the introduction of the integrated drug treatment system, which brings healthcare and CARAT (counselling, assessment, referral, advice and throughcare) teams closer together (Ministry of Justice and DH, 2009). This model has proved to be effective in that it differs from the other models; it is based on trust rather than criticism, reduction of harm rather than abstinence and looks at reducing anxiety rather than challenging denial (Abou-Saleh, 2004: 356). However, McMurran (2002: 18) has found that although some studies show integrated treatments to be more effective, the results of research findings were inconclusive, suggesting that it may be the intervention, rather than the service delivery, that is the effective element.

In order for interventions to be effective, they need to be delivered by well-trained staff who can effectively assess and match offenders to treatment (Falk, 2004). Given those with complex needs have a tendency to disengage from services, assertive outreach is effective in engaging and maintaining contact as well as providing intensive support, motivating people to change, having a broader focus on relationships, work, leisure and accommodation and taking a longitudinal approach to work with relapse of either mental health problems or substance misuse problems (McMurran, 2002: 18). Given that lack of motivation is one of the most common and pervasive problems among clients with dual diagnosis, motivation interviewing is effective in enabling those with substance misuse problems to identify commitments to change, set goals and achieve change.

For more information on motivational interviewing read: Fuller, C. and Taylor, P. (2003) *Toolkit of Motivational Skills: A Practice Handbook for Using Motivational Skills in the Work of the Probation Service*. London: NPD.

Summary of key points and future direction

- Due to a range of factors, from the separate development of service provision and policy developments through to the differing philosophies of individual services, those with complex needs have often had to endure a fragmentation in the provision of services.
- There is evidence that joint policy making has begun to develop a more coherent strategy to closer working between the mental health services and the Prison Service (Ministry of Justice and DH, 2009).

- Future developments of multi-agency joint working with those who have a dual diagnosis must be governed and driven by a centralised strategy and owned by those working on the front line. The government has made a commitment to build on Lord Bradley's recommendations for the development of a new National Programme Board and Advisory Group, which will bring together the range of departments from health, social care and the criminal justice system (Bradley, 2009; Ministry of Justice, 2009). The development of a national model of criminal justice mental health teams will provide the framework for a more coherent, effective intervention and continuity of care. This can best serve the complex needs of those who are dually diagnosed.
- The National Probation Service has implemented the Offender Management Model, which promotes engagement with other services. This has been developed to use scarce resources more effectively and placed the National Probation Service in a good position whereby offender managers can respond accordingly to those with complex needs.
- The key skills of core correctional practices have already been developed to effectively manage change. If resources, leadership and a commitment to joint training are put in place then a coherent service can be developed and be better placed to serve the needs of those dually diagnosed rather than the fragmented service currently in operation.

Points for further consideration

- Think of the cases you currently manage. Can you clearly identify those with:
  - substance misuse problems? Are there any signs of a possible undiagnosed mental disorder?
  - mental health disorders? Are they misusing substances as a coping strategy?
- If there are, who would you approach to discuss these concerns?
- In cases where there is no other agency involvement, the general practitioner (GP) may be your first point of reference. What if:
  - your client tells you they don't have a good relationship with their GP?
  - they don't give you permission to contact their GP?
  - following a successful discussion and referral to their GP, the client is told to go away, stop their substance misuse and come back when they are clean if the symptoms still exist? What is your next step?
- Both individually and as a team, map out a local directory of resources in your area for dual diagnosis by sharing resources and named contacts.

Further reading

Bradley, Lord (2009) *The Bradley Report: Executive Summary*. London: DH. Available at www. dh.gov.uk/en/Publicationsandstatistics/Publications/PublicationsPolicyAndGuidance/ DH_098694

Ministry of Justice and Department of Health (2009) *Guide for the Management of Dual Diagnosis for Prisons.* London: Home Office. Available at www.dh.gov.uk/en/Publicationsandstatistics/Publications/PublicationsPolicyAndGuidance/DH_097695

Watson. S. and Hawkings, C. (2007) *Dual Diagnosis: Good Practice Handbook.* London: Turning Point. Available at www.turning-point.co.uk/NR/rdonlyres/9D063EC0-1DF6-4F62-8E99-CFAADC4749BD/771/DualDiagnosisGoodPracticeHandbook.pdf

References

Abou-Saleh, M.T. (2004) 'Dual diagnosis: management within a psychosocial context', *Advances in Psychiatric Treatment*, 10, 352-60.

Afuwape, S.A. (2003) *Where Are We with Dual Diagnosis (Substance Misuse and Mental Illness)? A Review of the Literature.* London: Rethink.

American Psychiatric Association (2000) *Diagnostic and Statistical Manual of Mental Disorders* (4th revised edn) (DSM-IV-TR). Arlington, VA: American Psychiatric Association. Available at www.Psychiatryonline.com

Banerjee, S., Clancy, C. and Crome, I. (2002) *Co-Existing Problems of Mental Disorder and Substance Misuse (Dual Diagnosis): An Information Manual.* London: Royal College of Psychiatrists Research Unit.

Boardman, J. (2005) *New Services for Old: An Overview of Mental Health Policy.* London: Sainsbury Centre for Mental Health. Available at www.scmh.org.uk/pdfs/overview+of+mental+health+policy.pdf

Bradley, Lord (2009) *The Bradley Report: Executive Summary.* London: DH. Available at www.dh.gov.uk/en/Publicationsandstatistics/Publications/PublicationsPolicyAndGuidance/DH_098694

Buchanan, J. (2009) 'Understanding and misunderstanding problem drug use: working together', in Carnwell, R. and Buchanan, J. (eds) *Effective Practice in Health, Social Care and Criminal Justice* (pp 111-28). Milton Keynes: Open University Press.

DH (Department of Health) (1999) *The National Service Framework for Mental health.* London. Department of Health.

DH (2002a) *Mental Health Policy Implementation Guide: Dual Diagnosis Good Practice Guide.* London: DH Publications.

DH (2002b) *Models of Care.* London: National Treatment Agency. Available at www.nta.nhs.uk/publications/documents/nta_modelsofcare1_2002_moc1.pdf

DH (2007) *Improving Health, Supporting Justice: A Strategy for Improving Health and Social Care Services for People Subject to the Criminal Justice System: A Consultation Document.* London: Home Office.

DH (2008) *Refocusing the Care Programme Approach: Policy and Positive Practice Guidance.* Available at www.dh.gov.uk/en/Publicationsandstatistics/Publications/PublicationsPolicyAndGuidance/DH_083647

Drake, R.E. and Mueser, K.T. (2000) 'psychosocial approaches to dual diagnosis', *Schizophrenia Bulletin*, 26(1), 105-18.

Falk, C. (2004) 'Are DTTOs working? Issues of policy, implementation and practice', *Probation Journal*, 51(4): 398-406.

Gorry, A. and Todd, T. (2008) 'Overview of the NIMHE/CSIP National Dual programme in England', *Advances in Dual Diagnosis*, 1(1), 9-13.

Hawkings, S. and Gilburt, H. (2004) *Dual Diagnosis Toolkit: Mental Health and Substance Misuse: A Practical Guide for Professionals and Practitioners*. London: Turning Point and Rethink.

Hodges, C.L., Paterson, S., Taikato, M., McGarrol, S., Crome, I. and Baldacchino, A. (2006) *Substance Misuse Research: Co-morbid Mental Health and Substance Misuse in Scotland*. Edinburgh: Scottish Executive.

Home Office (1990a) *Partnerships in Dealing with Offenders in the Community*. London: Home Office.

Home Office (1990b) *Partnerships in Crime Prevention*. London: Home Office.

Home Office (2009) *Tackling Drugs Changing Lives: Drug Laws and Licensing*. London: Home Office. Available at http://drugs.homeoffice.gov.uk/drugs-laws/cannabis-reclassifications/

Khanom, H., Samele, C. and Rutherford, M. (2009) *A Missed Opportunity? Community Sentences and the Mental Health Treatment Requirement*. London: Sainsbury Centre for Mental Health.

McMurran, M. (2002) *Expert Paper: Dual Diagnosis of Mental Disorder and Substance Misuse: NHS National Programme on Forensic Mental Health Research and Development*. Liverpool: University of Liverpool.

Ministry of Justice (2009) *Lord Bradley's Report on People with Mental Health Problems or Learning Disabilities in the Criminal Justice System: The Government's Response*. London: Home Office.

Ministry of Justice and DH (Department of Health) (2009) *Guide for the Management of Dual Diagnosis for Prisons*. London: Home Office.

Minogue, V. (2009) 'Effective partnerships to assist mentally disordered offenders', in Carnwell, R. and Buchanan, J. (eds) *Effective Practice in Health, Social Care and Criminal Justice* (pp 210-26). Maidenhead: Open University Press.

Mueser, K., Drake, R. and Wallach, M. (1998) 'Dual diagnosis: a review of aetiological theories', *Addictive Behaviours*, 23(6), 717-34.

Nash, M. (2005) 'The Probation Service, public protection and dangerous offenders', in Winstone, J. and Pakes, F. (eds) *Community Justice, Issues for Probation and Criminal Justice* (pp 16-32). Cullompton: Willan Publishing.

Reason, P. and Bradbury, H. (2008) 'Introduction', in Reason, P. and Bradbury, H. (eds) *The SAGE Handbook of Action Research: Participative Inquiry and Practice* (2nd edn) (pp 1-9). London: Sage Publications.

Rethink (2009) *Cannabis and Mental Health: The Impact of Cannabis Misuse*. London: Rethink. Available at www.rethink.org/about_mental_illness/dual_diagnosis/information_pack_on.html

Rumgay, J. (2007) 'Partnerships in probation', in Gelsthorpe, L. and Morgan, R. (eds) *Handbook of Probation* (pp 542-65), Cullompton: Willan Publishing.

Volkow, N.D. (2008) *Co-morbidity: Addiction and Other Mental Illnesses.* National Institute on Drug Abuse, US Department of Health and Human Services. Available at http://drugabuse.gov/PDF/RRComorbidity.pdf

WHO (World Health Organization) (1994) *Lexicon of Alcohol and Drug Terms.* Geneva, WHO. Available at: www.who.int/substanceabuse/terminology/wholexicon/en/

WHO (2007) *International Statistical Classification of Diseases* (ICD-10). Version 2007. Geneva: WHO. Available at http://apps.who.int/classifications/apps/icd/icd10online

CHAPTER 15

Youth Offending Teams: a multi-agency success or system failure?

Nicholas Pamment

Aims of the chapter
■ To introduce multi-agency working within youth justice.
■ To critically assess its impact.
■ To consider the major barriers to effective multi-agency working.

Multi-agency working within youth justice

In 1996, an Audit Commission report argued that an immense amount of money had been invested into the youth justice system but nonetheless the interventions remained inefficient and ineffective. The Labour government capitalised on this finding and suggested that under the Conservatives the youth justice system was in disarray, and it proposed a radical change (Labour Party, 1996). After entering office in 1997, New Labour certainly embarked on what was a major reform (Home Office, 1997) and the 1998 Crime and Disorder Act was introduced. This put in place the specific requirement that youth offending is addressed through a multi-agency response, something that was suggested almost 10 years earlier by the Morgan Report (Home Office, 1991).

Youth Offending Teams (YOTs) were subsequently formed and they replaced social workers within local authority social services. They have been described as teams not belonging to a single department and consist of representatives from the police, probation, social services, health, education, drugs, alcohol misuse and housing (Souhami, 2007; YJB, 2009a). YOTs also work in conjunction with other statutory, voluntary and corporate services engaged within crime reduction strategies and, as Souhami (2007: 209) has previously suggested, they therefore embody multi-agency and inter-agency working. Staff can be seconded to YOTs by the varying agencies or they can be employed directly within the team by local authorities and they work towards the principal aim of 'preventing offending by children and young persons' (1998 Crime and Disorder Act, s 37). There is now a YOT in every local authority in England and Wales (YJB, 2009a) and they are centrally monitored and controlled by the Youth Justice Board (YJB), which was also set up as part of the 1998 Crime and Disorder Act.

The expansion of multi-agency working can be considered against wider developments in thinking with regard to crime and its management (Souhami, 2007: 209; Newburn, 2007: 726-31). For instance, a new 'corporatist' strategy for dealing with offenders appeared outside the traditional 'welfare' and 'justice' approaches at the end of the 1980s. This was primarily concerned with efficiently managing the offending population rather than offender rehabilitation. In fact, it has been strongly argued that multi-agency arrangements are merely utilised as a way of managing performance and monitoring cost efficiency (for a full discussion, see Pitts, 2001). Alongside the 'corporatist' strategy, evaluative research started to show that certain forms of criminal justice intervention could reduce recidivism and therefore there was a focus on 'what works' with offenders. It became accepted that offending should be combated at an early stage, as reflected in the principal aim of YOTs, through tough interventions as this was arguably more effective but also less expensive. Furthermore, it was acknowledged that crime is inherently complex with young offenders having multiple needs and these cannot be met by a single agency (Souhami, 2007: 209-10). Indeed, the Home Office (1997) argued that offending by young people is linked to a number of problems and it is important to bring experience and skills from varying agencies together. Furthermore, this approach would increase overall efficiency and avoid any duplication of effort.

During the early introduction of YOTs, the Home Office (1999) issued guidance on the roles of the different officers from the varying agencies but research suggested that YOT personnel were carrying out the same tasks, despite differences in professional background, training and qualifications (Ellis and Boden, 2005: 1). This raised concern that YOT personnel would not develop a 'fusion' or 'unifying' model of joint working (Burnett and Appleton, 2004; Ellis and Boden, 2005). However, research has suggested that this is not the case and Burnett and Appleton (2004), in their study of one YOT area, discovered that regardless of parent agency, there was a unifying social work ethic between the YOT staff. Furthermore, Ellis and Boden (2005) conducted a later study within a different YOT and also concluded that 'a social work ethic is alive and well' (2005: 19), indicating that they are generally working in a cohesive way, as desired.

The YJB suggests that YOTs are key to the success of the youth justice system and it claims that because they incorporate a number of representatives from a wide range of services, the needs of young offenders are addressed in a 'comprehensive manner' (YJB, 2009a). According to Souhami (2007: 208), multi-agency working has been most fully developed within the youth justice system and therefore one would expect that YOTs are successful in tackling the multiple needs of young offenders. In fact, the previous chair of the YJB, Professor Rod Morgan, stated prior to his resignation that 'this is one part of the criminal justice system that every informed commentator believes is fit for purpose' (Morgan, 2007).

Research regarding multi-agency working tends to centre upon the process of integration and the perceptions of professionals about the impact of the service (Blagg, 2000; Burnett and Appleton, 2004) and there exists only limited evidence on any outcomes (Brown and White, 2006). This chapter therefore critically assesses the impact that multi-agency working has had on the youth justice system and it investigates whether there has been a substantial improvement in outcomes for young offenders.

> How does multi-agency working within youth justice differ from adult supervision?

Multi-agency achievements?

Recently, the government's achievements with regard to the major youth justice reforms, of which multi-agency work forms a major part, have been called into question. Central to the argument here is Solomon and Garside's (2008) interesting and comprehensive audit of the government's record on youth justice, 10 years on from the 1998 Crime and Disorder Act.

The results are far from positive and the evaluation shows that most targets have been missed, youth offending has not declined and the principal aim of the youth justice system set out in the 1998 Crime and Disorder Act – to prevent offending by young people – has not been achieved (Solomon and Garside, 2008: 11). The evaluation explored a number of key areas of need for young offenders engaged within the youth justice system and these are explored below.

Accommodation

The YJB has described suitable and stable accommodation as a 'critical factor' in preventing offending as it helps maintain school attendance and employment, and offenders can engage with health services and other programmes to address offending behaviour (YJB, 2009c). The importance of suitable accommodation was tragically highlighted in the murder of Marian Bates, a jeweller who was killed in Brighton in 2004 by Peter Williams, a young offender under the supervision of Nottinghamshire YOT. The HM Inspectorate of Probation report into the murder criticised the lack of suitable accommodation and argued that Williams was unable to build his life on a secure base and it was difficult for the relevant agencies to work with him effectively (HMIP, 2005).

The YJB acknowledges that young people within the youth justice system have substantial accommodation needs (YJB, 2007a), and since 2002 there has been an ongoing target to 'ensure that YOTs have a named accommodation officer and all young people subject to community interventions or on release from custody have suitable accommodation' (YJB, 2003). While the former has been achieved (YJB, 2006), the latter has not. According to Solomon and Garside (2008: 54), there has been no improvement in the last three years and, while high, the proportion of young people gaining suitable accommodation rests at 93% or 94%. Furthermore, research conducted for the YJB also discovered that of a sample of 152 young people in custodial and community settings, all were in need of suitable accommodation (YJB, 2007a). It would appear that the role of the accommodation officer is primarily concerned with supporting young people on an individual basis at the operational level (YJB, 2007a). While this is laudable, they have a very limited impact at a strategic level and are unable to address the most important problem within this area: a lack of sufficient accommodation in the first place (Solomon and Garside, 2008: 55).

Education, training or employment

The YJB stresses that gaining the right qualifications and skills for employment are 'major protective factors' in preventing further offending by young people, especially in the long term (YJB, 2009c). The Home Office has previously argued that the chances of offending for young people who truant from school are three times higher than for those who do not and in 1995, 60% of convicted youths were unemployed and not in training or education (Home Office, 1997). More recently, the National Literacy Trust highlighted the extremely poor educational attainment of young offenders and discovered that over half of all young people serving a Detention and Training Order (DTO) had literacy levels below what was expected of an 11-year-old, although their average age was 17 (National Literacy Trust, 2009). Despite acknowledging the importance of education and ensuring that there are teachers and educational advisors within multi-agency YOTs (Solomon and Garside, 2008), only 69% of children currently under youth justice supervision are in full-time education, training or employment and this is far from Labour's target of 90% (2008: 11) (see Parkinson, this volume).

Mental health and substance misuse

The Mental Health Foundation argues that mental health problems among offenders engaged within the criminal justice system are three times higher than among the general population (Hagell, 2002). Furthermore, a study discovered that 60% of young offenders under YOT supervision had a drug problem (Pitcher et al, 2004). These are important issues that impact on the risks of offending and reoffending, as well as causing increased levels of self-harm or suicide (YJB, 2009b). Nevertheless, multi-agency YOTs have missed targets regarding substance misuse screening, assessment, intervention and mental health referral. According to Solomon and Garside (2008: 11), YOTs are struggling to ensure sufficient provision for a substantial demand (see Pakes and Winstone, Heath and Rees, this volume).

Reducing offending

As Burnett and Appleton (2004: 51) have already acknowledged, the ultimate test for the multi-agency approach to youth justice is in the reconviction rates for young people within the criminal justice system. However, it is difficult to make an overall assessment of these figures as targets have regularly been modified and changed over time, there has been confusion regarding the terms 'reconviction' and 'reoffending' and there has been an 'embarrassing' occurrence of overestimation on the part of the government (see Newburn, 2007: 720; Solomon and Garside, 2008: 50-1). According to the YJB, the reconviction rate in 2004 was reduced by 3.8% compared with 1997, but the 5% reduction target was not met (YJB, 2007b). Some of the most recently published statistics have also shown a slight 2.2% reduction in the reconviction rate of the 2002 cohort (YJB, 2008). Most importantly, it is clear that there has not been any significant or substantial reduction in reconviction rates since the introduction of multi-agency YOTs. This is perhaps unsurprising, given that the targets mentioned above have been missed. As has been previously stated, 'the government has been beset with problems in setting, revising and failing to hit its reconviction target for children' (Solomon and Garside, 2008: 51).

A damning verdict

With regard to multi-agency achievements, the highly negative verdict is best delivered in Solomon and Garside's (2008: 11) own words:

> The overall picture is of a youth justice system that was designed with the best intentions of providing effective multi-agency provision but that in practice is struggling to meet the needs of a group of vulnerable children and young people who require carefully co-ordinated specialist support. YOTs do not appear to be able to successfully meet the complex needs of children and young people.

Solomon and Garside's (2008) audit is not in isolation, in fact a number of other reports have drawn attention to the inability of YOTs to address individual needs. In a recent HM Inspectorate of Probation report (HMIP, 2007), it was found that despite young people having schooling difficulties (62%), emotional or mental health needs (40%), physical health needs (15%) and learning difficulties (15%), these are not met or addressed by the YOTs. Furthermore, the statutory entitlement to 25 hours' education for school-age children and young people is rarely achieved (HMIP, 2007).

The ISSP case study: another nail in the coffin?

The Intensive Supervision and Surveillance Programme (ISSP) is a community sanction aimed at severe and persistent young offenders and it is usually run by designated teams within YOTs. Young offenders on ISSP can be subject to monitoring up to 24 hours/seven days a week and should be subject to at least one form of direct surveillance (tracking, electronic tagging, voice verification) or intelligence-led policing (Gray et al, 2005: 28-9). Young offenders usually spend six months on the ISSP, with the most intensive supervision phase (25 hours a week) in the first three months, followed by a minimum of five hours a week and weekend support for a further three months. Offenders should receive five core intervention modules, including education/training, restorative justice, offending behaviour, interpersonal skills and family support (Gray et al, 2005: 18-27). The YJB set three objectives for the ISSP, one of which was to tackle young offenders' underlying problems effectively, and given the multi-agency make-up, coupled with increased contact time, this should be easily achievable. However, this is not the case.

The YJB commissioned an evaluation of ISSP in two stages (see Moore et al, 2004; Gray et al, 2005) and researchers discovered that there were many examples of homelessness, unmet mental health needs, ignored special educational needs and poor social work intervention. Furthermore, practitioners reported a number of difficulties in accessing education, accommodation, mental health and drug services (Gray et al, 2005: 32). Most importantly, however, a highly negative and perhaps unsurprising discovery, was the substantially high reconviction rates of 89% after 12 months, increasing to 91% after 24 months (Moore et al, 2004; Gray et al, 2005), hardly a ringing endorsement for intensive multi-agency working.

More recently, an independent study also explored the impact of the ISSP and reported similarly negative findings. It explored young offender and staff perceptions of the programme within two YOT areas and discovered that the ISSP is failing on a number of levels and is in danger of being abandoned (see Ellis et al, 2009). Young offenders were asked whether the ISSP addresses their individual needs and utilising a Likert scale data collection method (see Likert, 1932), 27 offenders responded with a negative mean score of 3.2 (7 being the best possible result). This negative score is best explained in the young offenders' own words:

> "I was given a school bullying pack to do when I was not even at school; the interventions are all based on the same thing."

> "I have to do teen talk packs which are really childish and nothing to do with me."

> "I was made to play with plastic men and told to move them through an imaginative grand chamber of feelings. I was embarrassed, coz I was nearly 18."

Throughout the study it was evident that much of the programme content was designed for a much younger age group and was not effective at addressing young offender underlying problems. This indicated that the foundation of the scheme was poor and that the multi-agency delivery would have very little effect (see Ellis et al, 2009).

Barriers to effective multi-agency working

It would appear, given all the evidence cited above, that multi-agency success within youth justice is insignificant and we certainly have not seen massive improvements that would perhaps have been expected with a 'comprehensive' multi-agency response. This is hard to fathom considering the clear benefits of this form of working, which have been comprehensively discussed elsewhere (see Souhami, 2007: 210-12). It has been argued that multi-agency working can lead to shared knowledge, easier access to other services, expertise and improved referral processes, all of which can contribute towards a 'seamless service' without communicational blocks or delays, bureaucratic divisions and defensive professional boundaries (Burnett and Appleton, 2004: 37). Indeed, it certainly has 'commonsense appeal' (Burnett and Appleton, 2004: 35), where the 'ideology of unity' (Crawford, 1994: 505) is generally considered an 'unproblematically good thing' (Blagg et al, 1988, cited in Burnett and Appleton, 2004: 35). Furthermore, for the government, it has the advantage of being extremely good for public relations (Gilling, 1994: 247) and, as Burnett and Appleton (2004: 35) state, 'there can be few more worthy sounding ideals than that of collaboration'.

In reality, joint working can be extremely difficult to achieve in practice and, interestingly, even before the introduction of the 1998 Crime and Disorder Act, incidents had highlighted difficulties faced with regard to multi-agency working. The National Society for the Prevention of Cruelty to Children (NSPCC) has argued that since the 1970s repeated inquiries into child abuse cases have exposed serious failings (Cloke, 2007). For instance, the report into the death of Maria Colwell argued that there was a lack of communication and liaison (DHSS, 1974). Furthermore, a report into child abuse in Cleveland discovered a lack of understanding between agencies and it was stated that 'it is unacceptable that the disagreements and failure of communication of adults should be allowed to obscure the needs of children' (DH, 1988) (see Watson, this volume).

Culture

According to Liddle and Gelsthorpe (1994), the most significant barrier to multi-agency collaboration can be found in the informal responses and complexities within the workforce. Indeed, the term 'culture' is regularly cited as having the most impact on the success of this type of working (see Gilling, 1994; Souhami, 2007: 220). Ogbonna and Harris (1998: 35) have described the notion of organisational culture as an enigma but it can be described as an umbrella term incorporating a number of aspects primarily centred on the idea of identity. Sergiovanni and Corbally (1984: viii) provide a comprehensive definition. They state that culture is:

> the system of values, symbols, and shared meanings of a group including the embodiment of these values, symbols, and meanings into material

objects and ritualised practices ... the 'stuff' of culture includes customs and traditions, historical accounts be they mythical or actual, tacit understandings, habits, norms and expectations.

When discussing 'culture' as a barrier to effective multi-agency working, it is argued that conflicts in the cultures of different agencies may negatively affect working relationships, thus obstructing any form of collaboration (Souhami, 2007: 220). Indeed, Sloper (2004: 572) argues that multi-agency working requires change at an individual and organisational level. This will inevitably challenge any existing culture and workers may fear such transformation, finding reasons for its failure (see Burnett and Appleton, 2004). In fact, it is not hard to find examples of cultural barriers within the youth justice system. For instance, Bailey and Williams (2000) discovered 'shotgun marriages' and 'turf wars' between different agencies in their study of early shadow YOTs. Furthermore, Holdaway et al (2001) discovered conflict over implementation of case working and obstructiveness regarding attempts to introduce evidence-based practice. Moreover, Burnett and Appleton (2004) also encountered underlying cultural issues with regard to appropriate language use within their study of an Oxfordshire YOT. These cultural issues will inevitably appear 'on the ground', in the form of communicational breakdowns and ultimately poor working relationships within YOTs. However, Crawford and Jones (1995) argue that conflicts in the workplace are always present and inevitable. Furthermore, Souhami (2007) suggests that these conflicts are 'integral' to multi-agency work as it is the merging of diverse approaches to work. Indeed, it must be remembered that culture can have both a positive and a negative impact. Nevertheless, it is perhaps all too easy to focus on culture as the main barrier to effective multi-agency working and this detracts from assessing whether our youth justice system is effective in the first place.

How might the cultures of the varying agencies differ?

The bigger picture?

Smith (2007) suggests that the public presentation of the youth justice reform programme is seamless, comprehensive and based on the best evidence about effective interventions; however, in reality, this is not the case. As mentioned further above, within the last few decades there has been a major shift from a 'welfare' approach to dealing with young offenders to that of a punitive response, where sanctions rely far more heavily on enforcement and punishment (Goldson, 2000; Pratt et al, 2005). As Solomon and Garside (2008: 66) highlight, it is therefore unsurprising that a labour target to halve the time from arrest to sentence has easily been achieved. However, through the 'tough on crime' standpoint (Newburn, 2007: 741) adopted by the current government, previous research evidence is ignored (see Goldson, 2000; Muncie, 2002). Instead, it would appear that there is a preoccupation with elections and the popular vote (Pitts, 2000; Burnett and Appleton, 2004: 48) and this is taking precedence over any research-led policy (see Henricson et al, 2000; Morgan and Newburn, 2007).

The ISSP is an excellent example of this, whereby it has been shown that the programme has no convincing evidence base, and a review of previous ISSP evaluations has shown, overwhelmingly, that they do not work, especially in reducing reconviction rates (see Ellis et al, 2009). Crucially, this evidence was available to policy makers prior to the introduction of the ISSP in England and Wales but faced with serious prison overcrowding and economic issues, the political attractiveness of intensive community programmes for persistent young offenders was overriding. In fact, intensive supervision provides a means for reducing the use of imprisonment and its associated costs without appearing 'soft on crime' (Corbett and Petersilia, 1994: 73). Tonry (1990) has supported this idea and argues that the goals of most intensive supervision programmes are indicative of the political environment of the time. Most importantly, however, we must have interventions that are based on sound evidence in order for multi-agency working to have the best possible foundation on which to operate.

However, through political expediency, we are also introduced to a further problem regarding the use of research, its reliability and the ensuing YJB gloss or 'smokescreen'. For instance, and with reference to the ISSP once again, in 2004 the YJB issued a press release stating that through the use of ISSP, reoffending was reduced (YJB, 2004). However, this was misleading, as both parts of the evaluation failed to demonstrate any real achievements (Moore et al, 2004; Gray et al, 2005). In fact, within one of the evaluations, the researchers make a rather revealing remark and buried at the end of a lengthy report they state: 'even though a number of methods were used, it proved difficult to establish if the ISSP has a beneficial impact on offending' (Moore et al, 2004: 321). The resulting negative publicity from *The Times* stated: 'when the main show is such a staggering flop, it takes some cheek to crow about the lighting' (Gibb and Ford, 2005: 12).

Within an issue of *Criminal Justice Matters*, Walters (2005) questions the independence of Home Office-funded research. He argues that studies are distorted and manipulated to demonstrate that some crime reduction initiatives are particularly effective, thus increasing political popularity. He further accuses Home Office research of 'rubberstamping' the political priorities of the government and even calls for a boycott of Home Office research. He states that 'its agenda is motivated by outcomes that are of immediate benefit to political demands and there is no independence' (Walters, 2005: 6–7). It is imperative that interventions are based on sound and impartial evidence and this is now long overdue.

Interestingly, YJB gloss has also been evident with regard to multi-agency working. After the introduction of the 154 YOTs, it was stated that joined-up working was an 'unqualified success' (*YJB News*, December 2000, cited in Burnett and Appleton, 2004: 48). Not only was this statement rather premature, but in making this claim, it has been argued that the YJB was highly selective of independent evaluations and ignored research that contained less positive results

(Burnett and Appleton, 2004: 48). As Burnett and Appleton (2004: 48) pertinently state, 'the unabated self-congratulation of the Youth Justice Board, endorsed by government ministers, has been hard to swallow'.

With the 'tough on crime' approach it is also argued that YOTs are failing to address the causes of offending. Solomon and Garside (2008: 65) argue that we have seen a degree of disinvestment in social responses to youth crime as substantial amounts of money have been transferred from policy areas critical to tackling the underlying causes of youth offending. Interestingly, a large proportion of funding for YOTs comes from the budgets of social spending, health, education and social services (Solomon and Garside, 2008). They also question whether YOTs can actually address the complex economic and social factors causing youth offending. It is suggested that a more effective solution may be found outside of the justice system in the delivery of coordinated services through mainstream local authority children's and young people's provision and more effective children's services that can effectively address the causes of offending (2008: 64). They state:

> After a number of years of expansion should youth justice be scaled back and social support-led prevention scaled up.... A decade on from the creation of the YJB and YOTs, and at a time of rising concerns about youth 'gangs' and violence involving guns and knives, the time has come to reappraise the role and purpose of the youth justice system and to consider what it can realistically achieve in addressing youth offending. (Solomon and Garside, 2008: 12)

What changes would you make to improve youth justice policy and why?

Conclusion

It has been suggested that multi-agency working has been most fully developed within the youth justice system (Souhami, 2007: 208) and through the utilisation of a recently published audit report (Solomon and Garside, 2008), this chapter has assessed its impact since its introduction. In 2004, Burnett and Appleton (2004: 36) argued that it was too soon to explore whether multi-agency reforms had reduced youth crime but now, several years on, it might be time to acknowledge that it has had very little impact. As shown above, despite the collaboration of a number of agencies within YOTs, the government has missed targets regarding accommodation, education, training, employment, mental health and substance misuse and there has been no significant decline in offending. Furthermore, the ISSP, which is meant to tackle underlying reasons for offending in a comprehensive and intensive manner, has produced an incredibly high reconviction rate of 91%, with several evaluations showing that it is failing to adequately meet the needs of young offenders. Solomon and Garside (2008: 48) have thus concluded:

When YOTs were rolled out across England and Wales it was widely expected that their multi-agency make-up would be a considerable advance over the previous arrangements ... the fact that nearly all the targets set by the YJB relating to each area of need have not been met suggests that the current arrangements are not necessarily working.

This overall finding is not in isolation. Sloper (2004: 571) found limited evidence regarding the effectiveness of multi-agency working in producing outcomes for children and families. Furthermore, Blagg (2000) has argued that in reality, and despite the rhetoric, not everyone benefits from the process.

Is it unfair to argue that multi-agency working is the failure? Certainly it is wrong to believe that crime can only be reduced through better coordination and cooperation, a belief that has been in existence for some time (Blagg, 2000). While it is acknowledged that multi-agency working can bring substantial rewards, through shared knowledge and speed efficiency (Souhami, 2007), it must be remembered that it is a process operating within the youth justice system, which needs to be functioning successfully. This means being based on impartial evidence of effectiveness, rather than political expediency, where underlying causes of offending are addressed in a comprehensive manner. We must be careful that the rhetoric of multi-agency working does not detract from building an evidence-led criminal justice system that is effective and fit for purpose.

Summary of key points

- Multi-agency working is yet to have a beneficial impact on youth justice.
- Better coordination and cooperation cannot solely address the complexities of youth offending.
- Youth justice policy must be based on evidence-based practice where the causes of offending are addressed.

Further reading

Burnett, R. and Appleton, C. (2004) 'Joined-up services to tackle youth crime', *British Journal of Criminology*, 44 (1), 34-54.

Solomon, E. and Garside, R. (2008) *Ten Years of Labour's Youth Justice Reforms: An Independent Audit.* London: Centre for Crime and Justice Studies.

Souhami, A. (2007) 'Multi-agency working: experiences in the youth justice system', in Green, S., Lancaster, E. and Feasey, S. (eds) *Addressing Offending Behaviour.* Cullompton: Willan Publishing.

References

Audit Commission (1996) *Misspent Youth: Young People and Crime*. London: Audit Commission.

Bailey, R. and Williams, B. (2000) *Inter-agency Partnerships in Youth Justice: Implementing the Crime and Disorder Act, 1998*. Sheffield: University of Sheffield, Joint Unit for Social Service Research.

Blagg, H., Pearson, G., Sampson, A., Smith, D. and Stubbs, P. (1988) 'Inter-agency co-ordination: rhetoric and reality', in Hope, T. and Shaw, M. (eds) *Communities and Crime Reduction*. London: Home Office.

Blagg, H. (2000) 'Multi-agency work, marginal communities and crime prevention'. Paper presented at the conference 'Reducing Criminality: Partnerships and Best Practice', Perth, 31 July/1 August. Available at ww.aic.gov.au/en/events/aic%20 upcoming%20events/2000/~/media/conferences/criminality/blagg.ashx

Brown, K. and White, K. (2006) *Exploring the Evidence Base for Integrated Children's Services*. Edinburgh: Scottish Executive Education Department. Web publication. Available at www.scotland.gov.uk/Publications/2006/01/24120649/0

Burnett, R. and Appleton, C. (2004) 'Joined-up services to tackle youth crime', *British Journal of Criminology*, 44(1), 34-54.

Cloke, C. (2007) *Safeguarding Children: The Importance of Multi-Professional and Multi-Agency Working*. London: NSPCC. Available at www.nspcc.org.uk/Inform/.../ SCImportance_wdf53655.ppt

Corbett, R.P. and Petersilia, J. (1994) 'Up to speed: a review of research for practitioners', *Federal Probation*, 58(3), 51-6.

Crawford, A. (1994) 'The partnership approach: corporatism at the local level?', *Social and Legal Studies*, 3: 497-519.

Crawford, A. and Jones, M. (1995) 'Inter-agency co-operation and community-based crime prevention', *The British Journal of Criminology*, 35(1), 17-33.

DH (Department of Health) (1988) *Report of the Inquiry into Child Abuse in Cleveland*. London: HMSO.

DHSS (Department of Health and Social Security) (1974) *Report of the Committee of Inquiry into the Care and Supervision Provided in Relation to Maria Colwell*. London: HMSO.

Ellis, T. and Boden, I. (2005) 'Is there a unifying professional culture in Youth Offending Teams? A research note', British Society of Criminology 2004 (Volume 7) Conference Proceedings.

Ellis, T., Pamment, N. and Lewis, C. (2009) 'Public protection in youth justice? The Intensive Supervision and Surveillance Programme (ISSP) from the inside', *International Journal of Police Science and Management*, 11(4), 393-413.

Gibb, F. and Ford, R. (2005) 'Row over tagging after fresh youth crime spree', *The Times*, October 28, p 12.

Gilling, D.J. (1994) 'Multi agency crime prevention: some barriers to collaboration', *The Howard Journal*, 33, 246-57.

Goldson, B. (2000) 'Wither diversion? Interventionism and the new youth justice', in Goldson, B. (ed) *The New Youth Justice*. Lyme Regis: Russell House Publishing.

Gray, E., Roberts, C., Merrington, S., Waters, I., Fernandez, R., Hayward, G. and Rogers, R. (2005) *ISSP: The Final Report*. London: Youth Justice Board.

Hagell, A. (2002) *The Mental Health of Young Offenders*. London: Mental Health Foundation.

Henricson, C., Coleman, J. and Roker, D. (2000) 'Parenting in the youth justice context', *The Howard Journal*, 39(4), 325-8.

HMIP (Her Majesty's Inspectorate of Probation) (2005) *Inquiry into the Supervision of Peter Williams by Nottingham City Youth Offending Team*. London: HMIP.

HMIP (2007) *Joint Inspection of Youth Offending Teams Annual Report 2006–2007*. London: HMIP.

Holdaway, S., Davidson, N., Dignan, J., Hammersley, R., Hine, J. and Marsh, P. (2001) *New Strategies to Address Youth Offending: The National Evaluation of the Pilot Youth Offending Teams*. Research, Development and Statistics Directorate Paper No 69. London: Home Office.

Home Office (1991) *Safer Communities: The Local Delivery of Crime Prevention through the Partnership Approach* (The Morgan Report). London: Home Office.

Home Office (1997) *No More Excuses: A New Approach to Tackling Youth Crime in England and Wales*. London: Home Office.

Home Office (1999) *Inter-Departmental Circular on Establishing Youth Offending Teams*. London: Home Office.

Labour Party (1996) *Tackling Youth Crime: Reforming Youth Justice*. London: Labour Party.

Liddle, M. and Gelsthorpe, L. (1994) *Crime Prevention and Inter-Agency Co-Operation: Crime Prevention Unit Paper 53*. London: Home Office.

Likert, R. (1932) 'A technique for the measurement of attitudes', *Archives of Psychology*, 140, 5-53.

Moore, R., Gray, E., Roberts, C., Merrington, S., Waters, I., Fernandez, R., Hayward, G. and Rogers, R. (2004) *ISSP: The Initial Report: Summary*. London: Youth Justice Board.

Morgan, R. (2007) Letter to all YJB staff, YOT managers, YOI governors, STC and LASCH managers and selected others, 26 January, Unpublished.

Morgan, R. and Newburn, T. (2007) 'Youth justice', in M. Maguire and R. Morgan (eds) *The Oxford Handbook of Criminology* (4th edn). Oxford: Oxford University Press.

Muncie, J. (2002) 'Policy transfers and "what works": some reflections on comparative youth justice', *Youth Justice*, 1(3), 27-35.

National Literacy Trust (2009) *Young Offenders*. London: National Literacy Trust. Available at www.literacytrust.org.uk/socialinclusion/youngpeople/offenders. html

Newburn, T. (2007) *Criminology*. Cullompton: Willan Publishing.

Ogbonna, E. and Harris, L. (1998) 'Organizational culture: it's not what you think ...', *Journal of General Management*, 23(3), 35-49.

Pitcher, J., Bateman, T., Johnston, V. and Cadman, S. (2004) *Health, Education and Substance Misuse Service*. London: Youth Justice Board.

Pitts, J. (2000) 'The new youth justice and the politics of electoral anxiety', in Goldson, B. (ed) *The New Youth Justice*. Lyme Regis: Russell House Publishing.

Pitts, J. (2001) 'Korrectional karaoke: New Labour and the zombification of youth justice', *Youth Justice*, 1(2), 3–16.

Pratt, J., Brown, D., Brown, M., Hallsworth, S. and Morrison, W. (2005) *The New Punitiveness: Trends, Theories, Perspectives*, Cullompton: Willan Publishing.

Sergiovanni, T. and Corbally, J. (eds) (1984) *Leadership and Organizational Culture*. Urbana, IL: University of Illinois Press.

Sloper, P. (2004) 'Facilitators and barriers for co-ordinated multi-agency services', *Child Care, Health and Development*, 30(6), 571–80.

Smith, R. (2007) *Youth Justice: Ideas, Policy and Practice* (2nd edn). Cullompton: Willan Publishing.

Solomon, E. and Garside, R. (2008) *Ten Years of Labour's Youth Justice Reforms: An Independent Audit*. London: Centre for Crime and Justice Studies.

Souhami, A. (2007) 'Multi-agency working: experiences in the youth justice system', in Green, S., Lancaster, E. and Feasey, S. (eds) *Addressing Offending Behaviour*. Cullompton: Willan Publishing.

Tonry, M. (1990) 'Stated and latent functions of ISP', *Crime and Delinquency*, 36, 174–91.

Walters, R. (2005) 'Boycott, resistance and the role of the deviant voice', *Criminal Justice Matters*, 62, 6–7.

YJB (Youth Justice Board) (2003) *Gaining Ground in the Community: Annual Review 2002/03*. London: YJB.

YJB (2004) 'Robust community programme for young offenders to go nationwide, ISSP: marked reduction in both frequency and seriousness of offending'. Press Release. 14 September.

YJB (2006) *Annual Report and Accounts 2005/06*. London: YJB.

YJB (2007a) *Annual Report and Accounts 2006/07*. London: YJB.

YJB (2007b) *Accommodation Needs and Experience*. London: YJB.

YJB (2008) *Youth Justice Annual Workload Data 2006/07*. London: YJB.

YJB (2009a) *Youth Justice System: Youth Offending Teams – Who Are They? What Do They Do?* London: YJB. Available at www.yjb.gov.uk/en-gb/yjs/YouthOffendingTeams/

YJB (2009b) *Health*. London: YJB. Available at www.yjb.gov.uk/en-gb/practitioners/Health/

YJB (2009c) *Accommodation: A Vital Need*. London: YJB. Available at www.yjb.gov.uk/en-gb/practitioners/Accommodation/

YJB (2009d) *Education, Training and Employment*. London: YJB. Available at www.yjb.gov.uk/en-gb/practitioners/EducationTrainingAndEmployment/

CHAPTER 16

The beauty of reflection and the beast of multi-agency cooperation

John E. Howard

Aims of the chapter
- To consider the aspects of what is variously termed 'reflection', 'reflective practice' or 'critical practice' in the arena of multi-agency working and to discuss:
  - why reflection is needed;
  - when it is needed;
  - how it can be done.

Introduction

Two monks are travelling together on a pilgrimage. Their sect forbids them having any physical contact with women. At a fast-flowing river crossing they encounter a woman who is having difficulty getting across. One of the monks, the older, offers to help her by taking her on his back as he wades across. This they do and she is set down on the other side. As the two monks go on their way in silence the younger is seething with anger and indignation at his companion's actions. The two men walk further together. After a while the younger can contain himself no longer and he accuses his friend of betraying the beliefs and values of their sect. The older monk turns to the younger and says: 'I saw a woman who needed help and I carried her across the stream. You, my brother, have been carrying her for the last ten miles'. Here we find the monks reflecting on their actions, values and possible consequences. This chapter deals with what Gardner (2005: 104) calls 'engaging with new realities', which includes acknowledging 'the compromise between retaining consistency and adapting to a changing context'.

An early question to be addressed is whether there are different skills for managers and practitioners within reflective, critical practice. One answer is that such a division is unhelpful as the issue may not be so much about different skill sets, but more about attitude, will and resolve. It will be argued therefore that reflection is a necessary aspect of joint working at whatever level of the organisation. At this point it is useful to make a distinction between the notion of puzzles and problems. In the former there is always a solution, as in crossword and Sudoku puzzles where there are answers that fit the clues. In the case of problem–solving in the sphere of human activity, solutions may not be so obvious, if they exist at all. Often, the most that can be expected is action based on the best available knowledge, which then leads to consequences, and outcomes that may or may not be positive. This is why Schön's (1983) 'reflection-in-action' and 'reflection-on-action' are useful tools in probing motivations, values and guiding principles. Moon's (1999) summary will serve as a working principle for this chapter. This is that 'reflection is a form of mental processing ... that we use to fulfil a purpose or to achieve some anticipated outcome. It is applied to relatively complicated or unstructured ideas for which there is not an obvious solution and is largely based on the further processing of knowledge and understanding and possibly emotions that we already possess'.

Reasons to reflect

One of the central features of this book is that, in the world of criminal justice and social welfare, little can be accomplished by one agency alone (Rumgay, 2003). Nash (2006: 147) points out that 'multi-agency working is now regarded as the only effective way to protect the public from dangerous offenders'. This is not to say that it is not important for each agency to have its own identity. For example, when applying for a job in the Police Service, applicants are unlikely to say that they wish to work in an holistic manner with suspects. They are more likely to seize on the public perceptions of the role, which includes fighting crime and disorder, and bringing criminals to justice. Each agency has its own specialised role: the police investigate and arrest, the Crown Prosecution Service does what it says on the can, the courts sentence, the Prison Service detains, the Probation Service supervises and the voluntary sector provides access to social capital and services for offenders. Bates (2004: 53) points out that each profession has its own duties, which do not normally apply across professional territories. To some extent, each agency relies on its comparison with other agencies for its sense of identity, purpose and importance within the hierarchy of the criminal justice system. It is the contrast that sets it apart from others. Paradoxically, however, if each agency works as though the other agencies do not exist then little will be accomplished by way of public protection, punishment or rehabilitation. It is these differences that provide a platform from which to build relationships with other agencies when it is clear they cannot work alone. However, even with a firm base, inter-agency cooperation is not a straightforward process and requires effort at levels where values, ideologies and organisational philosophies diverge.

Reflective practice is used widely in social work and associated professions such as nursing and teaching. Over 20 years ago, at a time of major changes in training for social workers and probation officers, Coulshed (1988: 160) argued that social work must maintain a balance between activity and reflection. Social work has ensured that reflective practice retains its place in the training of social workers. This has also continued into training for probation officers where the core curriculum contains provisions for trainee probation officers to prepare for practice by compiling reflective accounts. Based on iterative models of reflection, trainee probation officers write about their actions, consequences and how they think and feel about themselves in their engagement with offenders who may be vulnerable, shifty, deceitful, two-faced and sometimes dangerous people. When confronted with characteristics like this, trainee probation officers are brought face to face with their own values and ethical stances, and how they feel and deal with unpleasant people and despicable behaviour. Trainee probation officers are often confronted just as much with what offenders teach them about themselves and their attitudes as with what offenders learn from them. Bolton (1998) argues that reflection is an inward-looking process that encourages practitioners to ask questions about their way of doing things in order to become intuitive, wise and creative, which Whitehead and Thompson (2004: 36) term 'the key to professional artistry'. Kim (1999: 1207) refers to this as a method of research that is designed to discover 'various forms of coherence or incoherence and consistency or inconsistency between practitioners' beliefs and actions'.

> Think of who among your client group has presented the most challenges to your values and attitudes.

So when it comes to multi-agency working, what are the significant reasons as to why professionals engage in reflective practice? There are a number of reasons. First, there are differences between agencies around their histories and status within the criminal justice system's hierarchy of power and influence. When agencies are called on to work together they are confronted with differing professional agendas and driving forces, which influence their decision-making processes (Sloper, 2004: 574). Leadbetter et al (2007: 126) refer to Bines' (1992) observations that within multi-agency working there is the potential for conflict and territoriality as a result of agencies 'securing status through exclusive knowledge and occupation demarcation'. An agency such as the police, for example, with its long history, occupies a central role in the public's perception when it comes to law and order, but other more contemporary agencies such as those dealing with drug users may not rank as highly in the public's imagination. Although there are those who see power differences as a 'creative and productive force' (Crawford and Jones, 1995, cited in Crawford, 1998: 173), the uses and functions of power around issues of access to information in particular settings have to be understood and clarified. Sampson et al (1988, cited Crawford, 1998: 172) found that the police tended to set agendas and dominate inter-agency meetings. This might be due to power over access to resources and finance, or influence. As an example, when I was an assistant chief probation officer, and short of resources, I recall sitting on three separate steering committees in my area when Youth Offending Teams were being established. The police, on the other hand, had three separate officers on each of the committees. Sullivan (2002) argues that when autonomous organisations agree to work together to achieve shared goals they cede some of their power and influence over decisions in order that their chances of achieving their joint objectives are enhanced. However, if organisations have the power to give away power then it may not take long to take it back if events conspire against them.

> Think about how you rank the various statutory, voluntary and community agencies within the criminal justice system. Who do you think has the most/least power and influence? Are power and influence the same?

Second, agencies may have different values, attitudes and beliefs around their consumer group. For example, in working with victims of sexual violence, Robinson et al (2008) raise questions about different approaches between criminal justice agencies and the voluntary sector. The former may be concerned about increasing the number of convictions whereas the latter may be more focused on the needs of the victim. There may be congruence at times but the different value bases reflected in their aims and targets may be quite different. However, in this context we must not only talk of organisational values, we must also enter the murky world of our own personal values and attitudes to offenders and especially offences that fill us with horror and revulsion. Indeed, our own personal values are important in shaping our views about our fellow professionals whose personal philosophies may be at odds with our own. A recent European Social Fund intervention 'PS Plus' (PS Plus 3, 2008), which was designed to maximise offenders' employability, involved joint work between the statutory criminal justice agencies and the voluntary and private sectors. The Prison and Probation Services' offender managers discussed those using the services as 'offenders' whereas the employability providers described them as 'beneficiaries', emphasising their work to increase employability as most important.

Third, and closely related to the above, there are issues of professional cultures. This may best be illustrated by thinking about the ways in which agencies might describe offenders, either literally or metaphorically. Each agency will come with its own way of describing the 'subject' within its 'framing imagery' ('Everyday use of metaphor': http://changingminds.org/techniques/language/metaphor/everyday_metaphor.htm). After the 1991 Criminal Justice Act, probation officers were counselled against using the term 'client' and advised to use 'offender' to describe the recipient of their services. The use of language is important and reflects professional identities: social workers with medical overtones of diagnosis, treatment and prognosis; uniformed police officers talking about strategies and frontline tactics; prison officers with their emphasis on control and restraint, good order and discipline; and probation officers with their relationships with offenders – all will cross each other's paths hoping that along the way some common understanding will emerge.

Think of how you describe your 'consumers' to fellow professionals, and how they describe them to you.

What imagery is conjured up by words like stalkers, perpetrators, predators, treatment?

How do you perceive your work? Do you work *on* or *with* your 'consumers'?

Fourth, we come to managing dangerous offenders, where uncertainties and ambiguities are now commonplace. This is where we need to take time to think about what influences our decision making has, as this can be a means to preventing the development of a blame culture. Because in this context reflection has to be a joint effort and a joint responsibility, there may be a 'pay-off' in not taking time to reflect by absolving individuals and agencies from blame and shame as they can point to the inactions of others when things go wrong. Mackenzie (1991) states that no chief executive wants to face the press to explain why procedures were not followed when a disaster occurs. When managers and practitioners take time to analyse thoughts, feelings, perceptions and motives, this may assist in dealing with the 'daunting emotional and intellectual content of their work' (Mackenzie, 1999: 235). If they are left alone to work within a blame culture they may be 'more likely to deliver just those very disasters' (1999: 235). In the management of dangerous offenders there is the constant fear of making mistakes and wrong decisions (Parton and O'Byrne, 2000; Banks, 2002, both cited in Gardner, 2009: 180). This in turn can lead to an over-emphasis on the supposed worthlessness of an offender where it may be more comfortable to emphasise and heighten the risks being posed than introduce a value base that may be underpinned by a belief in the goals of rehabilitation or a rights-based approach when dealing with marginalised minorities. Those operating at this level of inter-agency cooperation need to ensure that their beliefs and motivations are explained, understood and challenged. Nash (2006: 149-50) refers to Lord Laming's inquiry into the death of Victoria Climbié and Parton's (2004) consequential argument that frontline staff should 'have the ability and authority to challenge other professionals'. He further cites Cooper's (2005) view that workers in the field of child protection, and here we can broaden this out to dangerous offenders, need to remain in touch with their feelings. This is so that they can confront their fears and anxieties before they lead to 'a form of paralysis' when confronted with 'unspeakable horrors'.

These reasons why managers and practitioners should think about the ways in which they operate together in multi-agency settings are summed up by Whittington (2003b: 52) when he refers to Miller et al's (2001) proposals for the right team approach, which includes 'a capacity among team members to understand and cope with group processes as they are affected by power, authority and professional culture'. As Huxman (1993, cited in Gardner, 2003: 153) argues, 'The more complex the issue … the greater the need of self reflection'. There has to be a willingness to understand one another to prevent inter-agency work descending into a 'mutual hatred in a desire to secure funding, and a scrabble for small scraps of money' (Robinson et al, 2008: 419).

When to use reflection

Leading up to the millennium, the Probation Service had to change its focus several times (Chui and Nellis, 2003). It moved from acting as the offender's friend, offering advice and guidance, to providing proper punishment in the community, and taking an active role in accommodating to the needs of victims (Spalek, 2003). It is now firmly at the centre of assessing, managing and supervising high-risk and dangerous offenders (Nash, 2006). It is during what Williams (2002: 130) calls 'paradigm shifts' that training and reflection is needed to refocus the perceptions of probation officers. This is important both in their own agency's approach but also when working across agency boundaries where roles and philosophies meet and clash. Cavadino and Dignan (2007: 132) compare the changes in community punishment to a 'seismic upheaval', which is marked by 'confusion and uncertainty'. Dugdill et al (2009: 125) refer to the daunting challenges of 'working without a blueprint', and in their research found that periods of reflection were rewarding in terms of how workers from different agencies bonded and supported each other. This may involve a time or period when professionals come together to examine the processes by which they operate in their decision making as much as the content of the decision itself, 'reflection ... is critical for sharing knowledge ... and learning from mistakes' (2009: 128).

This could also apply to a number of agencies, such as the police, who need to refocus on working with local communities under Partners and Communities Together (PACT), and drug agencies, where a culture of voluntarism meets the coercion of enforceable court orders for drug users (see Heath, this volume). A major paradigm shift for probation officers has been in the outlook and potential of their 'user group' – offenders. Under the National Offender Management System model, offenders are dehumanised as 'each case is a project' to be managed from sentence to discharge of a Community Order or period of licence. It is questionable whether the way the Probation Service currently operates sufficiently encourages a focus on the strengths and needs of the individual to reconstruct their identity through developing alternative narratives whereby they no longer perceive themselves to be an offender. Within a desistance paradigm, McNeil (2006) (see Parkinson, this volume) argues that the emphasis is too heavily weighted towards risk management, which conceptualises individuals as an amalgam of risks and problems from which society must be protected. Reflection at this point is needed so that managers and practitioners can question their expectations of offenders. Hardcastle (2004: 216) points out that professionals must have a belief that the group with which they work is 'worth the attention and capable of achieving goals'. He points to Furstenberg and Rounds' (1995) findings that professionals are more likely to achieve results if they believe in the potential of their group. We can see the potential for misunderstandings if one member of a joint agency approach has a positive attitude to change in the individual and another perceives that same person as a danger to be managed. Hardcastle (2004) cites Cox (1997) who argues that without reflection there is the potential for practice to become governed by preconceived ideas, and past habits of work.

> What are your definitions of a team, or a team approach to a problem?

When prisons, probation, the police and other agencies come together under Multi-Agency Public Protection Arrangements (MAPPA), it is open to question whether the professionals working across agency boundaries ever think of themselves as a team. Sloper (2004: 576) reports that studies have shown that barriers to effective multi-agency working revolve not only around a lack of clarity regarding roles and responsibilities, aims and lack of commitment but also around 'negative professional stereotypes and lack of trust and understanding between individuals and agencies'. However, by coming together and investigating themselves in a reflective manner there may develop a team ethos of mutual understanding, which may otherwise be narrowly confined to sharing information and taking responsibility for tasks and control. Sloper (2004: 576) also goes on to say that there is some evidence that shared learning between doctors and social workers 'is effective in reducing inter-professional stereotypes'. There are elements of reflective practice that require that we learn how to rein in our projections of what we impute to other professionals.

How to use reflection

If it is important for professionals to work as 'multi-agency entities' then it is equally important for those multidisciplinary teams to understand how they work together. Therefore reflection on the multidisciplinary teams' activities should occupy a focal point in the development of how those teams perform (Dugdill et al, 2009: 123). This might involve utilising Ghaye and Ghaye's (1998, cited in Bold, 2008) principles of effective practice, which require reflective practitioners to communicate and converse with the aim of disturbing their professional identity and helping them recognise and understand their existing conceptual frameworks. This will involve asking probing questions about attitudes, beliefs and assumptions (Bold, 2008: 258). Not only should practitioners be prepared to ask questions but by default they should also be prepared to answer questions about how they reach their conclusions, and how they explain and justify their decision making. Robinson et al (2008: 420), in their work on a Sexual Assault Referral Centre, noted that there were significant differences in culture and working practices and 'a lack of awareness of people's roles and issues within different partners' work places'. It is understandable in the rush to work collaboratively that there can be the temptation to 'think everyone has the same vision [but] when you get down to the practicality you have to explain that vision' (Robinson et al, 2008: 420).

So what does reflection call for from professionals? There are a number of themes to discuss here. First, Somers and Bradford (2006: 74) claim that this will involve thinking about how much of one's power is 'an illusion': that we are stronger than we think we are, and perhaps others are weaker than we think they are. This means asking colleagues where they think their sources of power lie, from where they take their mandate, and to whom they report in their own hierarchy. It is not uncommon at joint agency meetings to assume that one has less power than the others present.

> When you attend inter-agency meetings, who do you think has more influence than you? How do other professionals respond to your actions or decisions?

The second theme centres around the professional roles we play. Whittington (2003b) points out that we are more than the roles we play. These are influenced by our gender, race, religious beliefs, political stance and our socialisation. If we bundle these together then these will 'affect our perceptions and experience of our work' (2003b: 42). Boud and Knights (1996, cited in Dolan and Pinkerton 2005: 18) define the process of reflection as 'grounded in the personal foundation of experience of the learner, that is, those experiences which have shaped the person and have helped to create the person he or she now is and their intent'.

This raises questions of what sort of reflection is needed. Reflection itself must have an outcome. In a target-driven culture where managerialism is 'understood as a projection of state imperatives' (Somers and Bradford, 2006: 79), it will not suffice for it to be an end in itself. If it is it will run the risk of being seen as self-indulgent and self-serving and may only go to prove that professionals are engaged in contemplating their own navels (Bates, 2004: 62). The aim and outcome of reflection must be better outcomes for consumers no matter how they are defined. Robinson et al (2008: 416) in their work on victims of crime refer to complaints that services can become 'designed around professionals as opposed to being designed around service delivery'. This is where it is crucial in multidisciplinary teams as 'organisational scripts can dominate ... rather than the needs of the service users' (Bates, 2004: 61). This means that reflection should be structured in such ways that improve the outcome for offenders, victims and the public. Among Wood and Bradley's (2009) conclusions from their work on partnership policing is that it is important to develop understandings of the worldviews and perspectives that each organisation expresses around a problem. Work on reflection, they argue, should begin with new recruits in order to 'test the basic assumptions' and 'profound beliefs upon which their professional lives are based' (2009: 135).

> Think of why you joined your organisation and what values and attitudes influenced your decision. Have these changed over time for you?

The aim is to move away from managing through rules and procedures to creative problem-solving for the benefit of the wider community. This is a means to an end that Cartwright (2007) argues is paradoxical for Western cultures, which as a rule value quick decision making rather than the more deliberate and slow reflective approach. She argues that adopting the latter approach of deliberately slowing down and reflecting consciously actually helps to build our confidence in using our intuition and to gain trust in our decision making. Alvarez (2001), cited in Hardcastle (2004: 214), also urges practitioners to 'pause and reflect'. To this end she has developed a framework termed 'PRACSIS' (Practitioner Reflection on Actions, Characteristics and Situation, by Impact and Strategies). This involves taking an actual working situation and applying 'impact analysis'. The framework is designed as an invitation to think about how others perceive us. An example might be to consider how we think our skin colour, religion, gender, class, physical abilities and perhaps our qualifications are perceived by the communities in which inter-agency working takes place. This means sitting down with each other and beginning an exploration of our perceptions of others' perceptions of each of us as we represent our agency. We should not expect this be to be a comfortable experience. We shall be faced with our own prejudices and unravelling some of our dearly held interpretations and perceptions. Bates (2004: 61) refers to the way in which nurses embrace reflective practice as a means of moving from seeing their role as purely functional to one that 'emphasized the artistry of practice'. Not only should we examine our scientific knowledge – what we know – we should also ask questions of our own human agency, about how we know what we know, and the impact our human agency might have on those for whom we work. As Leadbetter et al (2007: 95) point out, this entails bringing organisations out of the box they exist in, where there are protections about their 'qualifications and skill base they think is theirs'. Whittington (2003a: 30) argues that it is a duty on those in the care professions to 'reflect as rigorously as possible' on their actions especially when partnership working carries 'a huge weight in policy objectives and official rhetoric'. We must talk about feelings we do not like, and strange though it may seem, how about our feelings about our feelings? If we are angry about the way colleagues might approach a sex offender, what do we feel about being angry? Disappointed at being angry, or pleased and self-satisfied that our anger only goes to show that we were right all along about our colleagues from other agencies? Somers and Bradford (2006) raise the question of whether some inter-agency work is a means to avoid taking action. We can see some logic in this. Meetings to discuss ways forward, strategies and future action can be a way of delaying actions when, for instance, resources are scarce, or the way forward is unclear and hazy. A commitment to reflection on action challenges motives, legitimacy and commitment to action and a review of that action (2006: 77), with a view to overcoming professional inertia.

Within this structure, how should managers and practitioners go about encouraging reflective practice? White (2001: 32) states that this begins with 'an assumption of trust, or the potential to build it'. Without this, reflection can be criticised for not having a sufficiently robust definition. Without a clear understanding of what reflection involves, managers and practitioners may open themselves to personal scrutiny as 'previously private thoughts ... enter the public sphere where they are subject to surveillance, assessment. classification and control' (Cotton, 2001: 512). Gilbert (2001) emphasises this point, arguing that governments operate through moral regulation rather than coercion 'when it comes to experts'. In the context of reflective practice, we can see an open door to moral inspection and scrutiny in front of us if it is not built on trust and a large measure of interdependence. Once we accept this premise, we move to a position in which we accept the validity of other professionals' experience, knowledge and interpretations, and interestingly that 'each partner has their own goals which they wish to pursue through the relationship' (White, 2001: 32).

Perhaps we can end on a micro-example of reflective practice in a multi-agency setting where we can see illustrations of how we organise our working lives around even the smallest of transactions. The example is a composite of my experiences while working in a dispersal prison where teams including probation officers, prison officers and education officers worked together. At times there were considerable tensions between the finely balanced dependence and interdependence of individuals and groups. Team members found that formal meetings were not really adequate to deal with some of the 'emotional business', which was seen as just as important as the daily routine of performing tasks. One of the middle managers suggested that the teams come together to reflect on the experience of their working environment. Over a period of months, as the teams' members became more prepared to face uncomfortable thoughts and relationships, some important themes emerged, which proved critical to the ways in which they worked. Among issues that were brought into the open were how gender affected the work with colleagues and prisoners, and the role played by power, status and vulnerability within the prison. One male probation officer talked about how he felt he was accepted by the prison staff due to having been in the Royal Navy, which was evidenced by the tie that he wore. He said he openly played on his sympathy with a uniformed organisation as this gave him better access to resources and 'inside information' within the prison as he was seen as 'one of the boys'. This opened the way for challenges from some of the female staff who asked how they could gain similar recognition. The officer began to appreciate how he might be disadvantaging his colleagues by 'pretending' to be more powerful than they were. Another topic was what staff thought they 'gave up' when they came through the prison gates each morning. One female said that when she exchanged – 'threw in' – her tally for her keys in the morning it was like throwing away her womanhood as she was constantly subject to sexist comments from prisoners and staff. This prompted another woman, who always wore an overcoat even in the height of summer, to talk about denying her femininity in the presence of violent sex offenders, and another to relate how she wore three sets of underwear on the grounds that if she were attacked 'the prisoner would soon lose interest'. There were also expectations of masculinity and one of the men admitted to being really frightened when asked to interview violent prisoners in the segregation unit. Being able to express his fears relieved him of the expectations that as a man he should be able to cope with anything thrown at him. There were team issues, too. One female probation officer was renowned for always taking on too much work and she was always under pressure. No matter what her colleagues did by taking work from her, and no matter how the allocation system was organised, she only seemed to end up with as many cases. This just made them more and more frustrated and feeling that their actions counted for very little. During one of the reflective sessions it emerged that she had had a still-born child. After some heart-wrenching discussion her colleagues were able to make connections with feelings of failure and the need to compensate by proving that she could cope no matter what demands were made of her. It is not hard to appreciate that issues like this had a profound effect on the way business was conducted, but once fears and anxieties, values and perceptions of power and influence had been brought into the open, there was a sense of support and working as a joint team in a hostile environment.

Multi-agency working within the criminal justice system can be characterised by differences in culture, attitudes, values, status and power at organisational and individual levels. Reflection calls on professionals to widen their perspectives to create 'the flexibility of mind deemed necessary to muster up the courage to change, adapt and expand [the] repertoire of responses to the world' (Costa and Garman, 1998, cited in Stroobants, 2009: 9). It has been argued that periods of professional reflection are necessary in order to prevent fragmentation and to produce more positive outcomes for offenders, and the public. Reflection is not an end in itself, but should be used in the constructive cooperation between agencies in an attempt to tame the beast of multi-agency working.

Summary of key points

- Reflective practice is essential to effective multi-agency working.
- Reflection allows us to broaden our perspectives, but ...
- Reflection is not a comfortable process and challenges professional identities and working practices.

Further reading

Hardcastle, D.A. (2004) *Community Practice: Theories and Skills for Social Workers*. Cary, NC: Oxford University Press.

Schön, D.A. (1983) *The Reflective Practitioner: How Professionals Think in Action*. Avebury: Ashgate Publishing.

References

Bates, J. (2004) 'Embracing diversity and working in partnership', in Carnwell, R. and Buchan, J. (eds) *Effective Practice in Health and Social Care: A Partnership Approach* (pp 51-64). Maidenhead: McGraw-Hill Education.

Bold, C. (2008) 'Peer support groups: fostering a deeper approach to learning through critical reflection on practice' (electronic version), *Reflective Practice*, 9(3), 257-67.

Bolton, G. (1998) *Writing as a Reflective Practitioner with Wisdom*. Sheffield: University of Sheffield. Available at www.shef.ac.uk/uni/projects/wrp/rpwrite.html

Cartwright, T. (2007) *Developing Your Intuition: A Guide to Reflective Practice* (electronic version). Greensboro, NC: Center for Creative Leadership.

Cavadino, M. and Dignan, J. (2007) *The Penal System: An Introduction* (4th edn). London: Sage Publications.

Chui, W.H. and Nellis, M. (2003) 'Creating the National Probation Service – new wine, old bottles?', in Chui, W.H. and Nellis, M. (eds) *Moving Probation Forward: Evidence, Arguments, and Practice* (pp 1-18). Harlow: Pearson Longman.

Cotton, A.H. (2001) 'Private thoughts in public spheres: issues in reflection and reflective practices in nursing (electronic version), *Journal of Advanced Nursing*, 36(4), 512-19.

Coulshed, V. (1988) 'Curriculum designs for social work education: some problems and possibilities', *British Journal of Social Work*, 18(2), 155-69.

Crawford, A. (1998) *Crime Prevention and Community Safety*. London: Longman.

Dolan, P. and Pinkerton, J. (2005) 'Family support: from description to reflection', in Dolan, P., Canavan, J. and Pinkerton, J. (eds) *Family Support as Reflective Practice* (electronic version) (pp 11-26). London: Jessica Kingsley.

Dugdill, L., Coffey, M., Coufopoulos, A., Byrne, K. and Porcellato, L. (2009) 'Developing new community health roles: can reflective learning drive professional practice?' (electronic version), *Reflective Practice*, 10(1), 121-30.

Gardner, F. (2009) 'Affirming values: using critical reflection to explore meaning and professional practice', (electronic version), *Reflective Practice*, 10(2), 179-90.

Gardner, R. (2003) 'Working together to improve children's life chances: the challenge of inter-agency collaboration', in Weinstein, J. (ed) *Collaboration in Social Work Practice* (electronic version) (pp 137-60). Philadelphia, PA: Jessica Kingsley.

Gardner, R. (2005) 'Safeguarding children through supporting families', in Dolan, P., Canavan, J. and Pinkerton, J. (eds) *Family Support as Reflective Practice* (electronic version) (pp 103-17). London: Jessica Kingsley.

Gilbert, T. (2001) 'Reflective practice and clinical supervision: meticulous rituals of the confessional' (electronic version), *British Journal of Advanced Nursing*, 36(2), 199-205.

Hardcastle, D.A. (2004) *Community Practice: Theories and Skills for Social Workers*. Cary, NC: Oxford University Press.

Kim, H.S. (1999) 'Critical reflective inquiry for knowledge development in nursing practice (electronic version), *Journal of Advanced Nursing*, 29(5), 1205-12.

Leadbetter, J., Daniels, H., Edwards, A., Martina, D., Middleton, D., Popovab, A., Warmington, P., Apostolov, A. and Brown, S. (2007) 'Professional learning within multi-agency children's services: researching into practice' (electronic version), *Educational Research*, 49(1), 83–98.

Mackenzie, G. (1999) 'Public protection, potentially violent offenders and the role of senior managers', in Kemshall, H. and Pritchard, J. (eds) *Good Practice in Working with Violence* (electronic version) (pp 231–40). Philadelphia, PA: Jessica Kingsley.

McNeil, F. (2006) 'A desistance paradigm for offender management', *Criminology and Criminal Justice*, 6(1), 39–62.

Moon, J.A. (1999) *Reflection in Learning and Professional Development*. London: Kogan Page.

Nash, M. (2006) *Public Protection and the Criminal Justice Process*. Oxford: Oxford University Press.

PS Plus 3 (2008) *Project Summary*. Available at www.psplus.org/Documents/PS%20Plus%203%20-%20Project%20Summary.pdf

Robinson, A., Hudson, K. and Brookman, F. (2008) 'Multi-agency work on sexual violence: challenges and prospects identified from the implementation of a Sexual Assault Referral Centre (SARC)' (electronic version), *The Howard Journal*, 47(4), 411–28.

Rumgay, J. (2003) 'Partnerships in the Probation Service', in Chui, W.H. and Nellis, M. (eds) *Moving Probation Forward: Evidence, Arguments, and Practice* (pp 195–213). Harlow: Pearson Longman.

Schön, D.A. (1983) *The Reflective Practitioner: How Professionals Think in Action*. Avebury: Ashgate Publishing.

Sloper, P. (2004) 'Facilitators and barriers for co-ordinated multi-agency services' (electronic version), *Child: Care, Health and Development*, 30(6), 571–80.

Somers, J. and Bradford, S. (2006) 'Discourses of partnership in multi-agency working in the community and voluntary sectors in Ireland' (electronic version), *Irish Journal of Sociology*, 15(2), 67–85.

Spalek, B. (2003) 'Victim work in the Probation Service: perpetuating notions of an 'ideal victim', in Chui, W.H. and Nellis, M. (eds) *Moving Probation Forward: Evidence, Arguments, and Practice* (pp 214–26). Harlow: Pearson Longman.

Stroobants, H. (2009) 'On humour and reflection' (electronic version), *Reflective Practice*, 10(1), 5–12.

Sullivan, H. (2002) *Working Across Boundaries*. Gordonsville, VA: Palgrave Macmillan.

White, V. (2001) 'Changing community care', in White, V. and Harris, J. (eds) *Developing Good Practice in Community Care: Partnership and Participation* (electronic version) (pp 13–33). Philadelphia, PA: Jessica Kingsley.

Whitehead, P. and Thompson, K. (2004) *Knowledge and the Probation Service*. Chichester: John Wiley.

Whittington, C. (2003a) 'Collaboration and partnership in vontext', in Weinstein, J. (ed) *Collaboration in Social Work Practice* (electronic version) (pp 13–38). Philadelphia, PA: Jessica Kingsley.

Whittington, C. (2003b) 'A Model of Collaboration', in Weinstein, J. (ed) *Collaboration in Social Work Practice* (electronic version) (pp 39-62). Philadelphia, PA: Jessica Kingsley.

Williams, B. (2002) 'Introduction', in Williams, B. (ed) *Reparation and Victim-Focused Social Work (Research Highlights in Social Work)* (pp 7-15). Philadelphia, PA: Jessica Kingsley.

Wilson, J.P. (2008) 'Reflecting-on-the-future: a chronological consideration of reflective practice' (electronic version), *Reflective Practice*, 9(2), 177-84.

Wood, J. and Bradley, D. (2009) 'Embedding partnership policing: what we've learned from the Nexus policing project, (electronic version), *Police Practice and Research*, 10(2), 133-44.

Conclusion: Does multi-agency working equate with effective practice?

Aaron Pycroft and Dennis Gough

As an advanced industrial society we are faced with a plethora of problems that are reflected in the operation of the criminal justice system, and form the day-to-day work of the professionals therein. This book has set out to highlight some of the key tensions and concerns involved in working within a criminal justice system that seeks to punish criminals and protect the public, but also rehabilitate offenders into becoming 'useful' members of society. While these aims are laudable and reflect the fundamental tenets of liberal democracy, they nonetheless give rise to a whole series of dilemmas that the contributors to this volume have reflected upon from a theoretical, policy and practitioner and ultimately ethical perspective.

This book has set out to demonstrate the ways in which multi-agency working has become a key feature of the criminal justice system and its correctional work. Developing out of a broader rationale for a mixed economy of public service provision, a rapid acceleration of multi-agency arrangements within the criminal justice system has reflected a need to build capacity to meet the ambitious targets set by New Labour and to demonstrate value for the public purse. In the inevitable tensions that arise from the New Labour project, the point is made by Taylor and Balloch (2005) that while we can bemoan the language of what works and evidence-based practice, this is not a reason to abandon the search for the ways in which 'truth speaks to power' (Pawson, 2006: 1).

Within this book there is a focus on the role of the Probation Service, and with good reason as it straddles the divide between punishment and rehabilitation within a public protection context. In this respect, it still remains a unique organisation despite experiencing an assault on its professional identity and practice in the wake of changes to the criminal justice system. It cannot be said that either the Prison Service or the police have had to contend with such changes in day-to-day practice as those experienced by probation officers. Likewise, it cannot be imagined that either the Prison Officers Association or the Police Federation would be as passive as the Probation Service in the face of such fundamental changes of role.

The reasons for that change are complex, presenting threats and opportunities to both probation and its partner agencies, who may on the one hand be competitors and on the other required to cooperate and work together to provide a package of support to an offender. This approach has been based on notions of New Public Management, which, as Pycroft (this volume) has noted, is coming under increasing scrutiny due to poor outcomes. These are summarised by Bovaird and Löffler (2003) as follows:

- Even economical, efficient and effective organisations appear unable to resolve so-called 'wicked problems', which cannot be resolved by improvements in organisational efficiencies.
- Competitive contractual arrangements have come to be seen as less important than ideas of trust between organisations.
- The role of the service user is too consumerist, and is seen purely as a consultative role, rather than genuinely democratising services and service delivery.
- In most countries, major scandals in relation to government performance have been about the ways in which ministers and officials have implemented policies and performance-managed organisations rather than being the fault of the contracted services.
- Long-term environmental, social and economic policies can only be sustained by looking at the whole structure of the delivery, rather than the performance of individual organisations. So failings within the criminal justice system in terms of serious further offences, for example, would consider the role that all agencies play rather than the failure of probation to perform in the way that it was expected.

The Probation Service exists within this context and is still poorly merged at a practice level with the Prison Service (the National Offender Management Service [NOMS] exists but at best represents a management take-over of probation by prisons) and the Offender Management Model (OMM) is at the heart of the new arrangements for correctional work in England and Wales. In considering the various contributions to this book, it is worth concluding with some final thoughts on the OMM and its context. The principles of the OMM are continuity, consistency, commitment and consolidation, and we suggest that you consider whether these can be/have been achieved by reflecting on the following questions.

1 How do contractual changes and changes in service providers help or hinder continuity of service?

2 Likewise, how does the involvement of a range of different professionals, working in a range of different agencies, help or hinder consistency of service delivery?

3 To what extent should the offender have a 'voice' in determining which services are received and the ways in which they are sequenced to fit with a Court Order?

4 Is there a potential for organisations operating in the correctional marketplace to put profit/winning contracts before a commitment to offenders/service users and, if so, what are the implications of this?

5 In what ways might a multi-agency response increase the complexity of an intervention and does this help the offender manager to consolidate the work that is undertaken?

References

Balloch, S and Taylor, D. (2005) 'What the politics of evaluation implies', in Taylor, D. and Balloch, S. (eds) *The Politics of Evaluation*. Bristol: The Policy Press.

Bovaird, T. and Löffler, E. (2003) 'Evaluating the quality of public governance: indicators, models and methodologies', *International Review of Administrative Sciences*, 69, 313-28.

Pawson, R. (2006) *Evidence-based Policy: A Realist Perspective*. London: Sage Publications.

Index

A

abuse *see* domestic violence; violence
Accelerate programme 59, 60
accommodation
  and dual diagnosis offenders 201
  and resettlement 82, 87, 157-8, 158-9, 160
  and women offenders 82, 87, 91
  and young offenders 219-20, 222, 226
accountability
  defensive practice 39, 128-9, 145, 192
  drug treatment partnerships 191, 192
  effect on risk assessments 97
  protection of multi-agency 'blanket' 111, 119
  and reflective practice 235
  and 'systems' response to failure 130
  and third sector involvement 42
Action Research 208
actuarial risk assessments 96-7, 100
administrative failure and risk 103-4
advocacy and mental health services 176
Afuwape, S.A. 202-3
age discrimination 55, 59
agencies as complex adaptive systems 12t
agency and successful resettlement 162
Alcohol Concern 188
alcohol misuse 172
  see also drug and substance misusing
  offenders
Alvarez's PRACSIS framework 239
Andrews, D. 161, 164
anti-discrimination legislation 52-3, 54-5,
  58-9, 83
anti-discriminatory practice 60-1, 75
Apena, F. 69
Appleton, C. 218, 220, 223, 224, 226
Asha Centre, Worcester 74, 84-5
Ashworth, Andrew 104
Askwith, D. 82, 91
ASPIRE managers 161
Assessment, Diversion and Liaison Schemes
  174, 176
assessment procedures
  drug misusing offenders 195
  dual diagnosis offenders 202, 208
  and mental health problems 174-5
  Probation Service and offender assessments
  23, 208
  risk management 96-7, 99-100, 117, 120,
  208

  child protection 126
  domestic violence 142
  see also Common Assessment Framework
Association of Chief Police Officers (ACPO)
  142-3
Audit Commission 217
Ayre, P. 119

B

Baby P(eter) case 4, 106, 119, 128-9, 133-4
Bailey, R. 67, 224
Baird, Vera 141
Balloch, S. 245
Banerjee, S. 204
barriers to multi-agency working
  communication failures 101-4, 106-7, 111-
  21, 126-30, 223
  language and terminology 65-6, 72, 156,
  207, 234
  and MAPPA framework 111-21
  mistrust between agencies 114, 115, 127, 237
  organisational culture 145, 170, 207, 223-4,
  232, 236-7
  in youth justice system 223-6
Bates, J. 232, 238, 239
Bean, P. 172
benefit sanctions for drug users 190
Bennett, T. 186, 187
Beveridge Report 10-11
bi-directional dual diagnosis models 205
Birch, P. 105
black and minority ethnic (BME) groups
  black voluntary and community sector 70,
  71, 72-6
  cultural diversity and segregated
  communities 57-8
  as offenders 3, 65-77
    experience of criminal justice system 66-8,
    76
    intervention approaches 68-71
    lack of research on women offenders 68,
    70, 74, 87
    and multi-agency working 71
    and resettlement 158
    and third sector providers 29, 71, 72-6
  and police attitudes 54, 66-7
  terminology use 65-6, 72
  women-centred initiatives 74, 91

W

Walklate, S. 10, 139
Wallis, Ethnie 28
Walmsley, R.K. 69
Walters, R. 225
Watson, A. 99
Webster, C. 67
Welfare Reform Bill 190
welfare state: historical development 10-11
'what works' service agenda 13, 218
  disappointing outcomes 14, 221, 226-7
  inflexibility 85-6
  see also evidence-based practice
Wheatley, M. 159-60
White, Elliott 101-2, 104, 107, 192
White, V. 239, 240
Whitehead, P. 36, 233
Whittington, C. 235, 238, 239
'wicked problems' 246
Williams, A. 106-7, 111
Williams, B. 224
Williams, Peter 219
Wilson, J. 111
Winstone, J. 174, 179
Witness Satisfaction Survey 146
women *see* domestic violence; women
  offenders
women offenders 3, 81-92
  complex needs and drug use 194
  diversity of needs 81-3
  lack of research on black and minority
    ethnic offenders 68, 70, 74
  lack of support for short-term prisoners 81,
    157, 158
  and partnership working 84-92
    funding restrictions 86-90
    requirements for good practice 90-1
    women-only centres and interventions
      84-6, 89, 91
women-only centres
  Women's Aid Refuge movement 140
  work with women offenders 84-6, 89
Women's Aid Refuge movement 140
Women's Offending Reduction Programme
  (WORP) 84, 85
Wood, J. 99, 100, 105, 238
World Health Organization (WHO) 203
Worrall, A. 85

Y

Youth Justice Board (YJB) 30, 217, 218, 219,
  221, 222, 225-6, 227
Youth Justice Teams (YJTs) 207
Youth Offending Teams (YOTs) and multi-
  agency working 5, 23, 217-27

and accommodation needs 219-20, 222, 226
barriers to effective working 223-6
and education and employment needs 220,
  221, 226
evaluation and outcomes for young
  offenders 218-22, 226-7
ISSP interventions 221-2, 225, 226
mental health and substance abuse needs
  220, 222, 226
organisational culture as barrier 223-4
and politics and policy 224-6
and reconviction rates 219, 220-1, 222, 225,
  226
research evidence and policy 224-6, 227